CONTENTS

PREFACE

Thomas Hobbes once made the indisputable obsrevation that you cannot predict the future, but that you produce the future in accordance with your idea of the past. It is unfortunate, therefore, that in Northern Ireland the Catholic and Protestant ideas of the past are so different. And it is worse than unfortunate that the general view is that this is an inevitable consequence of history. For, this being the case, the future of the sectarian division between Catholic and Protestant is assured.

There are certainly differences between the Catholic and Protestant communities on the "island of Ireland" (to use John Hume's phrase). Differences are natural, given the very different historical development and consequent distinctiveness of the two. But the communal divisions will not be broken down by teaching Protestants about Nationalist myths concerning them, or teaching Catholics about Unionist myths concerning *them*. It will only begin to break down when a common historical and political literature is written and made available to both communities. A literature which does not inevitably repel one side or the other because it gives a slanderous characterisation of one side or the other. What is necessary is a literature which is *national* in the true sense of the word.

It may suprise the reader to see the word 'national' used in talking about achieving the unity of Protestant and Catholic, since it may be presumed that the national issue divides Catholic Ireland and Protestant Ulster. But it is only surprising if you see national politics as being synonymous with Irish or Ulster nationalism.

A few years ago I realised that Nationalism was not about bringing about the unity of Ireland at all. It was merely about antagonising the Ulster Protestants and making sure that Catholics remained Nationalist in their politics, and not socialist or conservative. And, as a Catholic, I instinctively knew that the Unionist Party was not about reconciling Catholics to the Union at all, but about making life as difficult as possible for them within the United Kingdom. Both camps bothered not a bit about winning over a section of the other community to the desire of being part of the British or Irish nation, but sought merely to maintain their dominance over their own by propagating myths about the other. And, as a consequence, I ceased to be a Republican.

I came to this conclusion not by reading any Unionist histories (I could not find any), but by reading various articles and pamphlets by a Corkman, Brendan Clifford. And, being able to see in the experience of my own upbringing the Catholic-Nationalist society he described, I began to see the point of view of the Ulster Protestant. A point of view that no Unionist politician had ever got across to me.

I have no doubt, therefore, that a common or national literature and politics *can* be brought about between Catholic and Protestant Ireland. But only at the expense of Nationalism and Unionism. For, if a common understanding could develop between the two historic communities within the United Kingdom, would that not make the long-term prospects of Irish unity, in some form or other, that much better? That might be uncomfortable for the Unionist and Nationalist Establishments, but it is certain that that is how ordinary Protestants and Catholics could at last live at ease with one another. And who knows what the future might bring from there? Anything is preferable to the present communal certainty.

On that note of reconciliation let us turn to O'Neill.

Gerry Fitt used to say that the difference between Captain Terence O'Neill and his predecessors was that, while Craigavon and Brookeborough had walked over the Catholics with hob-nail boots, O'Neill walked over them with carpet slippers. It was probably the most astute thing Gerry Fitt said in his political career. And it just about sums up the beneficial aspects of O'Neillism for the Catholic community.

Captain Terence O'Neill is unique among Unionist politicans in having *benefitted* from Nationalist misrepresentations. It is usually the lot of the Ulster Protestant to be slandered and ridiculed by the sharp words of the nationalist propagandist or the sophisticated speech of Catholic politicians. But Terence O'Neill has even been given praise from a few **Irish News** editorials. And that is certainly saying something of the measure of misrepresentation which has gone into the creation of the O'Neillite myths.

While O'Neill was in power there was some reason for believing the O'Neill myth. Many did and had their expectations raised and then frustrated. And some went to war as a result.

But there is no justification whatsoever for maintaining the pretence today that O'Neill was a progressive reformer brought down by reactionary backwoodsmen. Though there is every reason indeed for Nationalism to maintain such a myth. For O'Neill is the proverbial exception that proves the rule. The rule being that the Ulster Protestant is a natural bigot interested only in keeping an 'ascendancy' over the Catholic. And O'Neill 'proved' it to be so because, in trying to end the ascendancy, he was brought down by the bigots for his pains.

That is the conventional Nationalist view of O'Neill. And it is a view that enjoys some credence in the Protestant community. The alternative Unionist view of O'Neill is that he was too soft on the Civil Rights movement. That he should not have abandoned the hob-nail boots for the carpet slippers. But these two views reveal more about the character of present day Unionist politics, than anything about O'Neill. For they reveal that, twenty years on, the Protestant community has failed to make sense of O'Neill. Or, more accurately, the leaders of the Protestant community have failed to make sense of O'Neill for their community. But that is only to be expected — O'Neillite as they all are to the core.

It is impossible for either Nationalists or Unionists to have a capacity for progressive politics while holding the conventional view of O'Neill. They must understand him more realistically, and go on from there. But as Goethe said in **Wilhelm Meister:** "Action is easy, thought is hard: action consequent on thought is inconvenient."

Davy Gordon describes O'Neillism for what it was (and is) — a deviation from the Unionism of Carson and Craigavon which led Catholics up the garden path and ultimately to war, just when they were forgetting about such things. He shows why the responsibility for the conflict lies squarely with the British government, which was the only agency in a position to prevent this happening. And, in dong so, he gives an explanation for the current conflict which is objective and is as meaningful to Catholic Ireland as it is to Protestant Ulster.

A national literature is emerging. The next step is national politics.

Pat Walsh
July 1989

Chapter One

Introduction

Northern Ireland is not a state. This comparatively simple fact should be the starting point for any serious analysis of the history of Ulster Unionism. The illusion that it is a state is a consequence of the pervasive and reactionary influence of the 1920 Government of Ireland Act.

The 1920 Act created a devolved sub-government in the province. This experiment in devolution was not a well-intentioned attempt to encourage peace and reconciliation between Protestants and Catholics in the six Ulster counties. The architects of the 1920 Act simply wanted to keep Northern Ireland at "arm's length" from Britain in the hope that it would gravitate towards the Irish Free State.

Nor was devolution introduced to satisfy the demands of the Ulster Unionists. The leaders of Ulster Unionism strongly opposed the idea of having their own parliament and they predicted that "Home Rule for Ulster" would exacerbate sectarian differences in the province. In May 1920 when the Government of Ireland Act was going through its Committee stage at Westminster, the Unionist leader, Sir Edward Carson, said:

> "It has been said over and over again, 'You want to oppress the Catholic minority, you want to get a Protestant ascendancy over there'. We have never asked to govern any Catholic. We are perfectly satisfied that all of them, Protestant and Catholic, should be governed from this Parliament, and we have always said that it was the fact that this Parliament was aloof entirely from these racial distinctions and religious distinctions, which was the strongest foundation for the Government of Ulster. Therefore, not only have we never asked to get an opportunity of dealing in a hostile way with the minority, but we have sought from the beginning to end of this controversy to be left alone and go hand in hand with Great Britain as one nation with Great Britain... We will do our best, but it is idle for any man to pretend that our Ulster Parliament, or any other Parliament in the midst of a community of that kind, will not... find very great difficulty in making progress as they would wish to do in the Parliament set up. No, sir, I urge even now at this hour that the proper course is that Ulster should remain as she is and that you should govern her, as you are governing her now, from here; there is very little difficulty about it, and that you should above all things have it as a place of your own with feelings towards you exactly like your own people... I say try to look ahead, and looking ahead, I believe the policy we have urged from the beginning of retaining Ulster as she is now as part of the United Kingdom, and treating the people of Ulster exactly as you treat the people of Great Britain, is the truest and surest policy for His Majesty's Government to pursue."

Carson's advice was ignored and the Ulster Unionist Party, which had only been an emergency all-class Protestant coalition against Home Rule, was handed responsibility for the Government of Northern Ireland. Unionists accepted this responsibility only because the alternative was Irish Unity. The Union was made dependant upon the periodical return of Unionist Governments at Stormont and the development of a "Protestant Parliament for a Protestant people" became inevitable.

Instability was almost literally written into the political framework established by the Government of Ireland Act. The creation of Northern Ireland as a 'political entity' was followed up by a rigid boycott of the province by the British political parties.

The Stormont set-up — devolution plus exclusion from UK party politics — placed both communities in the North of Ireland in an intolerable situation. Unable to participate in normal class-based politics, they stayed within their respective political ghettoes. The Protestant comunity was put in charge of a devolved sub-government it had never asked for, while the Catholic community was required to live as a permanent minority under Protestant rule.

That the Stormont system did not break down in sectarian chaos until the 1960s was due, at least in part, to the efforts of Northern Ireland's first Prime Minister, Lord Craigavon. After a prolonged struggle with Whitehall, he established the principle of parity with the rest of the UK in the vital area of social welfare. With the people of Northern Ireland paying the same taxes and receiving the same benefits as the rest of the UK, Stormont's potential significance was seriously reduced. The establishment of parity also frustrated the intentions behind the 1920 Act: devolution became redundant and incorporation into the Irish Free State was made impractical.

Having achieved parity, the Unionist leaders had little use for the political structures that had been imposed upon them. Under Craigavon and Lord Brookeborough, Stormont was commonly referred to as a "duplicating machine" or a "rubber stamp parliament".

Craigavon and Brookeborough, therefore, conducted government in Northern Ireland on a minimilist basis and, consequently, political activity in the province was kept to a minimum. Nothing much happened and expectations stayed low.

This uneasy equilibrium was ended in May 1963 when Lord Brookeborough was replaced as Prime Minister of Northern Ireland by Captain Terence O'Neill.

History books often portray Captain O"Neill as a reforming liberal who tried to modernise political life in Ulster. Paul Arthur and Keith Jeffery, for example, describe him as:

> "a man with a mission, an innovator who wanted to prepare Northern Ireland for the late twentieth century and its place in the affluent sun." (**Northern Ireland Since 1968**, Blackwell, 1988, p6.)

Likewise, Barry White, of the Belfast Telegraph, has stated that:

"O'Neill genuinely wanted to make Northern Ireland a model, modern province." (**John Hume — Statesman of the Troubles**, Blackstaff, 1984, p37)

F.S.L. Lyons, meanwhile declares in **Ireland Since The Famine**:

"Captain O'Neill set himself not only to divert domestic energies away from internecine quarrels and towards constructive policies but also to cultivate more amicable relations with the south." (London, 1971, p78.)

And W.D. Flackes in his Political Directory refers to O'Neill's "reformist course" and his desire to accommodate the political ambitions of an increasingly educated Catholic community" (**Northern Ireland: A Political Directory**, BBC 1983, p167).

It is the contention of this book that Terence O'Neill was, in reality, the most reactionary of all the Unionist Prime Ministers. Unlike his predecessors, O'Neill was an active devolutionist. He sang the praises of Stormont at every opportunity and spoke highly of the twisted form of politics the system had produced. For him, Unionism represented a coherent political philosophy which was infinitely superior to the left-right politics of Britain.

The entire Unionist Party followed their leader in this new direction. It was conveniently forgotten that accepting devolution had been the ultimate sacrifice for Unionists in 1920. In the minds of Unionists in the 1960s, defending the Union with Great Britain came to mean defending Stormont.

In reality, the O'Neill Government of 1963-69 actually did very little of substance. In spite of the rhetoric about the importance of Stormont, there was no serious attempt to tamper with the principle of parity established by Craigavon. Captain O'Neill simply busied himself trying to enhance the image of the pseudo-state at Stormont. His commitment to devolution expressed itself primarily through well-publicised gestures and a considerable amount of frenzied, purposeless activity.

O'Neill also indulged in a great deal of vague rhetoric about improving community relations. He raised expectations of change within the Catholic community, expectations which he did not even try to accommodate.

The resultant Catholic frustration produced the Civil Rights movement of the late 1960s. However, blind allegiance to Stormont rendered Unionists incapable of responding positively to the Civil Rights demands. In short, O'Neillism sparked off the explosion which had always been a possibility under the political framework introduced by Lloyd George.

This book is basically an examination of O'Neillism in action between 1963 and 1969. It demonstrates just how out of touch with reality the Unionist Government became and the extent to which the disentegration of Unionism under O'Neill contributed to the outbreak of a war which still shows no sign of ending after twenty years.

Chapter Two

1963

Terence O'Neill became Prime Minister of Northern Ireland on Monday, 25 March, 1963. No election took place within the Parliamentary Unionist Party although the then Chief Whip, William Craig, took "soundings" within the Party, which were said to have revealed "overwhelming support" for O'Neill as Brookeborough's replacement (Belfast News Letter (NL), 26.3.63). The News Letter which, as the Party newspaper, remained firmly O'Neillite right to the bitter end, greeted O'Neill's accession with the words, "as for the future, ...it is in safe hands" (ibid).

It did not take the new Premier long to make his presence felt. One of his earliest decisions was to appoint to senior positions what were described as "younger men with fresh ideas" (NL 28.3.1963). At Cabinet level, Brian Faulkner took over as Minister of Commerce, and William Craig became responsible for Home Affairs while, in the Civil Service, Ken Bloomfield and Jim Malley joined the Cabinet Secretariat. Although Craig and Faulkner are now remembered as bitter political enemies of O'Neill, all three men had a very similar outlook on the world. In particular, they were of one mind on the value of devolved government.

Less than a month into his Premiership, Captain O'Neill made his first grand entrance into the world of gesture politics. At the end of April, he decided to invite the United States President, John F. Kennedy, to open the Giant's Causeway as a Public Park. The News Letter positively glowed about the idea. Its editorial said: "the new O'Neill administration can take a bow here for this is the kind of imaginative public relations gesture that is needed if we are to claim our rightful place in the international picture" (NL 1.5.1963).

The Giant's Causeway idea was raised by O'Neill during his first meeting with the British Prime Minister, Harold Macmillan, in London. The account of this meeting in Captain O'Neill's **Autobiography** (p47-48) makes hilarious reading. Surprised that the Ulster Prime Minister wanted to "talk about anything other than the weather" (p47), Macmillan's response to the Kennedy invitation was to ask O'Neill why he wanted to make himself "unpopular with the Ulster Protestants". O'Neill replied by claiming "that by honouring an Irish-American president we might bring both sides together" (ibid).

In the event, Kennedy turned the invitation down, causing ungrateful Nationalists to sneer at the Prime Minister in Stormont. When the Republican Labour MP, Harry Diamond, described the Giants Causeway plan as a "political stunt that misfired", an upset Captain O'Neill replied, "I tried to show some statesmanship" (NL 16.5.63).

Although it may appear trivial, the Kennedy idea epitomised Terence O'Neill's entire approach to the Government of Northern Ireland. He attached immense importance to his regular journeys abroad, where he got the chance to shake hands with international statesmen and other famous people. Thus, in his first eighteen months as Prime Minister alone, he covered over 40,000 miles on official visits (NL September 16 1964).

However, due to an assassin's gun, Captain O'Neill never got the opportunity to shake the hand of John F. Kennedy. His reaction to the news of the United States President's death was the touching thought, "I would never meet Jack Kennedy now" (Autobiography p53).

Looking back, "I would never meet Jack Kennedy now" makes a fairly apt epitaph for O'Neill's entire Premiership.

The effect of all this globe-trotting and hand-shaking was to promote the dangerous illusion that Northern Ireland was a state. A powerless sub-government with the dubious privilege of having to rule over a sizeable and alienated Catholic minority was elevated into something of immense significance. And O'Neill thought he could keep Catholics happy and 'bring both sides together' with a few stunts like the visit of an Irish-American President. Thus, at a time when the Catholic community was eager for a slice of the political action, it got gestures and nothing else.

Apart from O'Neill's opening attempt at statesmanship, the new Government's enthusiastic attitude to devolution was noticable in a number of early administrative decisions. At the end of June, O'Neill introduced a new code of conduct regarding company directorships for Cabinet Ministers, in order to prevent conflicts between private business interests and public duty. Around the same time, a Select Committee was appointed to examine the salaries of Stormont MPs. It was also instructed to consider establishing a contributory pensions scheme for members of both the Commons and the Senate, and to examine the question of a salary for the Leader of the Opposition. Finally, the Government also decided to alter the rules of the House of Commons to enable it to sit an extra three hours per week.

Ralph Bossence, the News Letter's political correspondent, had this to say on the new changes:

> "There is a different spirit in the House today, a refusal to be content with doing things a certain way because they have always been done that way, and to its credit the Government has shown itself ready to meet the challenge.
>
> "The new code on directorships, the willingness to give the Opposition its proper place in the House and the allowance of more time to debate vital business are all signs that Captain O'Neill has responded to the change of feeling, and indeed he and his colleagues have sometimes helped to bring about the change." (NL 5.7.63.)

RECOGNITION OF THE ICTU

Unfortunately for O'Neill, progress to 'paradise' in an apolitical devolutionary arrangement was interrupted by a major controversy over the Unionist Government's refusal to grant official recognition to the Northern Ireland Committee of the Irish Congress of Trade Unions (NIC, ICTU).

In August 1963, the Government announced that the newly formed Economic Council was to have its first meeting in September. The terms of reference for the new body were to "consider and recommend a means of furthering the economic development of Northern Ireland with particular reference to the provision of employment, the promotion of economic growth and improved economic efficiency" (NL 18.8.63). The membership was to include six representatives of trade and industry, five trade unionists, two professors of economics and one accountant.

On the face of it, the Economic Council should have been completely untainted by controversy. Indeed, retrospectively, it is clear that, when it finally got going, the Council actually accomplished very little of substance. This is hardly surprising given Stormont's dependence on the economic policies implemented at Westminster.

The Government's problems with the Economic Council arose because the Trade Union nominees to the new body included William Blease, the Northern Ireland Officer of the ICTU. As it had been stipulated that the five trade union representatives should be full-time officials, Blease was unacceptable to the Government on the grounds that the ICTU was not a recognised body. His rejection led to an immediate boycott of the Economic Council by the other trade union representatives and the "Blease Affair" quickly became the central political issue in the province. The issue at stake in the affair was not the suitability of William Blease for the Council but the Government's refusal to recognise the Northern Committee. Acceptance of Blease's nomination by Stormont would have been regarded as de facto recognition of the NIC.

The non-recognition policy had been an integral element in the Unionist Party's election campaign in 1962. The Party Manifesto had stated bluntly that "the Unionist Party does not recognise the Irish Congress of Trade Unionists, but is prepared to recognise in N. Ireland a Committee of the British T.U.C." (Belfast Telegraph (BT) 11.5.62.) And in the Belfast Telegraph's Election Forum articles, the contribution from the Unionist Party dealt at some length with Unionist objections to the ICTU. Written by Isaac Hawthorne, Unionist Chief Whip, and MP for Central Armagh, it said:

> "As the Party which has always unequivocally stood for the British connection we cannot but view with deep suspicion a constitution [of the ICTU, DG] which talks of Ireland as one nation whereas there are two; that has a council which under the constitution must have a Southern Ireland majority although possibly more trade unionists are concentrated in the industrial North; which has fobbed off the gullible with a Northern Ireland Committee which is

not an autonomous body but merely executive and which must carry out the decisions of a Republican-dominated Congress; and which in general seems to us to be too much under Dublin.

"As a Party, we Unionists might be more ready to accept this Irish Congress if it were approved by what I might describe as a substantial majority of N. Ireland trade unionists. But they were never asked. This Congress was fashioned and imposed from above by a handful of leaders, mostly domiciled in Eire, and to this day the rank and file have had little say in its formation.

"From our extensive knowledge of the trade union movement in the North we are firmly convinced that had a free plebiscite of the trade union membership here been taken the scheme would have been decisively defeated.

"Are the Congress leaders afraid of such a free and unfettered vote in the North? Is that why it was never submitted to the constituent members of trade unions?

"We have said that any Unionist Government would be prepared to recognise a N. Ireland Congress trade union movement or a N. Ireland Committee of the British T.U.C. but remembering how hard was the winning of our constitutional liberty we are not prepared to undermine it, as we believe it would be, if we began negotiating with a body dominated by the politics and thinking of the Republic of Ireland." (BT 29.5.63.)

In the light of such forceful opposition, it is difficult to believe that, just two years later, the Unionist party meekly backed the O'Neill Government's decision to recognise the Northern Ireland Committee of the Irish Congress of Trade Unions. A brief summary of the developments which preceded this recognition provides a useful starting point for any analysis of the relations between Stormont and the ICTU in the 1960s.

In the very early days of O'Neill's premiership, there were some signs of a softening of the Unionist opposition to the NIC, ICTU. At the annual Unionist Party Conference on April 3rd 1963, the Government proposed a resolution incorporating the Manifesto position on recognition, but it was not passed. After 40 minutes of debate, the Conference decided to proceed to the next item of business without taking a vote.

Incidentally, the proposal to move to next business was made by a young (and upwardly mobile) Unionist named Robert Cooper. Although the 1963 Conference could not have known of the future in store for Bob Cooper in the Alliance Party and the Fair Employment Agency, it was probably aware that he was opposed to Government non-recognition of the ICTU. Cooper had publicly backed recognition in October 1962 in an article for a political commentary journal called **Review** (NL 28.8.63).

The spirit of compromise evident at the Unionist conference, however, was not evident once the controversy over the Economic Council began. The "Blease Affair" brought almost total unity to the Unionist Party. Groups like the Ulster Unionist Labour Association were quick to voice their unequivocal support for the Government line (NL 9.9.1963).

Indeed, the only dissident voice within the Party came from Robin Bailie, a former officer in the Ulster Young Unionist Council and an associate of Bob

Cooper. (Bailie had been a member of the Editorial Board of the political commentary, Review, in which Cooper's pro-ICTU article had appeared.) Bailie, who, like Cooper, was to become one of a number of young middle-class O'Neillites who grew disillusioned with the Unionist Party after O'Neill's departure, accused the Government of becoming "prisoners of reactionary elements among the backbenchers" over the issue (NL 28.8.63). Advising the Government to ratify Blease's nomination as a good-will gesture, Robin Bailie claimed that a solution of the problem of ICTU "will have to be found some time" (ibid).

Bailie received a harsh rebuke in a News Letter editorial which stated:

> "Anything in the nature of a compromise endangering basic principles could only be interpreted as weakness. Indeed, it would not be calculated to command the respect of the trade unionists themselves. The pity is that the Government did not ensure an adequate awareness of the complexities of the problem in the minds of all Unionists, young and old" (NL 29.8.1963).

The News Letter, in fact, published a considerable number of lengthy editorials on the subject. The first of these, entitled **Time To Face Hard Facts**, made some interesting points. It pointed out that, when the merger of the Irish TUC and the Congress of Irish Trade Unions, which resulted in the ICTU, was "first mooted, 175,000 of Ulster's 193,000 trade unionists belonged to British based unions, 10,000 of them to bodies with headquarters in the province and only 8,000 to Dublin-based organisations", and wondered how trade unionists in the North "allowed themselves to associate with the emerging ICTU" (NL 19.8.1963). The editorial also argued in favour of a Northern Ireland TUC, "co-operating on common problems with its counter-part in Eire but maintaining close association with the TUC in Britain with which its members have so much to share." The editorial ended by advising Northern Ireland trade unionists to demand a plebiscite to settle the whole issue.

Support for the idea of a plebiscite was a common theme in the debate about the issue which dominated the News Letter's Letters Page at the time. (See, for example, NL: 22, 27, 28 August, and 2 September). One advocate of a referendum, who signed himself as "Branch Secretary", recalled how the ICTU became responsible for Northern trade unionists:

> "As a branch secretary of the A.E.U., I remember at the time that the whole thing was foisted on the members of my union by outsiders who seemed to be in alliance with the Communists and Republicans" (NL 2.9.63).

Of the many letters published on the subject by the News Letter, the vast majority strongly backed the Government stance. The most coherent of these came from Edmund Warnock, the former Attorney General and the Unionist backbench MP for St. Anne's. His letter summed up Unionist apprehension about the ICTU. He claimed that the ICTU was "completely dominated by ardent Republicans", and that a "great majority" of its ruling Congress was "opposed to the the very existence of the N. Ireland Government or state". Warnock also pointed out the practical problems which the ICTU would have trying to co-ordinate trade union activity in the very different economic conditions which existed in the two parts of Ireland. For him, the solution lay in a Northern Ireland Committee of the British TUC:

"This is a great responsible body with fine traditions, vast experience in industrial relations and with an accumulation of wisdom acquired over years of negotiation. It is in the closest touch with the UK Government whose policies so vitally affect our industrial position at almost every point.

"The Irish Congress, whatever its merits, has no comparable standing and the trade unions and their officials and members would be in an infinitely stronger position if we had a local committee of that great body, the TUC." (NL 22 .8.63.)

The Warnock letter is worth quoting as it illustrates a crucial element in the whole history of relations between the ICTU and Stormont. It was argued at the time that the Unionist Party hostility to the NIC, ICTU stemmed from a general right-wing antipathy to trade unions. This myth, which still surfaces occasionally today, cannot be sustained in the light of the arguments used by Unionists like Warnock. Himself a former member of a Unionist Government, he was arguing that a link with the TUC rather than the ICTU would actually facilitate trade union activity.

The behaviour of the Unionist Government during the "Blease Affair" also contradicts the claim that it had ideological prejudices about unions. Indeed, in an early bid to end the trade union boycott of the Economic Council, the Government actually offered the unions additional representation on the Council. Likewise, a statement outlining the Government position at the end of September stated:

"The Government — and let this be clearly understood — has no quarrel with trade unionism. Day in and day out we work with unions in a spirit of good-will and cooperation" (NL 24.9.63).

The stalemate over the Economic Council was seven weeks old by the beginning of October 1963. And the situation could hardly have been helped by the ICTU announcement on October 1st that it had nominated two prominent Northern Ireland trade unionists for the Economic Council which was being established in the Irish Republic (NL1.10.63). To make matters worse, one of its nominees, Norman Kennedy, regional secretary of the Amalgamated Transport and General Workers Union, was also one of the nominated trade union representatives for the Economic Council in the North.

Nevertheless, the following day a development occurred which effectively marked the beginning of the end of the entire controversy over the NIC, ICTU. It emerged that, over the past six months, the Executive Committee of the Irish Congress and the British TUC had been involved in discussions aimed at securing greater autonomy for the Northern Ireland Committee of the ICTU (NL 2.10.63). Commenting on this news in an editorial entitled, **A Break In the Clouds**, the News Letter stated that, "if the formula which emerges is patently one which will give the Northern Ireland Committee complete authority in its own house, there would appear to be no reason why it should not bring the solution which the trade unionists of Northern Ireland and the Government are so anxious to find" (ibid).

This news abruptly ended the public controversy over Stormont relations with the Irish Congress. Months of behind-the-scenes negotiations followed involving the ICTU, the TUC and the Stormont Government. The compromise which emerged in the summer of 1964 consisted of an amendment to the ICTU Constitution on the question of the autonomy of the Northern Ireland Committee. It was eventually submitted by the ICTU Executive to a secret session of an ICTU Conference on July 28th 1964. It stated that:

> 'The functions of the Northern Ireland Committee of the ICTU shall be to implement in respect of N. Ireland decisions of annual and special delegate conferences, and of the executive council, on matters of concern to affiliated organisations having membership in N. Ireland and to recommend to the executive council policy on matters of concern to affiliated organisations having membership in N. Ireland, provided that, subject to the requirement that decisions reached have due regard to the position of members outside N. Ireland, the NIC shall deal with matters relating to the internal, industrial, economic, and political conditions of N. Ireland and of direct concern to N. Ireland members only and shall implement its decisions and the decisions of the N. Ireland conference on such matters" (NL 17.7.64).

The ICTU Conference's endorsement of this amendment was greeted by delight within Unionist circles. Herbert Kirk, who, as Minister for Labour had been involved in the lengthy negotiations with trade union leaders on the issue, said that he was "pleased to learn that the NIC of the Congress have now been gladly given that independence in industrial, economic and political affairs which they have for many years enjoyed in practice" (NL 29.7.63). Similarly, the News Letter editorial described the amendment's endorsement as "a milestone along the long road to the achievement of better understanding", and predicted that the Government would "quickly embrace this decision as a welcome opportunity to harness the full resources of the Province in the development of its progressive policies" (ibid). The subsequent formal recognition of the NIC, ICTU by the Stormont Government occurred on August 24th 1964.

Thus, the controversy sparked off in the summer of 1963 over the formation of the Economic Council ended. In the brief account of the ICTU recognition in his Autobiography, O'Neill comments that "the whole idiotic issue has long been forgotten" (p62), but adds that changing the Government position on the NIC involved "eighteen months of behind-the-scenes activity", and represented "one of the most difficult hurdles" of his premiership (p62-63).

To a minor aristocrat like Captain O'Neill, trade union disputes of any kind probably appeared "idiotic", but his comment on how the whole NIC, ICTU issue has been forgotten is certainly true. Consequently, the events which surrounded the eventual recognition of the Northern Committee are now shrouded in mystery for anyone without access to information on all the secret negotiations which occurred. The task of unravelling this mystery cannot be attempted here. This account of the developments which preceded the Government's recognition of the NIC, ICTU will, therefore, conclude by simply drawing attention to a few unanswered questions.

The first concerns the behaviour of the Irish Congress during the "Blease Affair". It is clear that details of the ICTU negotiations with the TUC over the autonomy of its Northern Ireland Committee were kept secret by the Irish Congress during the first seven weeks of the affair. Thus, in August and September, the Stormont Government was involved in a fierce controversy over an issue that was closely connected with the Constitution of the ICTU, while the ICTU itself had been secretly working on a relevant amendment to its Constitution since April. The obvious question is why did the Irish Congress conceal the facts which, after seven weeks, effectively ended the entire controversy?

The only logical explanation is that the Northern Ireland Committee must have engineered the whole controversy from the very beginning in order to strengthen its bargaining position with the Government. The NIC must have been aware that the Government would reject the nomination of Blease to the Economic Council. The trade union boycott of the Council which followed his rejection can only have brought deep embarassment to the Government by preventing the Council starting its work and by drawing public attention to the lack of proper arrangements between Stormont and the trade union movement. Consequently, the "Blease Affair" made the Government much more receptive to the ICTU "compromise solution" on the Northern Committee.

The second unanswered question concerns the readiness of the Unionist Government and the Unionist Party to accept the new terms of the Irish Congress. It was, of course, bizarre enough for a Unionist Government to hand over control of trade union affairs to the Congress of what it considered to be a foreign, hostile state. What is even more strange is that, in spite of the hostility to the ICTU expressed by Unionists during the "Blease Affair", the eventual recognition of the Northern Ireland Committee occurred without a voice of protest being raised by any Unionist.

It is true that throughout the controversy over the Economic Council, there were indications from some Unionists that autonomy for the NIC would settle the issue. For instance, in the News Letter editorial, **Time To Face Facts**, quoted above, it was claimed that in November 1962 the then Prime Minister Lord Brookeborough had "indicated that... if the Northern Committee were given a greater measure of independence by the Congress, the question of recognition might be re-considered." (NL19.8.63.)

Similar thinking was evident in a letter to the paper from Unionist Party member, Nelson Elder, which stated that "the Northern Ireland Committee of the ICTU have no autonomy and until the whole question of this is settled and they are allowed to act solely for the Ulster worker instead of being there only for the purpose of implementing the decisions of Congress, can they really speak for the Ulster trade unionist?" (NL 2.9.63.)

Support for the idea of NIC autonomy as the solution to the whole problem also came in a lengthy News Letter article by an "industrial expert", which appeared at an early stage in the "Blease Affair". The News Letter itself reported on September 24th that opinion among Unionist backbench MPs was that, "little progress will be made in reaching a settlement unless a greater measure of autonomy is given to the NIC of the ICTU" (NL 24.9.63).

However, it cannot be said that Unionist antipathy to the Irish Congress was solely due to NIC subservience to its Executive Committee. For example, there was a large body of opinion within Unionist ranks which thought that the whole issue should be decided by a plebiscite of trade unionists in Northern Ireland. The Stormont Government, it should be remembered, could not have set up such a plebiscite itself. However, it could have exploited the idea for propaganda purposes by refusing to even comment on the issue of recognition until the NIC, ICTU condescended to give the rank and file trade unionists a say on the issue.

Alongside the demands for a plebiscite were calls for alternative arrangements for the co-ordination of trade union activity in the province. For instance, the News Letter, which enthusiastically welcomed the ICTU compromise over its Constitution, had at the beginning of the "Blease Affair" advocated the formation of a Northern Ireland TUC. On the other hand, the senior Unionist backbencher, Edmund Warnock, had backed the idea of a Northern Ireland Committee of the British TUC. Such a Committee had been the official policy of the Unionist party as laid down in its Manifesto for the Stormont election in May 1962.

In short, it is clear from the controversy over the Economic Council that elements within the Unionist Party were opposed to recognition of ICTU for reasons other than the lack of independence of the Northern Ireland Committee. A typical example of Unionist resistance to the very idea of the Stormont Government giving its blessing to the Trade Union Congress of the Irish Republic came from the Unionist Senator, Sam Rodgers, who in September 1963 said that "no matter how much the Northern Committee whitewashes the problem, it remains a fact that their headquarters are in Dublin." (NL 13.9.63.)

The real mystery about Unionist acceptance of the NIC is not just that the dogmatic opponents of the ICTU were overruled by the rest of the Party. The fact is that, when recognition finally came in August 1964, not a single voice of protest was raised in public.

The comments made in O'Neill's Autobiography on the Unionist Parliamentary Party meeting which agreed to recognise the NIC simply deepen the mystery. According to O'Neill, the crucial meeting was only attended by a "small gathering" because "many MPs were too frightened to attend it" (Autobiography p63).

Nevertheless, in spite of the deep feelings which the issue had aroused in August and September 1963, and in spite of the uneasiness which apparently still existed over the ICTU in August 1964, the recognition of the NIC went ahead almost unnoticed. No Unionist at any level of the party spoke out against the decision and the whole issue was quickly and permanently forgotten.

The absence of any critical appraisal of the compromise solution reached in 1964 creates another problem. It leaves unanswered serious questions about the wordy amendment to the ICTU Constitution, which opened the door for recognition. Although the meaning of the amendment is hardly precise it does not appear to be granting the NIC the level of independence which the Government claimed it was. It states that "the functions of the NIC shall be to implement in respect of Northern Ireland decisions of annual and special delegate conferences, and of the executive council, on matters of concern to affiliated organisations having membership in Northern Ireland and to recommend to the executive council policy on matters of concern to affiliated organisations having membership in N. Ireland".

As the "annual and special delegate conferences" referred to are not specified as Northern Ireland-only conferences, they must be delegate conferences of the whole ICTU. Thus, the NIC function as laid out in the amendment is to implement decisions reached at all-Ireland ICTU conferences and at meetings of the Dublin-based Executive Council.

In judging the level of unfettered independence granted to the NIC by this amendment, note should also be taken of Clause 27 of the ICTU Constitution. This clause, which was not removed from the Constitution until 1970 (see ICTU Annual Report, 1970, p416), stipulated that over 50 per cent of the membership of the ICTU Executive Council had to be members of Irish-based trade unions. This obviously ensured the complete domination of the Executive Council by Southern Irish trade unionists, given that the vast majority of trade unionists in the North belonged to British-based trade unions.

Even a cursory glance at the present-day workings of the NIC, ICTU reveals considerable limits on its autonomy. For example, the present full-time official of the Northern Committee, Terry Carlin, was appointed to his position by the Executive Council. More important, the governing authority of the ICTU is still the Annual Delegate Conference, which is attended by delegates from both the Republic of Ireland and Northern Ireland. At the Annual Conference, delegates from the Irish Republic can vote on resolutions which are only of concern to trade unionists in Northern Ireland and vice-versa. Whatever the Unionist Government thought it was agreeing to in the mid-60s, the fact is that the ICTU Annual Delegate Conference is still the final authority on Northern Ireland affairs and the Northern Ireland Committee is subordinate to it.

Such matters of detail were of little interest to Unionists in August 1964. Even those who most strongly opposed to recognition of the NIC during the "Blease Affair" were probably motivated primarily by a gut reaction to the word "Irish" in the ICTU's name, rather than any actual interest in trade union affairs.

At any rate, the entire Unionist Party was obviously eager to extricate itself from the ICTU controversy and get back to the job of building Captain O'Neill's new Ulster. With such an important task on its mind, the Party had little desire to grubby its hands with the affairs of the working classes.

Chapter 3

1963/64
Forward To Wonderland

It is clear that the Prime Minister himself had little interest in the whole controversy over the ICTU. Although the question of recognition was one of the most significant issues to arise during the first year of his premiership, he made no reference to it in the many speeches which he made at the time. These speeches are nevertheless significant as they contain the basic tenets of Terence O'Neill's political philosophy. In 1963 and 1964, Captain O'Neill addressed meetings throughout the province, attempting to generate confidence in the institutions of Government at Stormont, and in the long term political future of Northern Ireland under a Unionist Government.

O'Neill's speeches between April 1963 and October 1964, therefore, provide a useful introduction to the politics of O'Neillism. In many ways these were the golden days of his premiership, as no one in the Unionist party at that time had any premonition of the crises which Captain O'Neill's approach to Government would inspire. In the calm before the storm, O'Neill outlined his comforting vision of the future.

Many of the early speeches centred on the need to improve Ulster's image. For example, after an eight-hour, 'meet the people', tour of Newtownabbey, O'Neill declared that the "the dreary, harmful picture of Ulster as a distressed, complaining backwater must be banished forever" (NL 15.8.63). Likewise, on September 20th, in the middle of the controversy over the "Blease Affair", the Prime Minister addressed delegates at a Conference of the Ulster Associations at Stormont. He said:

> "I think there is no doubt that in recent months we have been receiving a significantly better press in Great Britain and for this I hope that we in the Government can take some share of the credit. Nevertheless, I am convinced that part of the reason for the better Press lies in the better spirit which has begun to prevail recently among Ulster folk themselves." (NL 21.9.63.)

Northern Ireland expatriates living in Great Britain or abroad made up the membership of the Ulster Associations. The Associations worked in conjunction with the Stormont Government to promote the image and economic interests of the province. Needless to say, great significance was attached to their efforts by the Unionist Government in the 1960s. O'Neill told the delegates at the September 1963 conference: "Just as you look to us to keep Ulster in the van of progress, we look to you to project a favourable image of Ulster in the land of your adoption" (ibid).

There is no doubt that improving the performance of the Ulster economy was a principal element in O'Neillite government. Shortly before O'Neill became Prime Minister, the proposals of Professor Sir Robert Matthew's Belfast Regional Survey and Plan were published. The Matthew Plan sought to control the growth of Belfast, and "invigorate the economic development of the Province" (Richard Deutch and Vivien Magowan, **Northern Ireland A Chronology of Events**, Vol 1, p3, Blackstaff, 1973) by linking up the towns of Portadown and Lurgan to form a new town named Craigavon. As well as the creation of Craigavon (or as Sam McAughtry calls it, "Terence O'Neill's New Jerusalem"; **Down In The Free State**, p33, Gill and Macmillan 1987), the Unionist Government in the early 60s was concentrating heavily on economic planning. A new motorway, hospital and airport were among the more illustrious projects to be initiated.

A major concern of the Stormont Government at this time was the unemployment rate which, by the standards of the day at any rate, was quite high. The economic situation provided the Government with the opportunity to launch one of its first initiatives: the Economic Plan for Northern Ireland.

This plan was announced by O'Neill himself in October 1963 at the beginning of a new Parliamentary session at Stormont. A Belfastman, Professor Tom Wilson of Glasgow University, was appointed as economic consultant for the project. O'Neill's speech to Stormont graphically highlights the new sense of importance which the Prime Minister had brought to the Unionist administration. To illustrate the benefits of economic planning, he used the example of what had been achieved in France by a body called the *Commisariat Du Plan*, that had produced a "remarkable programme of development which encompassed hydro-electric power, railway modernisation, industrial rejuvenation and more modern methods of farming." (Hansard, 22.10.63 Vol 55, Col 31.)

The reference to France was followed up by a reminder that "Northern Ireland is not a sovereign country and cannot control the overall movements of the British economy" (ibid). Nevertheless, the whole tone of the speech, and the hype which accompanied the announcement of the Economic Plan, could only have given the impression that Northern Ireland was a sovereign state. O'Neill misleadingly claimed that, although Stormont's "efforts must obviously be more limited" than the those of the French Government, they could "still... be significant" (ibid). Having launched the Economic plan, O'Neill requested the "support of all sections of the community in taking an initiative which is directed to the national interest and to no other end" (NL 23.10.63).

The day after this speech at Stormont the News Letter's Political Correspondent reported that the new plan "was regarded in political circles yesterday as the most important decision taken since the new P.M. took office." (Ibid.) And the four Northern Ireland Labour Party (NILP) MPs were reported as feeling "that the Government had stolen their thunder" (ibid).

The increased emphasis placed on economic matters by the Stormont administration under O'Neill has led some commentators to concoct simplistic theories about the new style of Unionism introduced in 1963. For example, no less a person than Gerry Adams has claimed that the O'Neillite approach to government was based solely on the need to "attract multinational capital" (Gerry Adams, **The Politics Of Irish Freedom**, p24, Brandon 1986) to the province. Michael Farrell has also stated that, under "indirect pressure from the new class of managers of foreign-owned firms who were replacing the old Ulster industrial families, the Unionist Government under O'Neill made a few conciliatory gestures." **(Northern Ireland: The Orange State**, p329, Pluto Press 1980.)

Farrell's reasoning appears to be based on a belief in the innate morality of multinational companies who, apparently, never invest in countries where question marks exist over human rights issues. Leaving aside questions about multinational investment in such places as South Africa and Chile, or the less than spotless record of the multinationals themselves in the Third World, this whole theory actually understates the grandness of the O'Neillite project.

Captain O'Neill was certainly something of an economic determinist. In that respect, his premiership fitted in with the spirit of the times. Sean Lemass in the Irish Republic and Harold Wilson in Britain also believed in the primacy of the economy. O'Neill, however, had more on his mind than simply bringing foreign companies to Ulster to reduce the unemployment figures. He was a man of destiny who saw in the Stormont system a way of making his mark in the world. In particular, he believed that economic growth would make the National Question redundant in Northern Irish politics by copper-fastening the Union with Great Britain.

A classic example of such thinking came when O'Neill addressed the Mid-Antrim Unionist Association on 29th November, 1963. In a very gung ho speech he declared that "the development of Northern Ireland during the next ten years would be far beyond the reach of what the Irish Republic could achieve", and that "the situation would... reveal more and more clearly anti-Partition clamour as social and economic lunacy in Ulster." (NL 30.11.63.) He went on to say that the Unionist party intended "to write upon this Province with the hand of progress", by ensuring that Northern Ireland participated "fully in a social and economic revolution as far-reaching and overall more beneficent than the industrial revolution".

> "Only as citizens of one of the strongest and most prosperous nations on earth" he concluded, "can we hope to share in these immense benefits" (ibid).

This kind of heady rhetoric illustrates the extent to which O'Neillism was divorced from reality. It is difficult to believe that such grandiose declarations were made by the head of what was in reality a "rubber stamp parliament". More important, the extracts from the speeches quoted above contain early signs of two of the most reactionary elements in Captain O'Neill's political philosophy.

Firstly, there are some indications of a shift towards a vague form of Ulster Nationalism. There is, for instance, his claim that the Economic Plan was "an initiative... directed to the national interest and to no other end" as well as the claims that the Stormont Government was working to "keep Ulster in the van of progress". These themes were central to Captain O'Neill's entire approach to the government of Northern Ireland. He often preached the merits of an all-class Party governing in the national interest, and under his leadership the Unionist Party grew increasingly attached to the idea of "Home Rule for Ulster".

Some writers on the Nationalist Left have likened the fifty years of Unionist rule in Northern Ireland to fascism. Such a comparison is ridiculous, given the fact that the whole Stormont set-up was forced on the province by the British Government against the advice of the Unionist leadership. Nevertheless, it still remains a fact that the Stormont system of government did possess some of the outward trappings normally associated with fascism, with the most notable being continous single party rule. The fact that fascism did not develop in the province in the 1920s and 30s must owe something to the success of the then Prime Minister, Craigavon, in preventing the development of any popular enthusiasm for the Stormont arrangements. O'Neill, on the other hand, did everthing in his power to reverse Craigavon's achievement and the results can hardly be described as progressive.

Signs of an Ulster Nationalist direction in Unionist politics were evident in the first year of O'Neill's premiership. The most obvious occurred in January 1964 when Stratton Mills, the Unionist Party Westminster MP for North Belfast, called for the design of a new "emblem to symbolise Ulster", to be used by the province's commercial organisations when advertising outside Northern Ireland (NL 9.1.64). His idea received the firm backing of the News Letter, which stated that "the idea is a good one and particularly at a time when efforts are being made to encourage industrialists here to expand their export markets and to spread abroad the new spirit that is alive in this part of the United Kingdom" (NL 10.1. 64).

The new spirit alive in the province was the O'Neillite spirit, and it had Ulster Nationalist overtones. In his Autobiography, Captain O'Neill was able to claim that under his influence the Ulster Flag gradually replaced the Union flag as the symbol of the province (p64).

Aside from O'Neill's polite Ulster Nationalism, the speeches made in the early days of his premiership also brought into focus the nature of his Government's attitude to the Catholic community. His claim that growth in the province's economy would "reveal... anti-Partition clamour as social and economic lunacy" is both naive and intensely patronising.

It is still generally believed that O'Neill's premiership was based, above all else, on a policy of 'being nice to Catholics'. And it is suggested that his downfall occurred because everyone else in the Unionist party wanted to continue being nasty to Catholics. In reality, O'Neill's ecumenical niceness amounted to nothing more than a few pats on the head for Catholics, and a belief that an slight improvement in their economic position would make them forget all about a United Ireland. Hence the reference to "anti-Partition clamour as social and economic lunacy".

O'Neill, however, did not offer Catholics an alternative to the politics of Irish Nationalism. He made no attempt to encourage Catholics to join the Unionist Party, and he devoted a great deal of energy to preventing the Northern Ireland Labour Party developing into a significant political force. The NILP was already severely handicapped by its isolation from the socialist politics of the State, and by the absence of a normal Conservative opposition. The boycott of the province by the British Labour Party and the readiness of the Stormont Government to implement socialist legislation passed at Westminster restricted the room for manoeuvre of the NILP. Nevertheless, as a non-sectarian party, it could have performed a useful function in the 1960s, by reducing friction between Unionism and Nationalism. O'Neill, however, effectively smashed the NILP which he saw as a threat to his vision of uninterrupted Unionist Party rule at Stormont. The first sign of his campaign against the NILP was the attempt to steal "Labour's thunder" with the announcement of the Economic Plan.

O'Neill, therefore, expected Catholics to live as permanently frustrated Nationalists all their lives. And, as a reward for keeping their heads down, they might get better housing and a few more jobs.

O'Neill's reputation as a liberal came as a result of his occasional empty calls for better community relations and his claims that the Stormont Government was acting only in the "national interest". Better community relations simply meant apolitical gestures and statesmanlike posturing.

His first pat on the head for the Catholic community came early in 1964 when he made his first visit to a Catholic school (NL 25.4.64). In his account of the visit to Our Lady of Lourdes Intermediate School in his memoirs, O'Neill claims that the News Letter sent a photographer to the event to obtain a "shocking picture". Such a claim is difficult to believe as the News Letter remained firmly behind the Prime Minister and his policies throughout the 1960s. At any rate, the newspaper published a large photograph of O'Neill standing directly beneath a crucifix. Recalling the photograph, O'Neill writes that "in such ways was co-operation made almost impossible", and "in such ways reconciliation was bound to fail" (p59).

Thus, the objective of achieving "reconciliation" appeared on the political agenda for the first time. It is important to ask what he actually meant by the word. Was it reconciliation between Unionism and Nationalism? Such reconciliation is unachievable, as it is physically impossible to live in two states at the same time. Furthermore, a policy of achieving such reconciliation was not even on the agenda, for in the Prime Minister's scheme of things, the Unionist Party would always govern the province. It can also be taken for granted that the Unionist Government was not aiming for ecumenical unity between the Protestant and Roman Catholic faiths. Thus, it can only be concluded that reconciliation, in O'Neill's eyes, meant reconciling Catholics to being ruled by Prods.

As Brendan Clifford has pointed out (**The Road To Nowhere**, Athol Books 1987), the O'Neillite attitude to the Catholic community can be summed up in the phrase "Croppies lie down!" He ensured that Catholics had no alternative to being Croppies, and he then expected them to lie down.

Contrary to popular mythology, O'Neill's premiership did not fail because deep-dyed Protestant bigots objected to his overtures to Catholics. The Unionist Party, by and large, went along with his rhetoric about improving community relations. Moreover, it firmly attached itself to his vision of Wonderland under the Stormont system. Twenty years after his departure, although the man himself may be reviled in some circles, the Unionist Family is still firmly attached to the O'Neillite vision, thereby giving a whole new meaning to the phrase "the love that dare not speak its name". The fact that the Ulster Unionist Party ousted O'Neill from the leadership in 1969 was due primarily to his inability to deal with the fact that the Croppies were refusing to lie down. (To be fair, his successors have, with the partial exception of Brian Faulkner, been equally incapable of dealing with such an unpleasant reality.)

In the early days of O'Neill's premiership, however, no one in the Unionist Party seemed to be aware that the Catholic community might just possibly object to having to live without politics. Consequently, the Unionist Family approached the beginning of 1964 with the utmost confidence. This belief that they were entering a new era can be detected in the News Letter's Christmas message to its readers in 1963 which said:

> "As we approach the greatest day in our calendar there is much for which we can be thankful. While the dreaded scourge of unemployment is still with us there is a rising tide of optimism; hopes are high that it can be translated into terms of prosperity. There is another assessment too, from which we can draw comfort and satisfaction. The spirit of neighbourliness and tolerance which in recent years has been growing steadily between all classes and creeds in the Province has been more than maintained; 1963 has brought fresh evidence of a desire for a better understanding and for practical manifestation of it" (NL 24.12.63).

Such heady confidence was surpassed by the newspaper's political correspondent, Ralph Bossence, in his political review of 1963, which was entitled, **The Signs And Portents Of The New Ulster.** Referring to O'Neill, he wrote:

> "He is a young man, in tune with his age, forward looking and convinced of the necessity of positive planning. His accession to high office is, in its way, the most significant in the history of the Province, because of the break which it seems destined to make with many old and well-worn attitudes of mind.
>
> "He has surrounded himself in the Cabinet Office with young men who understand and sympathise with his objectives. In nine months he has not been able to do much more than lay the foundations of the new Ulster which will emerge from the Matthew Report and the economic blueprint being prepared under the supervision of Professor Wilson. But the signs and portents are there." (NL 7.1.64.)

Chapter Four

1964
Trouble In Paradise

UNGRATEFUL NATIONALISTS

On January 1st 1964, the news broke that the Nationalist Party was planning to lobby the Westminster political parties on the issue of discrimination against Catholics. Their campaign began with letters to the British Prime Minister and the Leaders of the Labour and Liberal parties. This particular lobby did not, by itself, achieve much for the Nationalist Party or the Catholic community. However, the hysterical reaction of Unionists to the very idea of such a lobby must have put some ideas in the heads of those who planned the Civil Rights agitation of the late 1960s.

The response of the Unionist Party to the allegations of discrimination in 1964 was a mirror image of its reaction to the Civil Rights movement in 1968 and 1969. Unionists made no attempt to positively counter the complaints of mistreatment and for the most part fell back on pompous expressions of disappointment at the behaviour of their opponents. A News Letter editorial summed up this attitude when it said that, "for those who would welcome political controversy on a broader plane with a really lively Nationalist Party making a worthwhile contribution to the welfare of the Province, there will be interest — and disappointment — in the latest surprise flurry of activity in that quarter" (NL 2.1.64). The editorial went on to whinge that the actions of the Nationalist Party were particularly out of place in "an age in which co-operation and friendship are common cause and the whole trend of policy from Stormont, under Captain O'Neill, is towards a society in which the fruits of economic planning and hard work are envisaged by every section." (Ibid.)

These feelings were echoed in another editorial two weeks later which stated that:

> "To the majority of thinking men in the Government Party... it is a source of grievous disappointment. There is no satisfaction in having to write 'off' a major opposition group. But how can it be otherwise when its principal resort is to 'discrimination' as the most powerful weapon with which to strike? It will indeed be a great day for Northern Ireland when the Nationalist Party re-captures its former stature, abandons propaganda and re-enters the field of politics" (NL 19.1.64).

The "grievous disappointment" displayed here is essentially disappointment over the fact that Nationalists wanted a United Ireland! It is difficult to imagine what the News Letter had in mind when it called on the Nationalist Party to re-enter "the field of politics", and make a "worthwhile contribution to the welfare of the Province". Under the existing political arrangements, the Nationalist

Party could do nothing but agitate against Partition. There was certainly nothing positive for it to do at Stormont, as it soon found out when it became the Official Opposition in 1965. Nevertheless, Unionists thought it unreasonable and indeed rather ungrateful of Nationalists to misbehave. Captain O'Neill was particularly unable to understand the basic realities of Irish Nationalism.

This inability is very obvious in O'Neill's Autobiography, where it emerges that a misunderstanding of Nationalism was an O'Neill family trait. In one of the many unintentionally hilarious parts of the book, the author recounts an episode in the life of his grandmother. This woman, it is claimed, was "strictly impartial in her employment policies because she pleaded that with her London and Scottish background she knew nothing about Irish affairs". Nevertheless, in 1922 the "Sinn Feiners set fire to the house", and at "the crucial moment of the fire the head forester, a Catholic, refused to ring the fire bell". The shock of this event caused the woman in her old age to often say to the young Terence: "After all that kindness they burnt down my home." (Autobiography, p13.)

In a statesmanlike comment on this event in his family's history, O'Neill said:

> "I was always determined that this early event in my life should in no way influence my outlook on Irish affairs, and it never did, though had I been a 'hardliner' I could certainly have pleaded special circumstances" (ibid).

Throughout his premiership, whenever developments disturbed his vision of the future, O'Neill's reaction always contained expressions of hurt and disappointment that people were behaving badly after all his kindness.

The Nationalist Party lobby of the British political parties also touched a raw nerve among Unionists concerning their attitude to the sovereign Parliament at Westminster. The rhetoric of their Prime Minister about the virtues of self-government had helped to foster delusions about the independence of Stormont. Although O'Neill himself seems to have been at times aware that there was no substance to his rhetoric, other Unionists took it more seriously and began to imagine that the Stormont Parliament possessed some form of sovereign power. With such a spirit developing in the Party, the faintest threat of Westminster interference in Ulster affairs immediately antagonised Unionists. Thus, a News Letter editorial in February 1964 declared that the Nationalist Party "had the effrontery to take their alleged grievances to London" (NL 15.2.64).

N.I.L.P. HERESY

In the same month, another troublesome development occurred, which evoked a similar response from Unionist ranks. On February 18th, the Northern Ireland Labour Party launched its Manifesto for the forthcoming Westminster election, which was entitled, **Signposts To The New Ulster**. This document is interesting in that it highlights something of a shift in the NILP's political direction. Having had their already severely limited room for manoeuvre restricted still further by the Unionist Party's new found enthusiasm for economic planning, the NILP appear to have attempted to move the emphasis to

Westminster and the British political scene. The Signposts To The New Ulster document was the result of discussions between the British Labour Party and the NILP which had begun in the autumn of 1963. Representing the Labour Party at these discussions were Ray Gunther MP, a Member of the Party's National Executive Committee, and Sarah Barker, the Party's National Agent. Among the NILP's representatives were its Secretary, Sam Napier, and its former Chairman, Charles Brett (NL 19.2.64). The Manifesto was drawn up in preparation for the forthcoming Westminster General Election, and was hailed as "the first detailed policy statement on Ulster by one of the National Political parties" (ibid).

The increased emphasis in the direction of Westminster was evident in a number of the document's proposals. It suggested, for example, that the Stormont Government should have a special Minister in London, who would be responsible for co-operation between the two Governments on economic and financial affairs. It also stated that, under a Labour Government, the economic development of Northern Ireland should be controlled by an Ulster Regional Board which would operate under a National Industrial Planning Board (NL 21.2.64).

The new Manifesto was given prominent attention at the NILP Annual Conference at the end of March. The final session of the Conference was addressed by Ian Mikardo, the then Deputy Chairman of the British Labour Party. Having described the twelve Unionist MPs at Westminster as "no more than a light-weight bunch of political nonentities", Mikardo claimed that "the Tories have neglected Northern Ireland more than any other region in the United Kingdom". This neglect, he argued, was possible because the Tories were "convinced that, however much they kick Ulstermen in the teeth, the Ulstermen will go on returning Unionist MPs." This was contrasted with the recent sudden interest in the North East of England by the Tory Party after "a number of Tory MPs up there told the Government that their seats were highly marginal". The lesson from this, he claimed, was: "If you want attention from the Tories you need a few marginal seats." (NL 31.3.64.)

The NILP's attempts to develop its relationship with the Labour Party in the 1960s can be seen as part of the process that culminated in its unsuccessful attempt to achieve a complete merger in 1970. There is no doubt that a sizeable section of the NILP would have welcomed the opportunity to play a full part in the state-wide struggle against the Tories at this time. However, this desire was only ever communicated in private, and no one in the Party openly protested about their exclusion from the socialist politics of the state. There is no knowing what might have happened if the NILP had thrown its not inconsiderable weight behind a demand for the British Labour Party to face up to its democratic responsibilities to the Northern Ireland working class by organising in the province.

Sadly, the NILP remained content to be patronised occasionally by figures like Ian Mikardo. Consequently, it was placed in an impossible situation in which it was held responsible for the policies of the 1964-70 Labour Government, despite the fact that it had no power over the formulation of these policies. In spite of Mikardo's rhetoric, the Labour Government found it just as easy as the Tories to ignore the needs of Northern Ireland, as it was not electorally accountable to the people of the province. And because it did not have to seek a mandate for its policies regarding Northern Ireland, it did not need to shape these policies in such a way that they would attract significant support at the ballot box.

The NILP Conference in March 1964 was obviously keen to share in the growing confidence felt by the British Labour Party in the wake of the Tory Government's embarrassment over the Profumo Scandal. Being able to bask in the reflected glory of Harold Wilson's 'Government in waiting' must have been something of a pleasure for the NILP, hemmed in as it was by the Unionist Government's commitment to parity in the field of social welfare provision. The possibility of a Labour Government coming to power at least gave them something to use against the Unionists. Thus, on the day following Mikardo's speech to the NILP Conference, the former Party Chairman, Charles Brett, declared that "A Labour government in Britain will have neither sympathy nor patience with legislative quibbling but will expect full and prompt co-operation from Captain O'Neill and his Government." (NL 2.4.64.)

Needless to say, this threat to the 'independent' functioning of Stormont immediately provoked rage amongst Unionists. Stratton Mills, the Unionist Westminster MP for North Belfast, responded to Brett by asserting that "Stormont has been given various powers of internal self-government by the Government of Ireland Act, and it really would be intolerable if our Government was to be subject to dictation and meddling by a future Labour government" (ibid).

The NILP's impudence in 1964 was not confined to its heretical belief that Stormont was subservient to Westminster. Some members of the Party also dared to pour scorn on Captain O'Neill's globe-trotting activities.

On March 23rd O'Neill returned from a visit to the USA, where he had achieved the next best thing to a meeting with Jack Kennedy: a meeting with his widow, Jackie Kennedy. He also met President Lyndon Johnson and the US Secretary of State, Dean Rusk. Once he arrived back in Northern Ireland, O'Neill held a press conference at Aldergrove Airport at which he boasted:

"It has been my aim since I became Prime Minister to try to raise the level of appreciation of Northern Ireland outside the Province. For a Northern Ireland Prime Minister to stay at the British Embassy and to have met Mrs. Kennedy, the President and the Secretary of State is a slight change." (NL 24.3.64.)

When Sam Thompson, the well-known playwright and NILP candidate for the Westminster Constituency of South Down, dared to dub this trip to the United States as a "blarney tour" (ibid), the Unionist Prime Minister was definitely not amused. He replied to Thompson by saying: "unlike the works of the playwright, the work of the politician is concerned with facts. On this visit to North America, I made a speech on Ulster which was broadcast throughout Canada from the Atlantic to the Pacific. I addressed one of the most distinguished business audiences in New York" (NL 4.4.64).

DIVIS STREET AND THE OCTOBER 1964 GENERAL ELECTION

Unionist Party irritation at NILP attempts to bring a bit of reality to Captain O'Neill's idea of the future featured prominently in the Unionist Westminster election campaign in September and October 1964. The News Letter devoted an editorial to the joint plans of the NILP and Labour Party regarding the economic development of Northern Ireland. It stated:

> "there is one plank in the Labour platform which raises grave doubts about the degree of freedom which would be left to the Northern Ireland government in the key field of planning if Labour were to win. 'Signposts to the New Ulster' published earlier this year jointly by the British and N. Ireland Labour Parties stated that Labour would set up a National Industrial Planning Board, with regional boards including one for Ulster, subordinate to it. How closely will the planning policy of the O'Neill Government... dovetail with Labour's programme; and if there are conflicts whose will be the deciding voice?" (NL 4.9.64.)

The editorial also asked if a Labour Government "would... over-rule decisions made at Stormont", and declared that "if the flexibility and freedom Stormont enjoys under the Conservatives are to be curtailed under Labour, the electorate are entitled to know about it." (Ibid).

The deep uneasiness among Unionists about Labour plans to set up an Ulster Regional Board as part of a National system again illustrates how the Unionist Family had become enmeshed in the form of government imposed on the province in 1921. On a similar theme, a strident editorial from the Belfast Telegraph asserted that "Northern Ireland cannot but resist anything which would reduce not alone the right of constitutional self-determination but the right of the House of Commons at Stormont to make up its own mind on administration." (BT 28.9.64.)

The News Letter also singled out the NILP for strong criticism over its decision to run a candidate in the constituency of West Belfast:

> "It is particularly regrettable that in West Belfast... the Northern Ireland Labour Party has now seen fit to divide the vote and thereby enhance the chances of those who favour a United Ireland. This can only be interpreted in one way, and the message will not be lost in the other... contests in which a Socialist will be participating." (NL 15.9.64.)

This theme was taken up by the Unionist Party candidate for West Belfast, James Kilfedder, who said in his first election address that, "if the Republicans captured West Belfast because of the intervention of the Labour Party, the people would not forget nor forgive" (ibid). Similarly, the Chairman of the Ulster

Unionist Campaign Committee, Lord Robert Grosvenor, claimed that the NILP's "intervention" in the West Belfast Constituency made a "mockery of their boast as supporters of Ulster's constitutional position", as it would assist "the cause of anti-partitionists" (ibid). The spurious and politically corrupt nature of these accusations against the NILP can be demonstrated by the fact that when the NILP decided not to run a candidate for the West Belfast seat in 1966, Unionists accused them of deliberately giving Republicans a "free run" (Roy Bradford, NL 30.3.66).

The fight for the West Belfast seat, however, is not remembered for the use by the Unionist Party of the "orange card" against the Northern Ireland Labour Party. The election campaign in this Constituency witnessed both the arrival of Paisleyism onto the province's political scene and the worst rioting seen in Belfast for twenty-five years.

The trouble began in West Belfast as a result of a tricolour being displayed in the window of the Divis Street election headquarters of the Republican candidate, Liam McMillen. On September 27th, the Rev. Ian Paisley declared that, if the Government failed to act, he and his supporters would march to Divis Street and remove the flag themselves. On the same day, Kilfedder, who was receiving active support from Paisley in his campaign, sent a telegram to the then Minister of Home Affairs, Brian McConnell, calling on him to "remove tricolour in Divis Street which is aimed to provoke and insult loyalists in West Belfast" (NL 28.9.64).

The next day, under the provisions of the *1954 Flags And Emblems Act*, the police removed the tricolour on the direct instructions of the Home Affairs Minister. McConnell also placed a ban on Paisley's protest rally and march, planned for September 29th. Paisley threatened to defy this ban and, that night, a crowd gathered in Divis Street to defend the area. Although the Paisleyite march failed to materialise, the crowds clashed with the RUC. The rioting continued on the following three nights, encouraged no doubt by a re-run of the flag incident on October 1st, when the tricolour re-appeared in the Republican HQ window, only to be removed again by the police.

For the record, when polling finally occurred on October 15, Kilfedder held the seat for the Unionist Party.

WESTMINSTER ELECTION 15th OCTOBER, 1964: RESULT		
Candidate	**Party**	**Vote**
J. Kilfedder	Unionist	21,337
H. Diamond	Republican Labour	14,678
W. Boyd	NILP	12,571
L. McMillen	Republican	3,256

It is interesting to compare this result with figures from the previous election in 1959:

WESTMINSTER ELECTION 1959: RESULT		
Candidate	Party	Vote
P. McLaughlin	Unionist	28,898
J. Brennan	Independent Labour	20,062
T.A. Heenan	Sinn Fein	4,416

Although any analysis of election results is little more than guess-work, these figures do reveal two interesting facts. Firstly, they show that, despite the best efforts of Kilfedder and Paisley, the Sinn Fein/Republican vote actually fell in 1964. The Divis Street riots, cannot, therefore, be attributed to a revival of Republicanism in Belfast in the mid-60s.

The West Belfast 1964 result also indicates a growth in the strength of the NILP. Even the News Letter described Boyd's vote as a "minor triumph" (NL 16.10.64), and from the 1959 figures it is clear that this vote was not just achieved at the expense of the Unionist Party. It can, therefore, be assumed that Boyd received a fair degree of Catholic support, despite the fact that sectarian tensions had been very high during the election campaign. Overall, the NILP received just over 103,000 votes in the ten constituencies it contested in 1964. In 1959, it fought only three seats and received 44,000 votes (see letter from NILP member, NL 9.11.64). The NILP showing in 1964 is certainly impressive for a Party with no prospect of state power and with no real Tory Party to campaign against. To put it into perspective, the NILP received more votes in the 1964 Westminster Election than either the Alliance Party or Provisional Sinn Fein have ever achieved.

Nevertheless, the election stands out only because of the controversy over the tricolour and the subsequent riots in West Belfast. Interestingly, in the Stormont Debate on the incidents in Divis Street, the unsuccessful Republican Labour candidate, Harry Diamond, claimed that the flag had been on display at the Republican Headquarters since September 6th, three weeks before it became an issue. Furthermore, the Flags And Emblems Act only made the display of a tricolour illegal if it was likely to cause a breach of the peace, and it is obvious that it was Paisley's and Kilfedder's opportunistic sabre-rattling which threatened the peace, rather than the flag itself.

It would, however, be as pointless to condemn the activities of Paisley, as it would to denounce those who took on the RUC in Divis Street. The truth of the matter is that the events which occurred during the West Belfast campaign represented a normal part of the political life of Northern Ireland. The exclusion of the province from the party politics of the UK state ensured the survival of the communal politics of Unionism and Nationalism and, throughout the world, sectarian friction and violence always accompany communal politics.

The Unionist Party, under O'Neill, was unable to cope with the events in West Belfast. O'Neill believed that Unionist politics were more dignified and less divisive than British politics. His lofty ideals counted for nothing, however, at election time in areas like West Belfast when the chief function of the Unionist Party was to get the Prods out to vote. And from this standpoint, Paisley made a good Unionist in 1964.

Even before any trouble had begun, the News Letter acknowledged that West Belfast "is a seat where it is supposed to be important to 'get the blood up'" (NL 8.9.64). Paisley's behaviour certainly achieved this and the riots he helped to provoke must have boosted the Unionist vote by persuading Protestants to stick with the Unionists, rather than vote NILP. Kilfedder was therefore only being honest when he said during his victory speech that, without Paisley's help, his victory "could not have been done" (Clifford Smyth, **Ian Paisley, Voice Of Protestant Ulster**, Scottish Academic Press 1987). A similar admission was made in the more liberal surroundings of a Young Unionist Conference in Derry the following year. There, a Young Unionist from Queens University, E.Curran, admitted that not only did "Mr. Paisley... give a considerable amount of support to the Unionists in West Belfast during the last general election", but that, "in fact... he won the election in West Belfast" (NL 1.3.64).

Throughout the sixties, the leadership of the Unionist Party made no attempt to develop non-sectarian political structures which would have made events like those which occurred in West Belfast in 1964 less likely. Instead, they stirred up political activity in a situation in which structures channelled political activity into communal conflict. Then they condemned the resultant expressions of communalism. O'Neill's speech in Stormont during a debate on the Divis Street riots is a perfect embodiment of this attitude. With its praise for the Churches, its claim that only a "tiny minority" was involved in the disturbances, and its call to all "men of good will" to work together, this speech was a forerunner of all the meaningless 'liberal' condemnations of violence that have been made over the last quarter of a century. As such, and also as a clear expression of the main tenets of O'Neillism, it deserves to be quoted in full:

"**The Prime Minister**: Mr. Deputy Speaker, with your permission I should like to start this debate.

"Since I changed jobs last year I have had two principal aims in view. I have wished to make Northern Ireland economically stronger and more prosperous, so that all our people may enjoy a fuller and richer life. I have wanted, too, to build bridges between the two traditions within our community. Though progress in this movement has been gradual, it has also been steady. More and more people have been feeling a pride in our community. That is why these incidents have been so deplorable and so disruptive. No one who wishes Northern Ireland well has gained anything from them. They can benefit only those who wish us harm, who seek to discredit us in the eyes of the world.

"As I think you know, Mr. Deputy Speaker, I received last Friday a letter from the hon. Member for Pottinger (Mr. T.W. Boyd) calling for an inquiry into these events. This suggestion may have been made with the best of intentions, but such an inquiry — whether held now or later — would in my view do no good and might even be harmful. There is no mystery about these disturbances; we all know their origins and subsequent pattern. What useful purpose would be served — particularly when peace has happily now returned to the area concerned — by a prolongation of public controversy? I might add that I can find no modern precedent in Great Britain for such an inquiry, although there too there have been in recent years a number of incidents of more or less serious civil disturbance.

"The House will, I know, feel greatly indebted to the various organisations who have contributed to the cessation of the disturbances. First the Churches themselves, both Protestant and Roman Catholic. They urged restraint. They spoke with the voice of charity and mutual understanding. The influence which they brought to bear was wholly beneficial. Then the Churches Industrial Council which pointed out the industrial harm which was being created, and last but by no means least the police, who in the most trying circumstances had the difficult task of enforcing law and order.

"We should also remember that only a tiny minority of the citizens of Belfast either provoked or took part in these disturbances. The great majority stood, as always, on the side of peace and order.

"While I can understand the provocation which exists where men associated with the I.R.A. offer themselves as candidates for a Parliament in which they do not intend to sit, equally no one can condone any utterance or action which wittingly or unwittingly contributes to a breach of the peace. Indeed most of us in this House would, I think, spend sleepless nights if we felt responsible in any way for the wounded now lying in hospital, and in particular the constable who so narrowly escaped death.

"Those of us responsible for the industrial development of this Province can only deplore world-wide publicity being given to events of this character when we have laboured to convince the world that Ulster is an ideal place in which to build a factory and give employment to our people. We cannot go back to the 1920s and 1930s when 100,000 unemployed were the order of the day and misery and privation stalked the streets of Belfast. I pray God that as we advance in wealth and education and maturity the dreadful scenes which we witnessed will never be repeated, and I trust that men of goodwill throughout our Province will work to that end." (Hansard, Vol 57, 7.10.64, Col 2835-2836.)

Thus O'Neill failed to face up to the events in West Belfast, putting them down to a throwback to the bad old days before he was Prime Minister. And he believed that a spot of economic growth and the resultant advances in "wealth and education and maturity" would turn sectarian politics into a polite affair and persuade Catholics to live forever as permanently frustrated but well-behaved Nationalists.

Doing its best to facilitate this retreat from reality, the News Letter said on the day after O'Neill's speech to Stormont that "the best thing that can be done about the Divis Street riots is to put them out of mind as quickly as possible — a bad dream, produced by a temporary indisposition" (NL 8.10.64). In line with this advice, the paper promptly closed down all correspondence on the subject in its letters page.

Chapter Five

1965
LEMASS AND O'NEILL

LEMASS

Following the October 1964 Election, political activity in Northern Ireland went into a lull. Such lulls were surprisingly common in the 1960s and it was a strange experience for this writer to come across periods of time when things like car accidents made the front page headlines in the News Letter.

Early in 1965, however, O'Neill did his very best to really stir things up. On January 14th, Sean Lemass became the first Taoiseach of the Irish Republic to visit Stormont. The extent to which this visit came out of the blue for everyone except O'Neill and his close advisers is captured in Brian Faulkner's account of the event:

> "One day in January 1965 at about 1 p.m. I was sitting in my office at Stormont working when the telephone rang. It was Cecil Bateman, then Secretary to the Cabinet, and he said, 'The Prime Minister is at the moment having lunch with Sean Lemass in Stormont House. He would like you to come over at three o'clock and meet him.' I think I said, 'You must be joking!' He soon convinced me that he was quite serious, and I arrived at the appointed hour to have tea and buns with the Taoiseach." (**Memoirs Of A Statesman**, p39.)

Following their meeting O'Neill and Lemass issued a joint statement which said:

> "We have today discussed matters in which there may prove to be a degree of common interest, and have agreed to explore further what specific measures may be possible or desirable by way of practical consultation and co-operation.
>
> "Our talks — which did not touch upon constitutional or political questions — have been conducted in a most amicable way and we look forward to a further discussion." (NL 15.1.1965.)

According to the standard version of the Lemass visit in the history books, the Unionist Party split down the middle, and O'Neill's premiership was doomed the moment the Taoiseach set foot in Stormont. This, in fact, is not an entirely accurate picture of the political repercussions of the event.

The truth is that doubts within the Unionist Party about O'Neill's leadership did not really surface until 1966. There were no strong feelings about the visit within the Protestant community and the initial reaction to it within Unionist ranks was generally favourable. The News Letter, for instance, greeted the event with a rare Page One Platform, which said that the Lemass/O'Neill meeting "must be hailed by all men of good will on either side of the Border" (ibid). The Westminster MP, Captain L.P.S Orr, who was certainly not a member of the liberal wing of the Party, stated that "the meeting is obviously to be welcomed", because it represented "a partial recognition of the Northern Ireland position on the part of Mr. Lemass", and a similar response was made by his fellow MP, Sir Knox Cunningham (ibid).

In fact, public criticism of O'Neill's initiative only came from Ian Paisley and three Stormont MPs: Desmond Boal, Dr. Robert Nixon and Edmond Warnock. Although Paisley did lead a 5,000 strong protest march against O'Neill at the end of February (NL 26.2.1965), no significant challenge to the Premier emerged from inside the Unionist Party. It was, therefore, no surprise when O'Neill received the backing of the Parliamentary Unionist Party in a two-hour meeting in early April (NL 8.4.1965). Indeed, the resolution passed by this meeting, expressing "overwhelming confidence in, and support for, Captain O'Neill", even received the support of Desmond Boal (ibid).

There is no real evidence to support the belief that the Unionist Party was immediately besieged by the "O'Neill Must Go" campaign following the first visit of Sean Lemass to Stormont. And while, in the wake of the visit, Paisley did call upon O'Neill to resign and go to the polls on the issue (NL 26.1.1965), this call received very little support at the time from other Unionists. When the province did go to the polls in November 1965, Paisley did not run a single candidate in any Constituency, while O'Neill's administration received a massive vote of confidence from the electorate.

The extent to which the O'Neill/Lemass talks were welcomed within Unionist ranks can be gauged from Mervyn Pauley's review of 1965 which was published in February 1966. Having summarised the various events of the year, Pauley wrote:

> "The history books, however, will give pride of place to the ice-breaking talks between Captain O'Neill and Mr. Lemass which took place on a sunny January afternoon and which were, it was generally agreed, fittingly preceded by a champagne luncheon at Stormont House... The meeting produced criticism from fairly predictable sources, but the weight of the praise diminished the dissidents' impact to that of irrational voices crying in the wilderness" (NL 2.2.1966).

It is, therefore, difficult to sustain the claim that O'Neill's premiership ran into its first major difficulties simply because the backwoods of the Unionist Party wouldn't wear the idea of establishing friendlier relationships with the Irish Republic. There was, in fact, a strong desire among Unionists in the 1960s to work with the Irish Government on economic matters, and to end what Faulkner called "the Cold War between North and South initiated by De Valera" (Memoirs, p39). A few days before the unexpected Lemass visit, for example, the Northern Ireland Cabinet had decided that Faulkner should meet the Minister responsible for tourism in the Republic to discuss co-operation on an all-Ireland basis (ibid).

Furthermore, the frequent meetings between Ministers from Belfast and Dublin, which occurred after January 1965, never provoked controversy. And it was William Craig and Brian Faulkner, the supposed backwoods enemies of O'Neill, who played the most prominent role in this area of cross-border co-operation. The most significant achievement of the North-South co-operation, the electricity grid link-up, was a product of negotiations between Faulkner and the Eire Minister, Erskine Childers.

Nevertheless, in spite of these favourable factors, the Lemass visit did eventually come back to haunt O'Neill. It is likely, for example, that doubts about North/South cooperation were a factor in the attempt to remove him as leader in September 1966. Part of the explanation for this must lie with O'Neill's style of leadership. The ridiculous secrecy with which he surrounded the whole Lemass visit certainly planted seeds of suspicion and mistrust about his intentions within the Unionist Party and the Protestant community. The decision not even to inform his Cabinet, let alone the Parliamentary Party, about the invitation to Sean Lemass was not just an unfortunate lapse of political judgement: it epitomised his entire approach to Government and society in Northern Ireland. Throughout his premiership he maintained a discreet distance between himself and the hoi polloi. He obviously saw no need to consult the Party rank and file over decisions and anyone who dared to question his word was simply branded as an irredeemable reactionary. This pompous posturing merely exacerbated the feelings of mistrust about him.

It is also true to say that mundane matters like electricity grid link-ups were not the only things on Captain O'Neill's mind when he invited Sean Lemass to Stormont. In his Autobiography he decribes the event as "a bold initiative", designed to "break Northern Ireland out of the chains of fear which had bound her for forty-three years" (p68). Central to this initiative was his desire to get the Nationalist Party to agree to become the Official Opposition at Stormont. In short, O'Neill thought that feeding tea and buns to the Taoiseach at Stormont was a major step towards solving the National Question for good and turning Stormont into a real Parliament.

If the intention had been to transform the nature of politics in the province, the Lemass visit might have been of some value, if it had been followed up by a real effort to provide Catholics with a political alternative to Nationalism. Under O'Neill's guidance, however, the "bold initiative" was designed solely to institutionalise the ghettoisation of the Catholic Community by making the Nationalist Party the Official Opposition.

The political stupidity of this approach may provide the best explanation for O'Neill's eventual problems over the Lemass visit to the North. O'Neill believed that Irish Nationalism had had its day and he acted accordingly. However, when the celebrations in Belfast for the fiftieth anniversary of the Easter Rising in April 1966 showed that Nationalism had not quite evaporated into the air, the Unionist Party began to have serious doubts about their leader. And this was when active support for Paisley really began to develop within the Protestant community

In a real sense, therefore, Terence O'Neill created the conditions which turned Ian Paisley into a functional politician. O'Neill unsettled the Protestant community for no real purpose other than to display his 'liberal' credentials.

He also raised the political expectations of the Catholic community without providing a political alternative to Nationalism. O'Neill believed that Catholics would not take their Nationalism seriously. Paisley, on the other hand, has never underestimated Catholic Nationalism and, shortly after the Lemass visit, he provided one of the best comments ever made on O'Neillism when he quoted the biblical prophet Jeremiah's statement: "Peace, peace, when there is no peace" (NL 26.1.1965).

O'NEILLISM MARCHES ON

Paisley's assessment of O'Neill, however, was not taken seriously within mainstream Unionism at the time. In the pages of the News Letter, for instance, the Prime Minister's status as a hero was enhanced by the Lemass visit. On January 18th, the paper published a lengthy interview with O'Neill by its political correspondent, Mervyn Pauley, which was entitled, **Ulster's Man Of The Year On Vital Issues** (NL 18.1.1965). During this interview, the Premier was kind enough to point out the unimportance of trifling things like politics compared to the glory of dear old Ulster:

"As for the divisions in our society, I sometimes wonder whether we do much good by so frequently talking about them. There are so many things which should unite all Ulster people. If we emphasise these things, the divisions will seem less significant" (ibid).

The most notable part of the interview came when Pauley put a very sharp question to the Prime Minister regarding the whole basis of his claims about the virtues of devolved Government. Pauley asked:

"With the expensive programmes planned for Ulster (in fields of transport, town planning and education) is there a danger that the self-help doctrine could develop a somewhat hollow ring about it, in view of the consideration that the British Government will have to subsidise heavily these ambitious plans?" (ibid).

In the face of such a perceptive point, O'Neill had no option but to retreat into an integrationist argument:

"I do not think 'subsidy' is... appropriate. You cannot talk about 'the British Government' as if it were some kind of external agency. We are part of Britain, we pay virtually the same taxation as the rest of Britain and we expect to develop our area to the highest British standards. It is true that we could not pay for all these ambitious programmes out of taxation raised in Northern Ireland; but you could probably say the same of an area such as North East England." (Ibid.)

On February 2nd, O'Neill's "bold initiative" with Lemass achieved its desired result. On the prompting of the Taoiseach, the Nationalist Party agreed to become the Official Opposition at Stormont. The decision was reached in Room 43 of Stormont buildings, which was, in fact, the Official Opposition room. For years, though, the word "Official" on the door had been covered by a strip of brown paper (BT 2.2.1965). The News Letter did not consider the removal of this paper to be important enough for an editorial. The comments of the supposedly more liberal Belfast Telegraph, however, reveal the breathtaking smugness of the O'Neillite middle class at the time:

"Captain O'Neill has a fair chance of changing the face of Unionism, as well as of the province.

"Already the Nationalist Party, in another rejection of the straitjacket of the past, has become the Official Opposition. Democratically this must be welcomed; in the same way there would be a welcome for its re-organisation on normal political lines instead of the present control by the few.

"In the train of the Lemass meeting, goodwill is accorded to Mr. McAteer and his colleagues on coming to the front. Their belief in a united Ireland is acknowledged, and it remains for them to fill their new role with respect for Parliament and the sense of responsibility proper to a Party which bids to be an alternative government .

"The point is important since Nationalists have seldom shown much appreciation of the problems of administration, or indeed of the way Northern Ireland has been transformed before their own eyes. In what has still to be done they must be builders, not wreckers." (BT 2.4.1965.)

It is difficult to comment rationally on these statements, other than to say that they help to explain why a war broke out in Northern Ireland in the late 1960s. It is unlikely that O'Neill spent much time thinking about the political position of Catholics. Then, as now, members of the Unionist Party seemed barely aware of the existence of the Catholic community and they certainly made no attempt to understand it. At any rate, whether it was intentional or not, O'Neill effectively gave Catholics no option but to stay with the Nationalist Party in the mid-60s. And while O'Neill was securing the permanent political isolation of the Catholic community, his supporters in the press were rubbing salt in the wounds.

Although there may have been a limited role for a Government in the Stormont set-up, there was certainly nothing constructive for an Opposition Party to do. There was also no likelihood of the Nationalist Party beating the Unionists at the polls, and even if such an unlikely event occurred it would have meant the end of "Northern Ireland", rather than Eddie McAteer becoming the Prime Minister at Stormont. Nevertheless, in spite of the fact that the Nationalist Party could never be more than a small and ineffectual protest group, the Belfast Telegraph declared that its new role as Official Opposition meant it had to behave with a "sense of responsibility proper to a Party which bids to be an alternative government". It would have been more honest if the editorial had just come out and said "Croppies lie down".

As might be expected, there were strong feelings of confidence and ambition about the Unionist Government in the months following the Lemass visit. O'Neill had just pulled off his biggest ever stunt by producing a Taoiseach almost literally out of a hat on the steps of Stormont. Then the Nationalist Party had agreed to add a touch of respectability to the Stormont arrangements by becoming the Official Opposition. Signs of the up-beat mood among Unionists can be found in a number of speeches made by the Prime Minister himself in the first half of 1965. On February 17th, for instance, he opened a Debate on a Government White Paper on economic development by saying:

> "If, in this day and age, we prove to be more devoted to local interests, to sectional interests, to class interests than to the overall Northern Ireland interest, we will never meet the targets of these plans, which we see merely as a first stage in Ulster's forward progress." (NL 19.2.1965.)

At the end of April, in his well-received speech to the annual Unionist conference, O'Neill told the delegates that "it was not enough to be just part of the United Kingdom", and that his administration was aiming to make Northern Ireland "a progressive part of that Kingdom" (NL 1.5.1965).

Captain O'Neill developed his vision of the future in a speech at the annual Lord Mayor's Show Banquet at the City Hall. He said that if he had to "sum up, in two words, the 'flavour' of the new Ulster" the Government was working to create, he "would use the words 'opportunity' and 'partnership'." (NL 24.5.1965.) He went on to claim that "when Ulstermen are united, they are a formidable force — as the history of this century has shown on more than one occasion", and to bemoan the fact that Ulster people too often dissipate their "energies in arguments about comparative trivialities." (Ibid.)

The first half of 1965, therefore, saw O'Neill reiterating some of the main themes of his political philosophy. An underlying hint of Ulster Nationalism and his belief in the primacy of the economy can be seen in his emphasis on the Ulster identity of the Northern Ireland people and his calls for "comparative trivialities" and "local", "class" and "sectional" interests to be set aside in the interests of the economic progress of the province. In short, O'Neill was appealing to everyone to forget about politics and give their uncritical support to the Unionist Government.

There is no doubt that the Prime Minister had his fair share of adoring fans within the Unionist Party at this time. In early April, for example, Robin Bailie, the Vice-Chairman of Belfast Central Young Unionist Association, sang his Leader's praises:

> "In the space of less than two years the Prime Minister has succeeded in solving the problem of the I.C.T.U. He has placed north-south relations on a reasonable basis and has taken the sting out of the community tension which was sapping the vigour of the Province... Above all, he has presented to every section of the community in Northern Ireland and to the people of the Republic of Ireland, Great Britain and throughout the world an intelligible and persuasive view of Unionism. The image of Ulster and Unionism is better now than it has ever been." (NL 8.4.1965.)

Bailie's speech was a response to criticisms of O'Neill that had been made by the Stormont MPs, Edmond Warnock and Dr. Nixon (NL 6 & 7.4.1965), who had raised a number of issues, including the secrecy over the Lemass visit. Nixon went as far as to call for O'Neill's resignation and replacement by Brian

Faulkner (ibid). However, as has already been stated, these calls came to nothing in the subsequent two hour meeting of the Parliamentary Unionist Party, which passed a motion of confidence in the Prime Minister. According to Faulkner, however, "there was some straight talking at the meeting" (Memoirs p40), with Faulkner himself stresssing his "continuing loyalty to O'Neill and saying quite frankly that many of his problems arose from lack of consultation." (Ibid.) The decision of the meeting to back O'Neill received a welcome from the News Letter. It published an editorial the following day which stated that "the Parliamentary Unionist Party has shown good sense in giving an expression of renewed confidence in its leader" and asserted that "there should be no doubt within the ranks of the Party either inside or outside Stormont where Unionists stand in regard to the progressive policies which have emerged since Captain O'Neill assumed office."

STRAWS IN THE WIND

The degree of confidence exhibited by the O'Neillites in the first half of 1965 seems to have created complacency about the future. For, at the same time as the Government was congratulating itself on provincial progress, a few signs of trouble were emerging.

The first of these was the controversial decision to site Northern Ireland's new University in Coleraine rather than Derry. Anger at this decision was evident on February 16, when 2,000 cars formed a "siege of Stormont" in protest (NL 17.2.1965). It is beyond the scope of this chapter to evaluate the claims and counter-claims concerning discrimination against Catholics and the North West of the province that were made about the siting of the University. It should be recorded, however, that the decision rankled with many in the Catholic community and certainly helped to fuel the resentment which eventually boiled over into the Civil Rights movement. The same can be said, though probably to a lesser degree, of the creation of the new town, Craigavon, in the East of the province and, indeed, of the decision to name it after a former Unionist Prime Minister.

In the month of March, the Unionist Party addressed itself to two of the issues which were later to become central to the demands of the Civil Rights movement: discrimination and reform of the franchise.

On March 15, the News Letter reported on a weekend conference on discrimination organised by the National Council of Civil Liberties which had been addressed by John D. Taylor, a member of the Executive Committee of the Ulster Unionist Council (now Official Unionist MP for Strangford). His speech vividly illustrates the political degeneration that was occurring within Ulster Unionism. He stated:

> "There is a new feeling of confidence in Ulster. We are preparing for the day when there will be no reason for discrimination. In other words, at this present moment, Ulster is solving its own community problems. We are determined that this Province shall maintain its position within the United Kingdom and on

that basis exercise its contribution to the conflict with international Communism. It is the intention of the Unionist Party to modernise this Province so that all, Protestant and Roman Catholic, will benefit from an improved way of life. In the society we see ahead there will be no place for second-class citizens." (NL 15.3.1965.)

This speech reveals that Taylor was an avid O'Neillite in 1965. He also told the conference that the "Government at Stormont is enthusiastically tackling the problems that challenge our whole society", and that the "Government of N. Ireland Act 1920 [sic] secures complete equality and freedom for all" (ibid). His belief that the problem of discrimination could best be tackled by a Unionist Government at Stormont reveals again the extent to which the devolutionary spirit was at large in Unionist ranks.

The truth is that discrimination was the inevitable accompaniment of the system of government foisted on Northern Ireland in 1920, rather than the product of the will or behaviour of the communal Party which had to govern under that system. The Stormont system reinforced all the pre-existing communal divisions by connecting them with the process of government. In the absence of the party politics of the state, the two communities could not divide and their elements recombine on the basis of class or social philosophy. And, while the two communities remained intact as political blocs, devolved government was, of necessity, continuous government by the same party, and the patronage network of that party naturally extended itself. In democracies the check on patronage is not moral restraint within a party, but the real prospect of electoral defeat. And in regions of England where Local Government has been dominated by one party for generations on end — as for example Labour Party predominance in the North East — party patronage was just as extensive as in Northern Ireland.

The Unionist Party should not have answered charges of discrimination by arguing that everything had been fine under its administration. It should have pointed out that it had never wanted to govern the province in the first place, and that the ill-effects of one party rule at Stormont were the responsibility of those who framed the 1920 Government Of Ireland Act. However, by the 1960s, as Taylor's speech illustrates, the overwhelming majority of Unionists had grown strongly attached to the arrangements imposed on Northern Ireland by the 1920 Act and, especially, to the belief that defending the Union meant defending the Stormont system of government. In short, they put themselves in the position of having to defend the indefensible. Anyone, therefore, who has ever wondered why the Unionist Government was so systematically hammered by the propagagandists of the Civil Rights movement need only look at John Taylor's attempts in 1965 to prove that "complete equality and freedom" for Catholics could be assured by a Unionist Government representing the Protestant community and under no threat of electoral defeat.

Later in March 1965, the Home Affairs Minister, Brian McConnell, reported that changes in the franchise for Stormont elections were under consideration.

He hinted that he was planning to abolish the business and special company director's votes and the University seats. These hints received enthusiastic support from the News Letter in an editorial, entitled **One Man, One Vote:**

> "In a democracy the principle of 'one man one vote' is a corollary of the ideology on which the system is based and this has operated in Great Britain for a number of years. That Northern Ireland has not followed the Westminster example conveys a reluctance to break with a practice which is regarded with some suspicion. The Government, backed so solidly as it is by the country at large can well afford to forgo whatever little advantage accrues to it from plural voting. Above all, a change would deprive enemies of Ulster of ammunition for sniping at the electoral system in Northern Ireland." (NL 25.3.1965.)

Significantly, however, McConnell had made no reference to the need for reform in the area of local government, where the ratepayers' franchise still existed. On this, the News Letter argued that "different criteria apply in the field of local government where it is a sound principle that not only should there be no representation without taxation, but that full recognition should be given to the stake in the community or village of those who pay the piper." (Ibid.)

Given the lack of controversy over the changes to the franchise for Stormont elections, it is more than likely that the Government could, at the same time, have also pushed through a reform of the Local Government franchise without it becoming a major issue. This the Government did not do, even though, as it found to its cost in 1968/69, the absence of "one man one vote" at Local Government level also provided "ammunition for sniping at the electoral system in Northern Ireland." Once again, the O'Neill administration had its mind fixed on higher things and failed to adequately address a practical political problem which existed in the real world.

THE SUMMER OF '65
The Twelfth

As ever, the summer of 1965 began for Unionists with the 12th of July processions. The "Twelfth" in 1965 provided further proof that the Unionist Party had not been overly concerned by the visit of Sean Lemass to Stormont. Thus, one of the Orange Order's resolutions on the day offered qualified support for O'Neill's attempts to promote cross-border co-operation:

> "We are conscious of the efforts the Prime Minister and the Government are making for a better understanding between the peoples of the island, which we trust will lead to an extension of the economy of the countries, to their mutual benefit, thus leading to more harmonious relationships between all men.
>
> "Whilst we welcome this new approach to advance the prosperity of our new country, we are also aware of the continuing assault on our constitutional position. This we will resolutely resist." (NL 13.7.1965)

The speeches made on the Twelfth which mentioned the Lemass visit were all favourable. For example, the Stormont MP, Walter Scott, said at Annalong: "It is no threat to Northern Ireland if we seek to improve our trade and commerce with the Republic." (Ibid.) And at Limavady, Joseph Burns MP claimed: "the O'Neill-Lemass talks have led to a recognition that Northern Ireland is a separate country with a right to govern itself [sic]", and therefore constituted "a major breakthrough in the thinking South of the Border." (Ibid.) Burns, incidentally, was later to become one of the Unionist MPs involved in the backbench revolt against Terence O'Neill in January 1969. From the remarks quoted above, it can be concluded that, whatever turned him against the Prime Minister, it was definitely not the Taoiseach's visit to Stormont in January 1965.

One of the more interesting speeches of the day was made at Augher by W.F. McCoy, QC, the Stormont MP for South Tyrone. McCoy, a genuine right-wing Unionist, had made a name for himself within the Party in the 1940s and '50s by advocating Dominion Status for Northern Ireland as a means of avoiding socialist legislation implemented at Westminster by a Labour Government. His calls went unheeded, largely because of the commitment of the then Prime Minister, Lord Brookeborough, to the principle of parity with the rest of the UK.

In July 1965, however, McCoy was still fighting the good fight only months before his retirement from politics. (He did not stand for re-election in the Stormont Election in November). In his speech to the assembled brethren at Augher, McCoy "described Ulster's constitution as a patchwork quilt and said that a new one was needed". To illustrate his point, he claimed that "by reason of the constitution, the capital gains tax had been imposed on Northern Ireland" earlier in the year. "Had we the necessary powers," he concluded, "that tax would never have been passed at Stormont" (ibid).

CONSERVATIVE BOW GROUP

Later in July, a very different criticism of the Stormont arrangements was made. The quarterly magazine of the Conservative Party's influential Bow Group, **Crossbow**, published an editorial on Ulster Unionism. Having noted a "new note of shrillness" in the propaganda of some Unionists (NL 20.7.1965). The editorial stated:

"Ulster Unionists have a perfectly sensible way out of their difficulties without having to wave the Orange flag quite so hysterically. By all means let them inveigh against drifting into union with the South — but let them at the same time call for a real union with England, Wales and Scotland.

"Instead of the 12 MPs who today represent some 900,000 voters at Westminster there should be 18, even if some of them are Nationalists, or, who knows (in time), Labour. Ulster should be treated by Westminster as a proper region, in the same way as the North-East or Scotland or Merseyside. How long would Sunderland or Glasgow or Birkenhead have tolerated Belfast's rate of unemployment?

"In return, Ulster should cease to cling to the shadowy illusion that it has self-government and a parliament of its own. We all know by now that Ulster will fight. Will it also be right?" (NL and BT 20.7.1965).

Not surprisingly, the Bow Group application of logic was not to the liking of the Unionist Family. The Westminster MP for South Belfast, Rafton Pounder, claimed that the article was "based on factual inaccuracies", and that its conclusions were "erroneous" (BT 20.7.1965). And, although the News Letter did not respond to the Bow Group arguments in its editorial columns, the Belfast Telegraph was quick to defend the honour of Stormont. Its editorial took particular exception to the Bow Group comments on the "shadowy illusion" that Northern Ireland has "self-government and a parliament of its own". In reply, the Telegraph claimed that "the Northern Ireland Prime Minister and Cabinet are under no illusion that they are at the head of a self-governing state." (Ibid.)

The Bow group article, therefore, brought into the open many of the contradictions in the Unionist attitude to devolution in the 1960s. In a sense, the Belfast Telegraph was correct to say that Terence O'Neill was under no illusion that Northern Ireland was a self-governing state. Throughout his premiership, he readily admitted that overall sovereignty rested with the British Government. Nevertheless, the logic of his whole approach to Government was that Northern Ireland was a state. He generated illusions about the autonomy of the Stormont parliament and claimed that the province benefitted from its exclusion from the centre of political power in the UK: the left-right party political conflict. For O'Neill, the attraction of devolution seems to have rested on little more than its capacity for generating political glory. Being Prime Minister of Northern Ireland may not have given him the opportunity to achieve anything in the policy sphere, but it gave him ample opportunity to jet round the world and put Ulster on the map and himself in the history books.

Others in the Unionist Party, however, were not content to indulge in spurious rhetoric about devolution and tried to follow O'Neillism through to its natural conclusion. This was particularly true of William Craig, a very close associate of O'Neill's for a large part of his premiership. As later events were to prove, Craig came to believe during the 60s that Northern Ireland had Federal Status within the UK and consequently, that the Stormont Parliament had full authority over Ulster affairs.

The split between O'Neill and Craig, however, did not occur until the end of 1968. In 1965, the Unionist Government had no intention of following the advice of the Bow Group; it was united in its desire to cling firmly to the "shadowy illusion" that it had self-government. Within months, though, the contradictions inherent in its commitment to devolution created problems for the Government.

LABOUR'S NATIONAL PLAN

The first of these problems arose in September following the announcement of the Labour Government's National Plan. The plan was introduced by Labour Minister, George Brown, and included a £900 million Development Plan for Northern Ireland. It also referred directly to the province in relation to what was being planned regionally in the areas of housing and education and named Northern Ireland as one of five areas where "the greatest scope for faster economic growth is to be found." (NL 17.9.1965.)

Because of the close financial relationship which existed between the British Treasury and the Northern Ireland Ministry of Finance, there was never any likelihood of Stormont doing anything other than fall in behind the Labour Government's Plan. Thus, the response of the Northern Ireland Government to the National Plan stressed that its own Wilson Plan fitted into the National Plan, while "still preserving its own identity" (ibid). And Captain O'Neill publicly welcomed the Plan at a North Belfast Unionist meeting where he said: "Make no mistake about it — Ulster intends to pull her full weight in the new Britain."

Such ready subservience to socialism was too much for the right-wing instincts of William Craig, who at that time was the Stormont Minister for Development. Craig's repressed Tory tendencies were released at a Young Unionist rally in Belfast where he described George Brown's plan as "nonsense". His speech also called on the Tory and Unionist MPs at Westminster to bring "the period of uncertainty" in the House of Commons to a quick end by accepting Harold Wilson's threat of an immediate election if they tried to interfere with Government plans (NL 29.9.1965).

Bill Craig's outburst produced a political storm, with George Brown himself reportedly "angry and astonished" at the remarks (ibid). There was anger too among the trade unionists from Northern Ireland who were attending the British Labour Party Annual Conference at the time of Craig's comments. After a meeting of Northern Ireland trade union delegates, a statement was issued which said:

> "We, the Northern Ireland members of trade union delegations attending the British Labour conference have heard with deep concern of the statements made by Mr. Craig which have caused embarassment to the N. Ireland delegates who feel that their efforts to achieve the utmost consideration for the people of N. Ireland by the Westminster government have been seriously retarded by Mr. Craig's statements. This speech surprised and shocked many people here and in our view has damaged the N. Ireland-Westminster relationship and introduced sharp political issues into this relationship between the two Governments, a situation scrupulously avoided by Labour Ministers visiting N. Ireland." (NL 2.10.1965.)

The controversy over the Stormont-Westminster relationship was deepened by O'Neill himself, during a visit to Northern Ireland by the newly elected leader of the Conservative Party, Edward Heath. Introducing Heath to an audience at the Institute of Directors in Belfast, O'Neill spoke of his delight at Heath's election as Tory leader, and described him as "the future Prime Minister of the United Kingdom" (ibid).

In response to the comments of both Craig and O'Neill, the maverick Unionist MP, Dr. Robert Nixon, said that he was "astonished that the harmonious relationship between Stormont and Westminster has been broken by political leaders in Northern Ireland", and claimed that "both Mr. Wilson and Mr. Brown could infer from these recent statements in N. Ireland that the people here wished to remain part of the UK only if a Conservative Government is in power." (NL 5.10.1965.)

In the event, the controversy over the anti-Labour comments was short-lived, and an NILP censure motion on Craig was defeated in Stormont by 28 votes to 8 (NL 8.10.1965). More important, the Tory sentiments of Unionist Ministers continued to count for nothing in the real world as the Stormont Administration went on implementing the policies of Harold Wilson's Government.

On the other hand, it is possible that the political repercussions of the comments were greater in Westminster than they were in Stormont. The Tory sabre-rattling by Craig and, to a lesser extent, by O'Neill, may have increased the feelings of antagonism towards Unionists that were developing on the Labour benches. This antagonism was directed mainly towards the 12 Unionist MPs at Westminster, who sat with the Conservative Opposition and could vote on any issue despite the fact that, by convention, the House of Commons did not even discuss Northern Ireland affairs. This anomaly annoyed many on the Labour side, particularly in the period between the 1964 and 1966 elections when Labour's majority was fragile, and led to calls for the placing of restrictions on the Unionist participation in the Commons.

O'NEILL ON DEVOLUTION

The issues raised during the public debate over Craig's remarks about the National Plan quickly surfaced again following a speech made by O'Neill to the Court Ward Unionist Association in Belfast on October 18. The Premier's speech dealt with the subject dearest to his heart: the virtues of devolution. His comments on the vital subject of parity with Westminster provoked an angry response from the Northern Ireland Labour Party, which accused O'Neill of wanting parity only when a Conservative Government was in power. When replying to criticism of his speech in Stormont, O'Neill claimed that it had not been fully reported in the Press and had been misunderstood. The full text of the speech suggests that he may have had a point.

> "The words 'step-by-step' and 'parity' have become a part of our political vocabulary in Northern Ireland. Unfortunately, those who use them do not always appear to have a real understanding of their meaning.
> "'Parity' in the widest sense is the overall aim of our policy. I would define it as the position which will be reached when the general level of services and amenities and the general standard of living in Northern Ireland are as high as in Great Britain. This is our long-term goal, which we are trying to attain by every means at our disposal.
> "'Step-by-step' is one of the means — but only one — which we use in working towards that end. It means that we offer our citizens the cash benefits of the Welfare State at the same level as in Great Britain, and that we seek to attain as high an overall standard in the social services generally. This does not mean that in the social services — other than the cash social services — we

must necessarily adopt the precise policies or financial methods used on the other side of the Irish Sea. We have, for instance, been free to spend twice as much per head on our hospitals, and in housing, to set up an agency — the Housing Trust — which has no English equivalent. We have been free to develop a system of education which we believe to be quite as good as any in the United Kingdom, but which recognises the existence of special factors here.

"Much of our capital expenditure has been not so much a case of 'step-by-step' as of 'step-ahead-of-step'. In those areas where we have leeway to make up, there has been a generous recognition by successive United Kingdom Governments that more than normal measures are needed to close the gap. This has applied, too, in the wider field of economic and industrial development, in which we have maintained since 1945 a more generous and flexible range of inducements than any other part of the country.

"There are still other fields where the concepts of 'parity' and 'step-by-step' do not really apply at all — nor should they. In purely social questions I believe that it is right that we should do what we think is best, taking full account of course of what is done in Great Britain, but also bearing in mind the particular circumstances of Ulster and —not least — the views of those who return us to Parliament.

"There are a good many members of the Opposition who want to have the best of both worlds. On the one hand, they want to be able to denigrate our political institutions by claiming that we are a mere 'rubber stamp' with no real powers. On the other hand, whenever some specific policy adopted in London happens to appeal to them, we are told that 'step-by-step' demands that we should follow suit.

"This is an age of 'regionalism', and it is a pretty fair bet that within Great Britain we will see further measures of decentralization on the executive, if not on the legislative, level. This whole process will be pointless, however, unless regional government is properly responsive to the special needs, the special traditions and, not least, the special views of its own area.

"I hope, therefore, that no one who hears about 'step-by-step' will see the Parliament of Northern Ireland as a kind of pet dog trotting at its master's heels. 'Parity', in the widest sense, is the end; 'step-by-step' is a part of the means; but in many fields we have the right and indeed the duty to go our own way.

"'Step-by-step' assures Northern Ireland citizens of the same pensions when they retire, the same benefits if they are unemployed, as are received by the people of Great Britain. Under our new legislation recently introduced at Stormont they will be assured of substantial help to tide them over any period of redundancy. In any society, there are always some industries which are contracting while others are expanding. This means that many people will have to contemplate a change of employment, and I think it is only right that society should provide a cushion against the hardship which can result from that process.

"But we should also consider some of the benefits which we in Northern Ireland enjoy which are outside the scope of 'step-by-step' but are rather the results of the forward-looking policies of our own Government. In housing, I have already mentioned the position of the Housing Trust, but in addition we have had special measures in Northern Ireland to encourage the owner-occupier, which have no counterpart elsewhere. I like to think that, just as the old Land Purchase Acts encouraged the farmer to take over the ownership of his land, so our housing policy has encouraged home-ownership. More than other parts of the United Kingdom, we have demonstrated our belief in the 'property-owning democracy.'

"In the attraction of industry, it is only very recently that anything similar to our Capital Grants scheme has been introduced in Great Britain, and the grant rates there are substantially lower. There is, understandably, a great deal of interest in new industry, but no one should overlook what has been done to modernise the older industries of the Province which still employ so many of our people. It is in no small degree due to these policies that such industries as linen and shipbuilding have made such a massive and impressive come-back from some of their earlier difficulties. In 1960 the British Government set up an office in New York to attract new American industries to this country. But it was not first in the field; the Northern Ireland Government already had an office there three years before the British office was set up.

"What all this means is that we need, more than ever, the ideas and hard work of this community. Our connection with Great Britain gives us the firmest of foundations, but it does not exempt us from the need to build ourselves. With our own Parliament and our own Government machine, we have built-in advantages over any region of Britain. We are close to the needs and desires of our own people, and can seek within Northern Ireland suitable Ulster solutions to the problems which face Britain today." (NL 19.10.65; see also, **Ulster At The Crossroads**, 1969 Faber and Faber, p85-88.)

It is essential at this stage to emphasise the fundamental difference between Terence O'Neill's conception of devolution and the normally understood meaning of the word. Those who have advocated devolution in Great Britain in recent decades have never suggested that the Labour and Conservative Parties should withdraw from a region once a devolved assembly was established. Consequently, if the people of Scotland and Wales had accepted Devolution in the 1979 referenda, they would have still been able to take part in the election of the sovereign government at Westminster. This was not the case, however, in the fifty years of devolved government in Northern Ireland. And that was how Captain O'Neill liked it. He believed in devolved government and devolved politics; a Stormont Parliament and Stormont politics. His influence lives on in those who nowadays reject the very idea of the people of Northern Ireland being able to join and vote for the Labour and Tory Parties in preference for the return of a devolved administration, where local politicians could make minor amendments to policies introduced at Westminster by an unaccountable government.

The speech quoted above represents Terence O'Neill's most detailed defence of the Stormont system of government. If the grandiose rhetoric is ignored, his list of the wondrous achievements made possible by 45 years of devolution is hardly impressive.

The most significant claim in the speech was that much of Northern Ireland's capital expenditure had been "not so much a case of 'step-by-step' as of 'step-ahead-of-step'". The latter phrase creates an impression of the Stormont Government bravely beating a path where Westminster feared to tread. In the next sentence, however, O'Neill explained the actual meaning of his claim:

> "In those areas where we have leeway to make up, there has been a generous recognition by successive United Kingdom Governments that more than normal measures are needed to close the gap".

In other words, thanks to the "generosity" of the British Treasury, Stormont had been able to spend more than the UK average in some areas in order to bring standards in the province into line with those in the rest of the state. O'Neill was, therefore, arguing that devolution was necessary in order to achieve integration! The phrase "step ahead of step" is not an apt description of this process. It was more a case of Northern Ireland taking some big steps to catch up with the rest of the UK.

This piece of verbal juggling was followed up by a reference to "purely social questions" where "the concepts of 'parity and 'step-by-step' do not really apply at all". In the Stormont Debate on his speech, O'Neill elaborated on this comment. He claimed that, if 'parity' applied on social matters, "Bills might... be expected to permit the Sunday opening of public houses, and to permit the operation of casinos in Northern Ireland" (21.10.1965 Col 2422).

Overall, Stormont's major achievements as listed in the Speech amount to: the existence of the Housing Trust; an education system which is "as good as any in the United Kingdom, but which recognises the existence of special factors"; and Northern Ireland having a promotional office in New York three years before Great Britain. The "Ulster solution" in the education field was the dubious achievement of segregated schooling. The other achievements listed in the speech (and the additions to the list by O'Neill in the subsequent Stormont Debate) raise two significant points. Firstly, it is highly questionable whether any of these policy differences between Northern Ireland and Great Britain required the existence of legislative devolution in the province. Parity, it should be remembered, does not mean uniformity and there have always been significant regional differences throughout the UK in areas like Local Government and education.

Secondly, it should be noted that all of the Stormont policies referred to by O'Neill had been introduced before he became Prime Minister. This lack of innovation by his Government was not corrected in the remaining four years of his Premiership. Ironically, despite all the pro-devolution rhetoric, the O'Neill administration did nothing new with the Stormont arrangements between 1963 and 1969. The only significant policy initiative was its recognition of the Northern Ireland Committee of the Irish Congress of Trade Unions in 1964.

The main impact of O'Neillism was its encouragement of a reactionary "little Ulster" outlook within Ulster Unionism. This devolutionary spirit made its presence felt, not in the implementation of new policies, but in a reluctance to follow Great Britain immediately in a number of areas of seemingly secondary importance.

Thus, O'Neill's controversial speech to the Court Ward Unionists was, in large part, just a response to demands for an Ombudsman for Northern Ireland. This was made clear by O'Neill himself in Stormont:

> "If I had one thing more than another in mind when I was speaking that night it was the question of the ombudsman which had been raised comparatively recently. As I understand it, there is a White Paper before the Westminster Parliament about an ombudsman. This, in time, will presumably lead to legislation and possibly in two years from now there will be an ombudsman in Great Britain. It is only reasonable that we in Northern Ireland should not rush into this experiment but that we should wait and see how it develops." (Hansard, 21.10.1965 Col 2417.)

(Ironically, the appointment of an Ombudsman suddenly became a matter of great urgency for the Unionist Government in the wake of the disturbances at the Derry Civil Rights march in October 1968.)

The reluctance of the O'Neill Government to bring Northern Ireland into line with Great Britain on policies like the appointment of an Ombudsman was drawn attention to by the NILP in its response to O'Neill's comments on devolution and parity. For example, Tom Boyd, the leader of the Parliamentary NILP, stated at a meeting of Clifton NILP:

> "Here's how the Unionists have made Ulster really different. We do not have compensation for victims of criminal violence; we have waited seventeen years for legal aid; we will not have an Ombudsman; our consumer protection legislation, particularly in weights and measures, is years behind Britain; on capital punishment our law is and will remain different; and on electoral reform, Britain has one man one vote for fifteen years and we are still without change." (NL 21.10.1965.)

The Unionist desire to keep Ulster a little bit different proved to be their undoing. The Civil Rights movement was based on a strategy of exploiting the differences between Stormont and Westminster. It would have had no impact, but for the attachment of Unionists to Stormont and its trappings. In short, O'Neillism left Unionism wide open for the assault which came in the late 60s.

Some of the issues referred to by Tom Boyd in his speech to Clifton NILP were to feature prominently in the demands of the Civil Rights agitators. Nevertheless, in spite of their eventual importance, none of the anomalies between Stormont and Westminster could form the basis for the development of class politics in Northern Ireland. Despite the rhetoric about "self-government", the Unionist Government had no intention of breaking with the principle of parity in social welfare legislation. Consequently, any significant achievement made by the Labour Party at Westminster automatically applied in Northern Ireland. And because of their exclusion from the Labour Party, Northern Ireland socialists could only engage in shadow-boxing and attempt to portray the Unionists as enemies of the working-class.

The NILP reaction to O'Neill's speech to the Court Ward Unionist Association represented such an attempt. But it was an extremely spirited piece of shadow-boxing, and it certainly irritated Captain O'Neill. During the

Stormont exchanges on his speech, the statesmanlike Prime Minister struck the Despatch Box forcibly on two separate occasions to emphasise his indignation.

These exchanges also contained two interruptions by the Nationalist MP, Patrick Gormley, which are worth recording. The first came when O'Neill declared that he would "fight a long way to maintain" the "separate and distinct benefits" made possible by Stormont. Gormley commented: "the Prime Minister is a good home ruler" to which O'Neill replied: "Maybe I am in a modified form; let us agree on that point at least" (Hansard, 21.10.1965 Col. 2421). The second interruption was in response to a claim by O'Neill that he was "solidly behind the British Welfare State" to which Gormley said: "The Prime Minister is a Socialist now" (Col 2427).

The forcefulness with which the Prime Minister attacked the NILP in this Stormont debate led more than one Opposition MP to conclude that an election was in the offing. They were right. Within days, November 25th, 1965 was announced as the polling day for the Stormont Election.

O'NEILL'S ELECTION TRIUMPH

During the election campaign, Captain O'Neill claimed that he had gone to the polls early in order to avoid a clash with a Westminster election and the highly charged atmosphere which might surround the celebration of the 50th Anniversary of the Easter Rising (NL 5.11.1965). A couple of months later, however, the Prime Minister told a meeting of North Down Unionists that he had "surprised the people of Northern Ireland with a pre-Christmas General Election" because he had become concerned at the gradual rise of the NILP over the preceding thirteen years and wanted to contain it (NL 12.2.1966).

O'Neill's worries about the growth of the NILP are also referred to in Brian Faulkner's memoirs which note that the Prime Minister was "very anxious to prevent it attracting any further support" (Memoirs Of A Statesman, p30). Such anxiety had no rational basis, as the NILP had only four seats at Stormont and posed absolutely no threat to the Unionist Government. Nevertheless, the Ulster Unionist Party devoted its entire election campaign in November 1965 to crushing this fragile base. Such behaviour represented the peak of stupidity, given O'Neill's determination to stir up political activity under the Stormont arrangements. Sectarian friction was always likely in these circumstances. But if anything could have lessened that likelihood it was the existence of a strong NILP as a non-sectarian, non-nationalist alternative to Unionism.

The 1965 Stormont election campaign saw O'Neillism at its zenith. It achieved a level of Unionist unity unheard of since, with members of the Unionist old guard standing on the same Manifesto as the Party's new Yuppie intake. And even on the hustings, loyalist backwoodsmen, like Johnny McQuade, preached the same politics as rising 'liberal' stars like Roy Bradford. Both men threw themselves wholeheartedly behind O'Neill's campaign against the NILP

This campaign received a couple of early boosts. Shortly after the election date had been set, the Government announced that it had learnt of an IRA threat against the Northern Ireland Cabinet. This timely reminder of the mortal threat hanging over the "beloved province of Ulster" also gave the Unionist Government a great deal of free publicity in the media. The News Letter exploited the fortunate coincidence to the full by giving front page headlines to the story accompanied by photographs of every single member of the Cabinet (NL 11.11.65).

The second boost came when Harold Wilson's Labour Government announced that the Sea Eagle Anti-Submarine Base at Derry was to be moved to Plymouth. This decision, of course, had nothing to do with the NILP. But that fact did not deter Unionist candidates from holding it responsible for the decision. Thus, Roy Bradford, the Unionist candidate in the Victoria Constituency, said :

> "Now that the Labour Government had decided to liquidate the Sea Eagle base, had Mr. Bleakley any inside information when Short and Harland could expect the Socialist chopper?" (NL 29.10.1965).

Overall, the Unionist Party launched a very effective two-pronged attack on the NILP. Firstly, Unionist candidates consistently stressed Government commitment to parity in the field of social welfare. Captain O'Neill, himself, declared, during a television election broadcast, that "the Unionist Party and the Unionist Government are all completely behind the Welfare State" , and that he had personally "gloried in the Welfare State" (NL 24.11.1965). Emphasis by Unionist candidates on their Party's commitment to parity was most common in Belfast, where the four NILP seats were held, and where no less than twelve straight fights between the NILP and the Unionist Party occurred.

In the campaign for the Woodvale constituency, for example, the Unionist candidate, Johnny McQuade, claimed that Belfast was the "cockpit" of the election, and that the main issue was the question of parity with Britain in welfare benefits. McQuade stated that "all along the Unionist Government has made it clear that it will never deviate from its policy of keeping step by step in this field" and that "this is only one of the reasons why the working man and woman should vote Unionist" (BT 18.11.1965). Similarly, the Unionist MP for Willowfield, William Hinds, said (during his election fight with Martin McBirney of the NILP) that his "chief aims" were to "cut down the unemployment figures and make certain that Northern Ireland remains part of the U.K. and enjoys all the social benefits which arise from that connection." (NL 20.11.1965.) And John Ferguson, the Unionist Party's candidate for the Oldpark seat held by the NILP, went so far as to claim the 1947 Education Act as an example of the Unionist Government's past achievements! (NL 18.11.1965).

The constant references to parity with Great Britain were not a clever piece of 'populism' designed to dupe the masses. They were reminders to the Belfast Protestant working class that voting NILP was really a waste of time as any social policies introduced by the Labour Government would automatically be implemented in the province by the Unionist administration at Stormont.

The second part of the assault on the NILP consisted of playing the "Orange

Card" for all it was worth. Despite the fact that it firmly supported Partition, the NILP's "loyalty" was repeatedly questioned. A number of Unionist candidates tried to make an issue of the fact that the NILP were not standing in Nationalist areas. Roy Bradford, for instance, claimed in a Unionist election broadcast that there were no Labour candidates up against Nationalists because "Labour would rather see a Nationalist returned than a Unionist" (NL 24.11.1965). When making this accusation, Bradford, for some reason, failed to mention that the Unionist Party were only running two candidates against sitting Nationalist MPs, while allowing five Nationalist Party candidates to be returned unopposed.

Walter Scott, the Unionist candidate for Bloomfield, tried a more direct approach than Bradford, claiming that the NILP had divided loyalties and asking:

> "Should the interests of Northern Ireland at any time conflict with the interests and aspirations of the Labour Government; where would the weight of the N.I.L.P. be placed?" (BT 16.11.1965.)

On a similar theme the Unionist MP for St.Annes, Edmund Warnock, said in his eve of poll message:

> "Tommorrow at the polls we shall teach the N. Ireland Labour Party that their duty is not to the British Socialist Government but to the people of their homeland [sic]. There is no room for fifty-fifty loyalty. We want 100 per cent loyalty to the men and women of Ulster." (NL 25.11.1965.)

And the ever subtle Sir Knox Cunningham, Unionist MP at Westminster for South Antrim, said while speaking on behalf of Captain Austin Ardill in Carrick: "If you want to aid Ulster's enemies, vote Labour" (ibid).

The "Orange card" tactic was not confined to occasional statements to the Press or on the hustings. As the election campaign progressed, Captain O'Neill spent more and more time in Belfast in an attempt to rally the Prods round to the Unionist cause. The Prime Minister had regained his Bannside seat without a contest and was therefore able to concentrate his efforts on the constituencies held by the NILP. Thus, the News Letter's report on the final day of electioneering stated:

> "Again underlining that Belfast is the flashpoint of the election tussle, Captain O'Neill returned yesterday to the city constituencies, concentrating on Pottinger, Victoria and Woodvale." (ibid).

In the Belfast constituencies, O'Neill employed all the traditional Unionist electioneering tactics. Sashes, Ulster flags, Union Jacks and flute bands were the order of the day, as the Prime Minister and the Unionist candidates marched at the head of processions. O'Neill's eagerness to literally beat the Orange drum against the four-seat strong NILP in 1965 has been conveniently forgotten by most 'historians'. Such behaviour, of course, is difficult to reconcile with O'Neill's image as a valiant liberal who struggled unsuccessfully to end sectarian politics. But O'Neill's alliance with Unionists like Johnny McQuade is still remembered in Belfast. And more honest writers like Sam McAughtry have recalled how O'Neill "went around in his Prime Ministerial car... telling people that the Northern Ireland Labour Party was anti-partitionist" (**Down In The Free State**, p111).

It is essential to recognise that the Unionist election campaign in 1965 was not an aberration in Terence O'Neill's otherwise progressive premiership. O'Neill's desire to destroy the fragile base of the NILP stemmed directly from his preference for single-party politics. Throughout the 1965 election campaign, therefore, O'Neill asserted that Unionism represented a higher form of politics than anything offered by his opponents. For instance, in an article for the Belfast Telegraph's Election Platform series, the Prime Minister informed the world:

> "Our opponents offer only doctrinaire ideas and threadbare policies. Socialism is rooted in the class struggle of the Thirties; Nationalism is bogged down in the emotions of the twenties; only Unionism turns its face to the promise and hope of the Seventies. As our election manifesto says: Forward, Ulster — to target 1970" (BT 23.11.1965).

By 1970, of course, Ulster had marched into a war and O'Neill, the brave liberal, had run away from the situation he had helped to create.

O'Neill's antagonism to the left-right politics which existed in the rest of the UK formed a central part of his approach to the politics of Northern Ireland. His dislike of class politics and his obsession with protecting the Unionist Party domination of Stormont even led him to tick off the Northern Ireland Committee of the ICTU. Having told a meeting in Ballyclare that divisions "between workers and bosses" could not be afforded in a "competitive world", O'Neill said:

> "We are all workers today and there is much for us to do. It is because I think we must move away from the politics of sectional interest that I regret the endorsement of the Labour Party by the Northern Ireland Committee of the Irish Congress of Trade Unions." (Ibid.)

The Northern Ireland Committee of the ICTU endorsement of the NILP, however, proved to be a mere dabble rather than the beginning of a sustained attempt to develop a political wing of the trade union movement in Northern Ireland.

The Northern Ireland Labour Party was unable to cope with this sustained attack from the Unionist Party. But, as it was being pounded, the Party's candidates made some telling comments about the true nature of O'Neillism. David Bleakley, for instance, said that the Unionist main aim was to "attack the candidates of the Labour Party and put them out of public life", and that this strategy represented a "return to the discredited Government claim that Stormont would be better without any effective opposition at all" (NL 17.11.1965). Later in the election campaign, Bleakley blamed O'Neill for the Unionist Party election tactics. He said that "the Nationalists had been let off nearly scot free by the Unionist machine" because the NILP was the "real mote" in O'Neill's eye and commented:

> "What a real changeling this Prime Minister of ours has become. At the beginning of the campaign he proclaimed himself as 'Mr. 1970'. Now we have the spectacle of a man who hopes to build a modern state with a Parliament devoid of those who beg to differ." (BT 29.11.1965.)

In the face of O'Neill's sustained attack, the NILP Parliamentary Party Leader,

Tom Boyd, actually ended up having to defend basic tenets of British democracy in the Party's Election Platform in the News Letter:

> "The two-party system, with its inherent dependence on a strong and active Opposition to provide a spur, is one of the elements of British democracy as it is understood throughout the world... It is Captain O'Neill who has now chosen to wage this election campaign primarily against Labour in an attempt to deprive it of the four seats it holds... We believe most earnestly that Ulster can only head for disaster if it remains, as at present, a one party state; that political monopoly is dangerous." (NL 22.11.1965.)

It is significant that Tom Boyd made no reference to N.Ireland's exclusion from the British party system. In the 1960s, the NILP behaved as if it was the Ulster wing of the British Labour Party, and tried to portray the Unionists as Tories. This strategy failed miserably in the 1965 Stormont election. At the end of the campaign, the NILP produced an eleventh hour leaflet entitled, **What Harold Wilson Has Done For You** (NL 24.11.1965). It listed such government policies as a £450,000,000 investment in Ulster's economic development, an increase in old-age pensions, the abolition of National Health Service prescription charges, the raising of ex-Service pensions and National Assistance rates, the abolition of the earnings rule for widows' benefits and the introduction of redundancy payments. But Harold Wilson's Labour Government had no real interest in the fate of the NILP. If it had been concerned about the Labour vote in Northern Ireland in November 1965, it would surely have postponed the announcement of the closure of the Sea Eagle Base in Derry until after polling day. And despite their claims to be Harold Wilson's representatives in Ulster, the NILP received no public support from the British Labour Party during the election campaign. No Westminster Labour MP, let alone a member of the Cabinet, appeared on the hustings for the NILP, or even visited the province to boost the socialist vote.

The impact of the NILP's eleventh hour leaflet on the achievements of the Labour Government was minimised further by the fact that all the policies it listed had been "rubber-stamped" without hesitation by the Unionist Government. Thus, the Unionist Party could claim the credit for policies like pension increases and the abolition of prescription charges. Deprived of any great policy issues to use against the Unionists, the NILP was reduced to accusing the Stormont administration of placing a strain on its relationship with the Westminster Government. The Unionists had little difficulty countering this accusation, armed as they were with a quote from the then Labour Home Secretary, Sir Frank Soskice, who had said that "the picture which presents itself when one looks at the happenings in Northern Ireland is one of substantial progress" (BT 23.11.1965).

The political conditions which had developed in Northern Ireland since 1921 were not conducive to the development of a provincial Labour Party. But, in 1965, the NILP also had to contend with a Unionist Party determined to exploit its weaknesses and play the Orange Card in order to wipe it off the political map. This combination of factors certainly took its toll on the NILP vote. The overall figures for the Stormont elections held on November 25 1965 were:

STORMONT ELECTION 25.11.1965: RESULT

Party	Seats	Uncontested	Change From 1962
Ulster Unionist Party	36	14	+2
Nationalist Party	9	5	0
NILP	2	0	-2
Ulster Liberal Party	1	1*	0
National Democrats	1	1	+1
Republican Labour	2	0	+1**
Independent	1	1*	0

* Queen's University; ** Republican Labour 'gain',
as a result of Gerry Fitt's switch from Eire Labour.
(Election figures compiled from the results given in BT 26.11.1965 and NL 27.11.1965.)

These results represented a personal triumph for Captain O'Neill. His vigorous electioneering in Belfast resulted in a 6% swing to the Government in the city. The two seats gained by the Unionist Party at the expense of the NILP came in the constituencies of Victoria and Woodvale. In the former, Roy Bradford overturned David Bleakley's 1,214 majority to win by 423 votes. And in Woodvale, where the previous NILP majority had been 2,157, Johnny McQuade defeated the sitting MP, William Boyd, by 1,724 votes. The NILP did manage to retain two of its four seats, but with reduced majorities. In the Oldpark constituency, Vivian Simpson's majority fell from 3,404 to 1,989, while Tom Boyd's majority in the Pottinger constituency fell from 1,852 to 874.

Reporting on the results, the News Letter stated that depression was pervading NILP headquarters, while in Glengall Street, it was a "case for 'champagne for all'" (NL 26.11.1965). The paper's editorial asserted that "the extent of support for Captain O'Neill gives him the go-ahead signal to get on with the job to which he and his Party are pledged." (Ibid). It was with this mood of confidence that the O'Neill Administration approached 1966.

Chapter Six

1966
REALITY DAWNING

CATHOLICS AND THE UNIONIST PARTY

By 1966, O'Neill had deliberately increased the Unionist Party domination of politics in Northern Ireland. In the light of this 'achievement', the onus should have been on the Prime Minister to encourage Catholic membership of the Ulster Unionist Party. O'Neill shirked the responsibility.

It is easy to underestimate the difficulties which a sustained effort to attract Catholics to the Unionist cause would have encountered in the 1960s. According to a myth still prevalent in 'liberal unionist' circles, the problem could have been solved by the Unionist Party breaking its links with the Orange Order. This myth vastly underestimates the extent to which sectarian divisions became entrenched in the political life of Northern Ireland as a result of its exclusion from the politics of the UK state from 1921 onwards. The truth is that the Ulster Unionist Party developed links with the Orange Order because it was a Protestant Party. It did not develop into a Protestant Party because of its links with the Orange Order.

It must be remembered that, in political terms, the Catholic and Protestant communities in Northern Ireland have only ever known each other as enemies. Consequently, Catholics interested in joining the Unionist Party have been deterred by the notion that they were moving over to the 'other side'. And those that did join up have often encountered suspicion from Protestants, anxious because 'aliens' were breaking into their Party.

Nevertheless, despite the enormity of the task, O'Neill's failure to even make an attempt at facilitating Catholic membership of the Unionist Party still stands out as a major indictment of his premiership. He sought to stir up provincial political activity in Northern Ireland and to ensure that this activity was completely dominated by the Unionist Party. In these circumstances, bringing Catholics into the Unionist Party should have been his number one priority. Instead, all that O'Neill and his colleagues did was to repeat, parrot-fashion, that Catholics would be more than welcome in their Party, and to believe that that was all that was required on the matter.

The O'Neill Government, therefore, attached little importance to the question of what Catholics were supposed to do in the political environment of Northern Ireland. The issue of Catholic membership of the Unionist Party only ever came up when it was raised by the media. On these occasions, the Government simply nodded patronisingly in the direction of the Catholic community. One such nod came from William Craig in January 1966. Craig told a Sunday News interviewer that he "deplored the present division in which many Catholics had found political expression only in the Nationalist Party", and added:

> "I am hoping that Catholics will be interested from now on in other parties... Naturally, as a Unionist, I am hoping that my own Party will receive increasing support from the Catholic community. In fact, there is at present a greater measure of support from Catholics for the Unionist Party than is generally realised. I see no reason why a Catholic should not join the Unionist Party or even become, eventually, a member of the Cabinet" (NL 17.1.1966).

Given the liberal posturing of the O'Neill Administration, Craig could hardly have said anything different to the Sunday News reporter. Nevertheless, his remarks went a little too far for the liking of the News Letter which commented that, while "Craig was not breaking new ground when he hoped that an increasing number of Roman Catholics would identify themselves with Unionism", it was still true that "the overwhelming majority of Roman Catholics hold that a United Ireland under a Dublin Parliament is preferable to a partitioned country with dual loyalties". The editorial also claimed that the rank and file of the Unionist Party were not convinced that there had been any "change of heart" by Catholics on the question of Partition (NL 18.1.1966). The paper returned to this theme a week later in an equally sniffy editorial entitled, **The Hard Facts Of Ecumenism:**

> "...we have advocated caution and warned against haste. The rank and file of the Unionist Party... are not convinced of any change of heart in Roman Catholic voters. To Unionists their objective is and has remained consistently a United Ireland" (NL 24.1.1966).

Alongside this editorial, the News Letter published a very different article on the subject by its former political correspondent, Ralph Bossence. Although an NILP supporter, Bossence had been fulsome in his praise of O'Neill in the early days of his premiership. Disillusionment with the new administration, however, set in around the middle of 1965 and, by 1966, Bossence was clearly aware of serious flaws in Government thinking. His article on the issue of Catholics and the Unionist Party must rank as one of the sharpest pieces of political analysis published in the News Letter in the 1960s.

The article began by noting that there was "little evidence of a fearful rush by Roman Catholics to join the Unionist Party", and that there had been no reports of "Orangemen, Apprentice Boys or Episcopalian company directors being jostled out of their place in the queue by a green wave". On a more serious note, the article referred to comments made on Ulster Television by a Catholic named Brian McGuigan, who said that "no-one wanted to join a party in which he would be a second class member with the faintest of hopes of being selected as a Parliamentary candidate", and had also noted that "all the present members of the Ulster Government" were Orangemen. Bossence commented:

> "Some things are established here by the Government of Ireland Act, and others by custom, and it is a toss-up which are the harder to get round... on the whole I agree with Mr. McGuigan that it is awfully difficult for a person of his faith to join a party in which the other members will be more equal than he is.

This poses a problem for those Catholics who are convinced Conservatives and who acknowledge that they are better off economically than they would be in a united Republic."

"...If these people are to be persuded to become Unionists, it is not enough for Mr. Craig or any other Minister to say: 'Of course Catholics are welcome to join the Unionist Party'. Catholics must be shown that, if they do, they will not merely be tolerated but will be admitted to the innermost councils of the party and, if they have the ability, seconded to the hustings.

"It is here, admittedly, that the progressives in the Unionist Party have a task that would have made Sisyphus' look a sinecure. Already, indeed, they have rolled the stone part way up the hill several times and had to begin all over again" (ibid).

Bossence concluded by claiming that, if the Government continued to shirk its responsiblities on the issue, Catholics would "stay out of the Unionist Party", and the province would remain "as far away as ever from that happy day when political parties in Northern Ireland will divide on rational lines" (ibid).

It was certainly over-optimistic to believe that the normalisation of politics in Northern Ireland could have been achieved by the influx of a significant number of Catholics into the Unionist Party in the 1960s. However, if the Government had at least demonstrated that it was serious about the subject, it might have done something to reduce the frustration which was building up in the Catholic community and which eventually spilled over into the civil disturbances at the end of the decade.

The Government, however, does not even appear to have been aware that there might just possibly be a problem with the fact that Catholics were isolated from the Party which totally controlled the Stormont apparatus. This inability once again contradicts the myth that Terence O'Neill attempted to develop non-sectarian politics in Northern Ireland. And it demonstrates, yet again, that O'Neill's strategy could only have produced stability if the Catholic community in the province had been prepared to put up with its complete isolation from meaningful politics.

DR. NIXON UTTERS HERESY

In February 1966, the controversial Unionist MP for North Down, Dr. Robert Nixon, created something of a stir within Unionist circles. During a Debate in Stormont, he complained of the increasingly excessive cost of bureaucracy in Northern Ireland and suggested a remedy for the problem:

"Ever since Northern Ireland came into being we have watched this form of devolutionary Government with the greatest of interest over the last 45 years. Here we have within the Six Counties a Government with all the offices — indeed a Governor as well. We have a build-up of establishment which is really terribly complex. If we had to pay for it we could not do it.

"The position is such that, with the sort of Government we have, if we are going to duplicate everything that is done at Westminster — and we must duplicate it to provide the services that are necessary for our people — we are going to create a Civil Service which will be fantastic. My solution is to pass it back to Westminster." (17.2.1966 Col. 1225.)

Nixon's heretical call for the abolition of Stormont provoked an immediate response from the Unionist MP, Nat Minford, who exclaimed "No, never" (ibid). Nixon replied to Unionist criticism of his comments by saying:

> "The point is that the administration at Westminster deals with Scotland, England and Wales and only very little work would be entailed in carrying out what we do here. They have all the machinery that is necessary. I suggest that many people in Northern Ireland will agree with what I say, that... our greatest safeguard would be — back to Westminster." (17.2.1966 Col 1227.)

The North Down MP was also criticised by Herbert Kirk, the Minister of Finance, who said that the majority of Stormont MPs disagreed with Nixon ,and claimed that "many members of the the Scottish and Welsh communities admired devolution in Northern Ireland" (NL 18.2.1965). A different response, however, came from the Nationalist MP, Austin Currie, who said of Dr. Nixon:

> "I am very glad to see that he realises the complete waste of having this Parliament here... It is good to know that he realises that this Parliament is nothing better than a glorified county council with no real powers but to give jobs to civil servants, Cabinet Ministers and Back Benchers." (Hansard 17.2.1966 Col 1227.)

Austin Currie was speaking here from from first-hand experience. Over the previous twelve months, his Party had discovered the truth about Stormont in its farcical position as the "Official Opposition" in a rubber-stamp Parliament. (Ironically, Currie later became one of the few remaining devolutionists within the SDLP. In 1989 he left Northern politics to join Fine Gael and was elected to a real Parliament, Dail Eireann.)

Dr. Nixon's unsporting attempt to bring reality into the proceedings at Stormont earned him a sharp rebuke from the News Letter, which accused him of "stretching the process of independent thinking too far", and asked:

> "Has Dr. Nixon, one wonders, considered seriously what the consequences would be of a return to Westminster? His memory cannot be so short that he has forgotten the 1949 Act which laid down that no change was to be made in the constitutional status of Northern Ireland without the consent of Stormont. If the Parliament of Northern Ireland is to be abolished at once the decision would revert to Westminster and the destiny of the province would be taken out of its own hands." (NL 22.2.1966.)

This editorial is an accurate reflection of Ulster Unionist thinking on devolution in the 1960s. Stormont had become increasingly attractive to Unionists because of their unwillingness to trust "British politicians". They had come to believe that devolution was their only safeguard against Irish unity and that the Union with Great Britain depended on the survival of Stormont. The logic behind such thinking was seriously flawed. As has already been stated, Northern Ireland is not, and was not, a state. Consequently (and contrary to the claims of the News Letter), the devolved Government which existed between 1921 and 1972 never had control over the "destiny of the province". A Northern Ireland Government could only ever have such control in an Independent Ulster. The News Letter's reference to the safeguards in the *1949*

Ireland Act was simply nonsensical. This Act was the work of the Labour Administration at Westminster and could have been repealed at any time, if a British Government so desired.

The News Letter's editorial on Dr. Nixon's heresy was wrong too in its prophecy about the terrible things which would befall Ulster if Stormont was ever abolished. When the unthinkable finally happened to Stormont in 1972, the Conservative Government introduced the *1973 Northern Ireland Constitution Act* which provided a much more straightforward safeguard for the province's Union with Great Britain than the 1949 Ireland Act. Under the 1949 Act, a change in Northern Ireland's status within the UK could only occur with the consent of the Stormont Parliament. Under the 1973 legislation, such a change required the direct consent of a majority of the Northern Ireland electorate in a referendum.

UNIONISTS AT WESTMINSTER

The relationship between Stormont and Westminster was again brought into focus less than a fortnight after Dr. Nixon's integrationist remarks. At the end of February, Harold Wilson set the date for the General Election that became memorable for Gerry Fitt's victory over Jim Kilfedder in West Belfast. At the beginning of the election campaign, it was reported that strains had developed in the relationship between the Stormont Government and the twelve Unionist MPs at Westminster. On February 28, the News Letter reported that the Stormont administration was facing a dilemma about the "Unionist 12":

> "The dilemma is whether to let the 12 Ulster Unionist MPs fight their own battle for their return to Westminster. Or to give them the traditional full support of the Premier, Captain Terence O'Neill and other Ulster Cabinet Ministers in their campaign... Some Unionists take the view that Ulster Unionism should mean union with Britain, irrespective of whether a Labour or Conservative Government is in power there. The task of trying to return the 12 Ulster MPs to Westminster is thought to be one which could very well be left to themselves while they accept the Conservative Whip, and some contend that the Conservative Party should give them organisational support and not Glengall Street." (NL 29.2.1966.)

The following day, the News Letter commented:

> "No matter what difficulties there may be in the relationship between the Northern Ireland government and the British Labour Party, no good purpose can be served by any reluctance to use to the full the machinery at the disposal of the Ulster Unionist candidates... whether the loyalties of the 12 M.P.s appear to lie with Mr. Heath or with Stormont, the primary claim on them is with the voters" (NL 1.3.1966).

The entire issue quickly faded away following a statement by the Unionist Party Secretary, Jim Bailie, which "refuted a suggestion that the party was facing a dilemma as to whether campaigning for the Unionist candidates should be primarily a matter for the Conservative Party Headquarters rather than for Glengall Street" (NL 2.3.1966). Bailie also revealed that he "had had talks with Senator John Drennan, Chairman of the Standing Committee of the Ulster Unionist Council and Mr. Drennan had declared, 'We are 100 per cent behind our twelve candidates and we will do everything we can to make sure that the electors return them.'" (Ibid.)

This brief controversy throws further light on the bizarre relationship which used to exist between the Ulster Unionist Party and the Conservative Party. These links only ever had any real meaning at Westminster, where all Unionist MPs took the Tory whip until 1974. These MPs, however, played a largely peripheral and anomalous role within the overall Ulster Unionist Party during the Stormont years. With the Party primarily interested in what was going on in the local parliament, Westminster functioned mainly as a stomping ground for the more right wing members of the Unionist Family. And, in the "Imperial Parliament", these right wingers regularly voted with the Tories against Labour legislation and then watched as the same legislation was introduced in Northern Ireland by their Unionist Party colleagues at Stormont.

(The right-wing instincts of Unionists at Westminster have been of significance on one major occasion in the post-war era. That was in March 1979 when eight of the ten MPs tipped the scales in favour of Margaret Thatcher in the crucial vote of confidence in the Callaghan Government. Ironically, their decision to follow their Tory hearts on this occasion opened the door for the Government which eventually introduced the Anglo-Irish Agreement.)

The reported strains between the Unionist 'teams' at Westminster and Stormont in February 1966 may have owed something to differences of opinions about Captain O'Neill's leadership of the Party. Later in the year, it became clear that the Imperial MP for South Antrim, Sir Knox Cunningham, was strongly opposed to aspects of O'Neill's policy on cross-border co-operation. However, if the reports in the News Letter were accurate, it appears that the primary reason for the strains lay in the concerns of the Unionist Administration about its relationship with Harold Wilson's Government in London. The Stormont Government seems to have been concerned that the behaviour of their Party colleagues at Westminster was stirring up greater antagonism towards Ulster Unionism on the Labour benches. At the back of all this concern, no doubt, was the fear that the "enemies of Ulster" in the Labour Party might persuade Harold Wilson to interfere in the affairs of Stormont.

EASTER AND AFTER

1966 is primarily remembered as the year when things started to go badly wrong for Captain O'Neill. 1966 saw the rise of Paisleyism, the emergence of the Ulster Volunteer Force in Belfast, and a serious challenge to O'Neill's leadership from within the Parliamentary Unionist Party. In his Autobiography, O'Neill blames the celebrations of the Fiftieth Anniversary of the Easter Rising for the difficulties which developed in 1966 (p76). His comments on these celebrations highlight the extent to which he underestimated Irish Nationalism:

"With the approach of Easter it became obvious that the Catholics in Belfast would insist on celebrating the Dublin Rebellion of 1916. Considering that Belfast was not involved in that event fifty years previously one might have hoped that those so minded would have contented themselves with attending the ceremony in Dublin, less than a hundred miles away [sic]. But all the indications were that there was no prominent Catholic prepared to give a lead in the interests of peace." (P79.)

O'Neill's hope that the Easter Rising celebrations would be restricted to Dublin was based upon the assumption that Irish Nationalism had nothing to do with the North of Ireland! When O'Neill was proved wrong, his Government was totally incapable of dealing with the situation.

Paisleyism, in fact, first made its presence felt in 1966, in mid-February, during a controversy over the naming of a new bridge in Belfast. On February 14th, Belfast City Council chose the name "Carson" Bridge. This led to an intervention by the Governor of Northern Ireland, Lord Erskine, who lobbied for the less controversial name, "Queen Elizabeth II" Bridge. Erskine's wish eventually prevailed, but both he and the Stormont Government were heavily criticised by Paisley over the issue.

During his campaign of protest against Lord Erskine's intervention, Paisley brought Edward Carson, the son of Lord Carson, over to the province to address loyalist rallies. Both Paisley and Carson appear to have been planning to stand in the General Election in March against the sitting Ulster Unionist MPs. Carson, in fact, actually announced that he was standing in North Belfast while Paisley was reportedly considering standing in East Belfast. Eventually, neither stood and Edward Carson Jr. quickly withdrew from the provincial political scene.

February 1966 also witnessed a number of incidents of violence. On February 18th, the Unionist Party headquarters in Glengall Street was petrol-bombed. A meeting of eight of the twelve Westminster MPs was in progress at the time but no one was injured (NL 19.2.1966). Three days later, the News Letter reported on Ulster's "weekend of shame", in which three Catholic schools were attacked and a window was broken at premises belonging to Paisley on the Albertbridge Road in Belfast. Two of the Catholic schools attacked were also in Belfast; one, on the Falls Road, was petrol-bombed, and the other was daubed with political slogans. The third, in Crumlin, was damaged by fire (NL 21.2.1966). A possible explanation for the attacks on Catholic schools emerged early in March when it was reported that the police were investigating rumours that the UVF had been re-formed to oppose IRA and Republican plans to hold parades at Easter (NL 2.3.1966).

These developments were generally believed to reflect a heightening of tension in the province in the run-up to the commemoration of the Easter rebellion. On the Sunday night of the "weekend of shame", Ian Paisley had addressed a rally in the Ulster Hall on the forthcoming commemoration. During his speech, he had warned the thousands of people expected to converge on Northern Ireland from the Irish Republic to "stay away".

When the Easter parades finally began, Paisley held another Sunday night rally in the Ulster Hall, where he spoke on the theme, "The Resurrection of the Redeemer, not the insurrection of the rebels" (NL 19.4.1966). The most significant Unionist speech in this period, however, had been made two days earlier by the Prime Minister himself at a joint Protestant/Roman Catholic Conference in the Corrymeela Centre, Ballycastle. The subject of O'Neill's speech was **The Ulster Community**:

"This Conference has been arranged in the spirit in which Easter ought to be celebrated in a Christian community. It is more concerned with our common Christianity than with our conflicting points of view. Such a meeting can do much good, and I consider it a privilege to be the first speaker.

"But the Conference will not achieve its potential without frank speaking, and an admission of differences of principle. The avoidance of controversial issues may be comfortable, but it makes no real contribution to better understanding. In speaking frankly tonight, I am sure that I will offend no one here.

"The Ulster community is a place in which two traditions meet — the Irish Catholic tradition and the British Protestant tradition. In India the place where two great rivers join together is often considered to have a particular sanctity — but it is also often a place of turbulence, as the currents from opposite directions swirl around each other.

"By and large these religious traditions have also been synonymous with political views. This correspondence of religion and politics has, in the past, created certain peculiar frictions in our public affairs, and prevented us from mounting a united effort to surmount other social and economic problems.

"A major cause of division arises, some would say, from the de facto segregation of education along religious lines. This is a most delicate matter, and one must respect the firm convictions from which it springs. Many people have questioned, however, whether the maintenance of two distinct educational systems side by side is not wasteful of human and financial resources, and a major barrier to the promotion of communal understanding.

"One must face also the fact that political divisions become unusually sharp when the argument is not about means, but about ends. Thus, in most countries political parties differ merely about the methods to be used for the achievement of certain accepted national goals — economic stability and prosperity, higher living standards and so on. Disagreements of this kind admit the possibility of compromise. While the extreme positions, for instance, may be those of untrammelled private enterprise or complete state control, what in fact has emerged in the United Kingdom under governments of different complexion is a 'mixed' economy.

"Here in Northern Ireland, however, disagreement has been centred not around the activities of the State, but around its very existence. Now it would be all too easy at a gathering such as this to speak soft words on this subject, and to give the impression that all that is needed to overcome every difficulty is goodwill. But that would be less than honest. I must say clearly that the constitutional position of Northern Ireland is not a matter on which there can be any compromise, now or in the future, and I must say, too, that I believe we have a right to call upon all our citizens to support the Constitution. The whole concept of constitutional government would be debased if the State were not to expect of its citizens at any rate the minimum duty of allegiance.

"When I say that there can be no compromise on this issue, I have clearly in mind the welfare of all our people. In seven years as Minister of Finance, I came to know very well the inescapable logic of our financial arithmetic — the plain fact that any break in the British connection would condemn our community to an intolerable reduction in its living-standards.

"Our political divisions of opinion will no doubt continue, but I would like to see them moved on to a new basis of rational argument. I have enough confidence in the economic and social advantages of my own political philosophy to be prepared to argue it on its merits, and without catch-cries or cheap slogans. I want the community to advance to achievements of which all its members will be proud. This has been my consistent aim as Prime Minister. I have spoken of the 'duty of allegiance' which the State expects; but I accept readily those obligations which the State owes in return.

"I defer to no one in my readiness to practice and defend my own deeply held Protestant beliefs, but I recognise and respect the rights of others to practice and uphold theirs. And all of us have a wider Christian duty to practise our religion 'with malice towards none, with charity for all'.

"One of our major difficulties is, that in an age of mass communications, the raucous sound of extremism is often heard much more loudly than the steady ground-swell of moderation. A bombing or a gimmicky demonstration provides a better headline or a more dramatic picture than the dignified expression of moderate opinion. This is a problem we have got to face, because no democratic society can afford to allow itself to be intimidated by violence or pushed around by noisy minorities. I can assure you that the Government intend to stand up to these people from whatever section of the community they may come — but it ought not to stop at that. I think there is also a job here for every organisation of moderate opinion, and above all for the Churches.

"There are certain challenges at certain times which must be met, whatever the cost. The real authority of the Christian Churches is a moral authority, and it is within their power to deploy that immense authority for the good of the community as a whole. The Government will speak clearly in terms of public order; I hope that the Churches will speak equally clearly in terms of moral order. Those who speak by word or deed to incite hatred and widen divisions in the community can be crushed by the universal disapprobation and distaste of decent people!

"We in Ulster today have much to work for, and much to hope for. Last month's unemployment figure was the lowest for any March since the War, and our economy grows steadily stronger and better balanced. The physical development of the Province proceeds apace on every side. A great new industry has chosen our new City in County Armagh as the location for a massive factory. The Vice-Chancellor of our second university has been appointed, and planning is far advanced. Driving around Ulster, one encounters almost everywhere new or improved roads and motorways.

"The future is full of promise for the people of Ulster. I believe that only two things can possibly stand in the way of full realization of that promise.

One of these — a serious economic set-back for the United Kingdom as a whole — is not a matter within our control, although we can join our efforts with those of our fellow citizens in defending ourselves against it. The other — which is very much within our control — is the danger of self-inflicted wounds. It is easy to be impatient with the pace of change in 1966, but it is no answer to return to the mentality of 1926. We may not have achieved perfection in our affairs, but in the words of the song we are 'Forty years on', and have built up material and other assets which this generation must not squander.

"If we cannot be united in all things, let us at least be united in working together — in a Christian spirit — to create better opportunities for our children, whether they come from the Falls Road or from Finaghy. In the enlightment of education, in the dignity of work, in the security of home and family there are ends which all of us can pursue. As we advance to meet the promise of the future, let us shed the burdens of traditional grievances and ancient resentments. There is much we can do together. It must - and God willing — it will be done."   (NL 9.4.66; see also Ulster At The Crossroads p113-116.)

The most important section of this speech is its appeal to the Catholic community to accept the "minimum duty of allegiance" to the Northern Ireland "State". The schoolmasterly tones in which this appeal was delivered were probably a reflection of O'Neill's disappointment over the decision to hold Easter Parades in Belfast. The requirement of "allegiance" is a peculiarly Ulster Unionist concept. In the rest of the UK, millions of people, who would never declare their "loyalty to the Crown", play a full part in the political life of the State. But the exclusion of Northern Ireland from such politics has drastically narrowed the horizons.

O'Neill's patronising appeal to Catholics to fulfill a "minimum duty of allegiance" was effectively a request to them to become token Nationalists. The most significant part of the Corrymeela speech is the statement:

"Our political divisions of opinion will no doubt continue, but I would like to see them moved on to a new basis of rational argument."

This totally disproves the notion that O'Neill tried to eradicate the ghetto politics of Nationalism and Unionism. He simply believed that a spot of economic progress would create a more polite expression of this politics. His Government never even attempted to develop alternative political structures that would take sectarian enmity out of the political arena. O'Neill believed that sectarian conflict was a thing of the past and when events threatened to prove him wrong, all he could do was make ecumenical noises and call for apolitical displays of 'moderation'. Thus, in Easter 1966 he was confidently declaring that "those who seek... to incite hatred and widen divisions in the community can be crushed by the universal disapprobation and distaste of decent people".

In Northern Ireland, expressions of "good will" tend to come to nothing, because they lack a functional political expression. This was vividly highlighted in the 1970s by the movement of the "Peace People" when thousands marched to demonstrate their rejection of violence. Violence could not be wished away, however, while the communal structure of politics remained.

In the mid-1960s, despite the continued existence of communal politics, O'Neill believed that his Premiership had ushered in a new age in community relations. And the confidence evident in the final paragraphs of his Corrymeela speech stayed intact over the Easter period.

In the event, the commemoration of the 1916 Easter rising passed off relatively peacefully. The most significant marches took place on Sunday April 17th when, according to the News Letter's estimates (NL 18.4.1966), 28,000 people lined the streets to watch the 8,000 people taking part in the 1916 march. 30,000 were said to have lined the route of the 5,000 strong Paisleyite counter-demonstration. Although at one stage, the rival parades passed within 200 yards of each other, no clashes occurred. The most serious incidents of the day occurred when crowds gave chase to people with tricolours. A bus was chased and caught when crowds saw a passenger waving a tricolour but the police intervened; five people were arrested and the passenger was taken into "protective custody". On another occasion, two girls with tricolours had to be ushered into a house by the police. A loyalist crowd broke windows in the house and clashed with police (ibid).

In its editorial on the following day, the News Letter stated that "Belfast's day of tension" had "passed off without any major clash if not entirely without incident". On the whole, the News Letter was very satisfied with the way events in Belfast had turned out:

> "It would not be out of place... if the city allowed itself some self-congratulation. By refusing to be stampeded into a reversion to uglier days, the citizens showed a maturity of outlook and a spirit of tolerance that augurs well for the future of Belfast and of Northern Ireland." (Ibid.)

The assumption that politics in Northern Ireland was becoming a dignified affair under Captain O'Neill soon took a severe jolt. On May 7th, a petrol bomb intended for a Catholic-owned pub set fire to the house next door. The elderly owner, Martha Gould, a Protestant, later died from her injuries. And on May 27th, a Catholic named John Scullion was stabbed on the Falls Road. He died in hospital on June 11th.

It appears that not everyone was aware at the time that these attacks were the work of the recently formed UVF. At any rate, both deaths were overshadowed in the press by the incidents which occurred before and during a Paisleyite demonstration at the General Assembly of the Presbyterian Church. This protest was primarily aimed at the Governor, Lord Erskine, who was attending the Assembly, but Paisley also claimed that it was directed against "Romanising tendencies in the General Assembly" (NL 7.6.1966).

On their way into the Assembly, Lord Erskine and his wife, and the Presbyterian Moderator, were loudly jeered by protestors. The most serious incidents of the evening, however, were provoked by a Paisleyite march to the General Assembly which deliberately passed through the Catholic Cromac Square district. An attempt by locals to intercept the march at this point was thwarted by the police, but some bottles were thrown at marchers.

In the subsequent Stormont Debate on the incidents, the O'Neillites queued up to condemn Paisley. Nat Minford referred to him as a "big wind-bag from the Ravenhill Road", and Roy Bradford urged the Government not to be stampeded by a "Latter Day Luther of the lumpen proletariat" (NL 16.6.1966). Captain O'Neill claimed that the activities of the Paisleyites had a "parallel in the rise of the Nazis to power", and a Unionist motion was accepted without a division. It condemned the events of "the evening of 6th June, 1966, the acts of provocation, the violence which ensued, the deliberate insults offered to Her Majesty's representative in Northern Ireland and the gross discourtesy to the General Assembly of the Presbyterian Church", and called upon the Government to "take whatever action may be necessary to ensure that law and order are preserved and these and similar acts are not repeated". (15.6.1966 Col 297.)

The only discordant note in the proceedings at Stormont was struck by Desmond Boal, the Unionist MP for Shankill, who attacked the motion for containing hysterical recitals, and claimed that the right to hold demonstrations and parades was a principal democratic liberty. Two days after he had made these comments the Government removed Boal from his £2,000 a year post of Counsel to the Attorney General (NL 18.6.1966).

The extent of the antagonism towards Paisleyism on the Unionist benches during the Stormont Debate on 15th June inspired the News Letter to declare:

> "Extremism, whatever form it takes, has no contribution to make to the new Ulster which is the objective of the O'Neill administration. We have not heard the end of Mr. Paisley's activities, but the forces now ranged against him are strong, determined and irresistible. They will not be beaten down. The House declared itself yesterday. It is for every man and woman to examine their conscience today" (NL 16.6.1966).

Within a fortnight of this editorial, the News Letter's confidence about the future was badly shaken. On the night of June 26th, a Catholic barman named Peter Ward was shot dead on Malvern Street, off the Shankill Road in Belfast. Two other Catholics, Andrew Kelly and Liam Doyle, were injured in the same attack. The News Letter editorial on the killings stated:

> "Recent armed attacks in Belfast have led, with a tragic inevitability, to a killing... The time has come for the Government and the people to call a halt to a drift of events that, unchecked, can only take the city and Province back to a period that lingers like a nightmare in the memories of the older generation of Ulster people." (NL 27.6.1966).

Peter Ward's murder was, in fact, the third killing to have taken place in the City inside eight weeks; Martha Gould and John Scullion were the other victims. But it seems that it was only after Ward's death that many people realised that a Protestant murder gang was operating in Belfast.

On the night after the Malvern Street attack, the police charged five men with murder. Two were charged with killing Peter Ward and three with the murder of John Scullion. The next day, O'Neill informed Stormont that the Government had proscribed the UVF. His speech concluded with an appeal for calm:

"We stand at the crossroads. One way is the road of progress which has been opening up before us with all its promise of a richer and fuller life for our people. The other way is a return to the pointless violence and civil strife of earlier years. We must not let anyone push us down that road. For myself, I do not seek the political company of anyone who would condone or justify recent events in the slightest degree. I will not stand idly by and see the Ulster which we love dragged through the mud. Every person who has a shred of influence has a duty to use it wisely and responsibly. Above all else, I appeal for a spirit of calm and restraint. If we were to experience a series of reprisals and counter-reprisals, the consequences could be grave indeed for us all. The battle against these evil forces must be waged throughout the community; but it must begin here, in this House, today." (NL 29.6.66; see also, Ulster At The Crossroads, p122.)

O'Neill, therefore, attributed all the blame for the emergence of the UVF to "evil forces". His comments illustrate how little has changed in the political life of Northern Ireland. Nowadays, nearly a quarter of a century after the Malvern Street murder, politicians and clergymen still greet each new murder with condemnations of the "evil men of violence". Blaming everything on external "evil forces" is, of course, convenient for those with a vested interest in the existing political framework. Viewing sectarian violence as if it was an unavoidable environmental hazard enables people to avoid the conclusion that it might just possibly have something to do with the continued existence of sectarian politics in the province.

The random sectarian attacks on Catholics in 1966 appear to have been inspired by paranoid fears of a resurgence of IRA activity in the wake of the Easter Rising celebrations in Belfast. This is not to say that the IRA threat was real in 1966 but simply to note that such fears did exist. Seemingly irrational communal fears are, in fact, a normal accompaniment of communally based politics.

There is no doubt that the Unionist Government must bear some of the responsibility for the development of paranoia within sections of the working class Protestant community. O'Neill often claimed that he was leading Northern Ireland in a new direction but he never bothered to explain exactly where he was leading it to. Anyone who dared to question his approach to Government was simply branded as a bigot. The way he handled the visit of Sean Lemass demonstrates his incompetence as a leader. In 1963, O'Neill ruled out a meeting with a Taoiseach until the Irish Republic recognised Northern Ireland's status within the UK. But less than two years later, he arranged the Lemass visit without even a hint of warning to his own Cabinet. Such behaviour can only have generated suspicion and confusion about his intentions among the more excitable members of the Protestant Community.

A fortnight after the Malvern murder, the Minister of Commerce, Brian Faulkner, pointed to a number of reasons for the uncertainty that had developed within the Protestant community. He claimed that the "spate of speculation" in the province had been triggered off by "the meeting between the Prime

Ministers of Northern Ireland and Eire, the discussions on cross-border trade, celebrations in Northern Ireland of the Easter Rising and the reaction of the Protestant churches in Ireland to the world-wide ecumenical movement." (NL 1966). Faulkner, it should be noted, was not passing judgement on any of the points mentioned in his list. This is hardly surprising as he himself was heavily involved in the "discussions on cross-border trade".

In his Autobiography, Faulkner also referred to the Protestant fears which he claims Paisley was able to exploit:

> "fears that better North/South relations might undermine Ulster's position as part of the United Kingdom; fears that the South was only trying to find a new way of effecting its claim on our territory; fears aroused by the massive republican celebrations of the fiftieth anniversary of the 1916 Rising and the accompanying riots; and fears that the ecumenical movement was in Northern Ireland designed to reduce opposition to a takeover by the Catholic Irish Republic." (P42-43).

Brian Faulkner was the only member of the O'Neill adminstration with any kind of grip on reality and his comments do provide some clues as to what was going on in the minds of some Protestants in 1966. He did not refer, however, to what was arguably one of the greatest factors behind the development of Protestant paranoia: the fear that the O'Neill Government was 'soft' when it came to the traditional task of "defending Ulster". This fear was evident in 1966 in the criticism made in some quarters of the Government's entirely practical decision not to ban the 1916 processions in Belfast. A ban on all parades at Easter would have been impossible to enforce and, consequently, counter-productive. Characteristically, the Government did not bother to spell out the unfeasibility of such a ban in public.

There was, in fact, more than a grain of truth in the accusation that Terence O'Neill was complacent about Irish Nationalism. Just seven months into his premiership he was boasting that the economic development of Northern Ireland was exposing "anti-partition clamour" as "social and economic lunacy" (NL 30.11.1963). Thus, on the eve of the first Easter parades, O'Neill was swanning about at Corrymeela and stating that, while the existing "political divisions of opinion" would "no doubt continue", Catholics still had a "minimum duty of allegiance" to the pseudo-State at Stormont.

O'Neill's high-sounding Corrymeela speech had absolutely no connection with the reality of Belfast in April 1966. The thousands of Catholics who marched in the 1916 commemoration parades, and the many more who turned out to watch them, certainly had no intention of abiding by a "minimum duty of allegiance". And to the Protestants who feared that the Republican parades signalled the beginning of another assault on Protestant Ulster, O'Neill must have sounded like a visitor from a different world.

1966 was the year in which reality really caught up with O'Neillism. In his Autobiography, O'Neill notes that "the co-operation which had started with the visit of Sean Lemass in 1965 had been shattered by the insistence of the Belfast

Catholics in celebrating the fiftieth anniversary of the Dublin Rebellion", and that "it was 1966 which made 1968 inevitable and was bound to put the whole future of Northern Ireland in the melting pot" (Autobiography, p87). In other words, 1966 was the year in which it became clear that, despite all Captain O'Neill's kindness, the Croppies were not going to lie down.

Chapter Seven

1966
LEADERSHIP
QUESTION MARKS

THE TWELFTH

The problems encountered by O'Neillism in 1966 led to the emergence of serious doubts about O'Neill's position as Leader of the Unionist Party. At the beginning of July, these doubts were reflected in one of the Orange Order's traditional resolutions for the 12th of July demonstrations. These resolutions normally contained a declaration of support for the Stormont Government, but in July 1966 the reference to the Government contained a veiled criticism of the O'Neill administration:

> "We wish to express our gratitude and congratulations to Worshipful Brother Captain Terence O'Neill D.L. M.P. and his Cabinet colleagues on their determined and successful endeavours for the material prosperity of Northern Ireland; and we urge them to have no hesitation in devoting the same determination in preserving our Constitutional integrity, as well as the peace and good order of Northern Ireland within the United Kingdom, in which task we pledge to them our steadfast support." (NL 11.7.1966.)

This resolution was read out at the nineteen demonstrations that took place throughout the province. 100,000 Orangemen reportedly took part in the marches (the largest number since the war) and, apart from the heckling of many of the speeches, the day passed off without incident (NL 13.7.1966). As for the speeches themselves, the only criticism of the O'Neill Government was made at Derriaghy by the Westminster MP, Sir Knox Cunningham, who attacked the policy of cross-border co-operation, saying:

> "I believe that we are embarking on a dangerous policy for Ulster. I am opposed to the policy and to the various comings and goings that are taking place. In Lord Brookeborough's words — I believe in good neighbourliness and then I stop." (ibid.)

Ironically, in his speech at Lisnaskea, Lord Brookeborough actually gave his blessing to the policy of cross-border co-operation. The former Prime Minister said: "I for one welcome an easing of tension and more co-operation from the South. I am convinced that this does not and will not mean any change in our constitutional position." (ibid.) Among the other speeches made at demonstrations, there were enthusiastic affirmations of support for O'Neill from Roy Bradford, Stanley McMaster and Senators Nelson Elder and Daniel McGladdery.

EVERYTHING UNDER CONTROL?

In the remainder of the summer, O'Neill and his colleagues sought to disprove the accusations that they were weak. On July 19th, Ian Paisley and two of his supporters were fined £30 each for unlawful assembly outside the Presbyterian General Assembly in June. All three refused to pay their fines, or to enter into bail to keep the peace for two years, and on July 20th they were arrested and taken to Crumlin Road prison. Defending his decision not to pay the fine, Paisley said:

> "The day is coming when, with the help of God and the Protestants of Ulster, I will be in the House of Commons. It seems to me that the only way the Protestant people are going to be able to answer the ruling junta of Lundys in Stormont is to have someone there to rid it of the nest. Captain O'Neill thinks that Paisley is finished but he hasn't heard the end of it. I am going to jail but I refuse to surrender the right to protest. The Ulster people are rising, not as gangsters but in a lawful spirit to protest against the fascist O'Neill" (NL 21.7.1966).

Paisley's imprisonment led to two consecutive nights of rioting outside Crumlin Road jail. On the night of Friday, July 22nd, the police baton-charged a crowd of 2,000 and 16 people were arrested. During the disturbances which followed the baton-charge, five public houses were looted and other properties were damaged (NL 23.7.1966). The troubles continued on the Saturday night with more arrests and some rioting around midnight (NL 24.7.1966).

On the Monday after these disturbances the Cabinet took measures to restore order. It placed a three month ban on all processions and outdoor meetings within a fifteen mile radius of Belfast (NL 25.7.1966). The ban, and Paisley's imprisonment, had the effect of cooling things down in Belfast for the time being.

Within a fortnight of Paisley's imprisonment, O'Neill made a very obvious attempt to prove that Ulster's "constitutional integrity" was safe in his Government's hands. In a message to the Ulster Unionist Council, O'Neill stated that he resented any suggestion "that the present Government is less than 100% firm on the constitutional issue". The Prime Minister quoted one of his constituents, whom he described as "one of those decent, sensible Orangemen who have long been the backbone of Ulster", as follows:

> "Everything seems to be changing these days. Nothing is the same as it used to be. How can we be sure that those great landmarks we always used to hold on to are not going to be swept away? We had the Unionist Party to defend the constitution and the Orange Order to defend our Protestant religion. Are those things still safe in Ulster today?" (NL 3.8.1966.)

Captain O'Neill's response to such fears was to say that "there can be no move away from London and towards Dublin because our people do not wish it. So, too, on the religious issue, the choice in the Protestant churches is ours. There can be no move away from Protestant principles and towards Rome unless our own people should wish it." (Ibid.) O'Neill also added that the Constitution was safe "unless we allow an irresponsible minority to bring such discredit upon us that the British Government will want to wash their hand of us" (ibid).

LEADERSHIP CRISIS

O'Neill's attempts to project a firm image did not remove the question marks about his Premiership which existed within the Unionist Party. At the end of August, twelve leading members of the Unionist Party met at Glengall Street to "discuss the present situation and how best to support the Prime Minister and the Government" (NL 3.8.1966). After the meeting one of those present, James Chichester-Clarke, the Government Chief Whip, said:

> "The meeting was entirely my own idea and was not prompted by pressure of any kind. I am not unduly worried by the situation but we must try and foresee what the opponents of the Government's policies may do next — and take precautions. It is an unusual step to take, but then we haven't had an attack on the party of this sort for about thirty years." (Ibid.)

It is unclear from the press reports whether this group was formed in response to Paisley's "O'Neill Must Go" campaign or whether it was also intended to counteract opposition to the Government from within the Parliamentary Unionist Party. At any rate the "back the Government group", as it became known, held two further meetings in the month of September. Whatever function this group fulfilled it certainly did not prevent a plot within the Unionist Party to topple O'Neill.

The news of this plot was made public on September 23rd and the Prime Minister immediately made it clear that he had no intention of resigning:

> "On returning from a very brief holiday, during which I carried out several official engagements, I find that a conspiracy has been mounted against me in my absence. I have only this to say — I will fight this out; I believe that my policies represent the best safeguard to our constitutional position and our best hope for prosperity. I believe, too, that the people of Ulster support them. I do not intend to desert all those who have backed me. I fought for my country in time of war, I have fought to maintain our constitution in time of peace." (NL 24.6.1966.)

Two different accounts of the plot can be found in the memoirs of O'Neill and Faulkner. Their versions of events highlight the antagonism which existed between the Prime Minister and his Deputy. O'Neill's description of the attempt to depose him reads as follows:

> "September saw Jean [his wife] and I setting out for the Ulster Societies' Annual Meeting in Manchester, and after ten days holiday in England we were due to go to Newcastle upon Tyne for one of our Ulster Trade weeks. While in Norfolk news began to filter through about a back-bench conspiracy. It was alleged that a member called Boal, who represents the Shankill Road, was collecting signatures of those who wanted me to resign. As a piece of paper had received ten signatures in my predecessor's day, and only shortly before he resigned, I felt that this was possibly true and moreover that probably the same people would sign it. My first reaction was to return home, but I was advised that the best method of dealing with the situation was to play it cool. In Lincolnshire, our next port of call, there were more messages of more

signatures, and this continued while we spent two nights at the Mansion House in Newcastle upon Tyne as the guests of the Lord Mayor, for the Ulster Week.

"On our return from England I was given a list of those who were supposed to have signed this mysterious piece of paper. The trouble was that officially no one knew anything about it. The next morning when a Cabinet meeting was over, I threw down the gauntlet and told my colleagues that I was going to fight this conspiracy. It was interesting to watch the faces of my colleagues: most were glad that I had spoken out, but some were surprised — perhaps even dismayed.

"Mercifully there was not long to wait, for a back-bencher soon informed the press that he had been asked to sign the 'piece of paper' and had refused. As soon as the news broke, the Chief Whip, Major Chichester-Clark, issued a statement supporting me. At the same time I recorded a statement on television, standing in the hall at Stormont Castle, in which I made it plain that though the conspirators pretended that they wanted a new Prime Minister what they really wanted were different policies. From this moment on the conspiracy began to crumble and Mr. Faulkner, who had postponed a trip to America, decided to leave.

"Later at a meeting of the Parliamentary Party stories emerged of a meeting at Brian Faulkner's house [he was than Minister of Commerce] at which Harry West [Minister of Agriculture] had been present. What, however, sticks out in my mind was my predecessor's contribution, which went approximately as follows: 'Once a General loses the the support of his troops he should go. In this case I would suggest he should have six weeks in which to repair the damage by touring Unionist Associations and explaining that he really is a true blue Unionist of the old type. If at the end of the six weeks the Party is not satisfied, he should resign.'

"In rather different circumstances, before World War 1, Carson described a statement by Asquith's administration involving delay over an intended action as 'sentence of death with stay of execution'. Brookeborough also knew perfectly well that during that six weeks Paisley would emerge from jail and that there could well be further disturbances during the autumn. The man who had taken so few courageous steps during twenty years of so-called power was quite willing to lay the head of his successor on a delayed-action guillotine.

"One Belfast MP, who had undoubtedly signed the 'piece of paper', issued a statement saying he had withdrawn from his position. One sentence in that statement was most revealing. 'He regretted that because of the indirect pressure of extremism, democratic decision within the Party was made more difficult.'

"There was a tailpiece to 'the conspiracy'. When Brian Faulkner returned from America I had a little chat with him. I explained that I had no intention of staying on for a long time and that if, for instance, I retired when I was sixty, he would then be 53, the exact age of my predecessor when he had become Prime Minister. But I said that, in fact, I expected I would go long before that. I had actually already decided to retire in September 1969. By that time the Parliament would be nearly four years old and it would give my successor over six months to play himself in before he need have an election. Moreover I would then be 55 — an appropriate age to start a new life. For six months after this chat co-operation was wonderful and when it ceased I didn't really blame

Brian. I knew the dominant power in his family was his father who was desperately anxious to see his son as Prime Minister while he was still alive." (The Autobiography Of Terence O'Neill, p84-86.)

In his account of "the conspiracy", Faulkner wrote:

"In September 1966 there was a major leadership crisis which brought to the surface many of the tensions which had been simmering in the party since Lord Brookeborough's resignation. A group of backbenchers, led by Desmond Boal, MP for Shankill, moved to oust O'Neill from the Leadership. They asked me to resign and spearhead the move, but I refused. They then asked whether I would take on the leadership of the party if asked to do so. My reply was, 'Only if that is the wish of a majority of the Parliamentary Party.' They held various meetings before a group came down to see me at home one evening and tried to persuade me to resign and contest the leadership. Again I took the line that a change of leadership was a matter for the majority of the Parliamentary Party. I was supported in this by Harry West, who was visiting me with his wife. Harry argued strongly that O'Neill should be given a fair chance to prove himself. I think it was the next day that they showed me a list of names totalling one less than a majority against him [i.e., O'Neill, DG], but I refused again. I had already notified the Chief Whip, James Chichester-Clark, that there were moves afoot to oust Terence, and he had simply thanked me and left it at that.

"I left for the United States on a Ministry of Commerce visit, but the matter continued to develop in my absence and Terence O'Neill held a Party Meeting at which he got majority support. Local journalists rang me in America when news of the crisis became public and asked if I supported the Prime Minister. I said I stood unequivocally behind the policies of the Prime Minister and the Government and was not interested in personalities. This was presented in the media as an ambiguous reply, and when I returned to Belfast, Terence told me he disapproved of it. He also said that he did not intend to stay on as Prime Minister indefinitely but only for a few years." (Memoirs Of A Statesman, p40).

It is implied in O'Neill's account that Faulkner was directly involved in the plot to oust him from the leadership. This is also heavily implied by the 'historian' Andrew Boyd in his poisonous little book, **Brian Faulkner And The Crisis Of Ulster Unionism** (Anvil Books, 1972). The most notable point made in this book is in the author's introduction which claims that "Northern Ireland would now be reformed", and the "country would be at peace", if the British Government had devoted sufficient attention to the task of "ensuring civil rights and equality for Catholics during Terence O'Neill's moderate [sic] premiership" (p10). Boyd's book attempts to portray Faulkner as the world's greatest bigot, but the assessment turned out to be badly flawed, and the book was not destined to be a best seller. Not long after its publication, Brian Faulkner joined forces with the SDLP in the Power-Sharing Executive. He was then hailed as a moderate, and Boyd's book quietly disappeared from sight.

With regard to the plot against the Prime Minister in 1966, Boyd, like O'Neill, tries to make insinuations about the meeting which took place in Faulkner's house:

"In private Faulkner was not above plotting with the Paisleyites against O'Neill. It was... revealed that Boal... and other dissidents met in Faulkner's house to discuss a plan to overthrow O'Neill. Faulkner later denied, when asked about this meeting, that he had taken part in the discussion. He said he left the room when Boal and his friends were talking" (p56-57).

In fact, Faulkner's account of the meeting in his house was verified in 1969 by a supporter of Captain O'Neill. The 1966 plot became an issue in the Stormont General Election, which took place in February 1969. During the election campaign, Sam Magowan, the Unionist MP for Iveagh, revealed that he had been present at Faulkner's house, but had eventually decided not to back the plot. Magowan, who stood as a "Pro-O'Neill" candidate in 1969, said:

"I want to make it absolutely clear that Mr. Faulkner himself never put pressure on me. He was not in the room at the time. Mr. Faulkner did not put the question of the leadership to me at all." (NL 12.2.1969.)

Harry West also commented on the 1966 leadership crisis during the 1969 election campaign. He claimed that "if Mr. Faulkner had yielded to pressure at that time he would undoubtedly have become Prime Minister", and stated:

"As I remember it, there were 17 members of the Parliamentary Party who wanted to overthrow the Prime Minister, and if I had put my name to the document it could have tipped the balance for the Parliamentary Party then had 35 members" (ibid).

Faulkner's refusal to lead the challenge to O'Neill's leadership in 1966 did not prevent speculation in the press about his intentions. And this speculation was not quelled by the comments which Faulkner made during the leadership crisis. On the day the details of the plot were made public, Faulkner confirmed that discontent about the Prime Minister within the Unionist Party was "strong" and "growing". He told the News Letter that he "would not be making any comment at this juncture", and claimed that he had no intention of becoming "involved in any kind of intrigue, now or at any other time" (NL 24.9.1966). Two days later, Faulkner stated, "I would not be a member of the Government if I did not support the policy of the Government and up to date I have wholeheartedly supported all the Government's policies" (NL 26.9.1966). On this occasion, he also referred to the "serious discontent" within the Party which, he said, was "a product of months rather than weeks" (ibid). Faulkner's final comments came a fortnight after O'Neill had received an overwhelming vote of confidence from the Parliamentary Unionist Party. In response to reports in some sections of the press that he was a rival to O'Neill and had been encouraging criticism of the Prime Minister, Faulkner said:

"I am quite satisfied that the Party has now expressed its confidence in the leadership of the Prime Minister. While serving in his Government, I shall continue to support his policies in the future as I have done in the past." (NL 11.10.1966.)

Prior to the crucial meeting of the Parliamentary Unionist Party on September 27th, various leading Unionists declared their support for Captain O'Neill. These included: John Drennan, the Unionist Party Chairman; Lord

Brookeborough, the former Prime Minister; Brian McConnell, the Minister for Home Affairs; Isaac Hawthorne, the Deputy Chief Whip; James Chichester Clarke, the Chief Whip; and William Craig, the then Minister for Development (NL 24.9.1966). The latter two did, however, refer to the problems which existed within the Party. Bill Craig admitted that O'Neill had been "slightly out of touch" (ibid), while Chichester-Clarke said:

> "There is perhaps a feeling of unease. There have been a great many events during the course of the summer and I think these have caused unease." (NL 26.9.1966.)

Ironically, support for O'Neill also came from Edward Carson Jnr., the one-time associate of Ian Paisley. On the eve of the Parliamentary Party meeting, Carson sent the Prime Minister a "Red Hand" tie-pin which Lord Carson had worn throughout his political career (NL 26.9.1966).

O'NEILL TRIUMPHS

On September 28th, the News Letter carried a front-page report of the Parliamentary Unionist Party meeting under the banner headline, **Day of Triumph For Captain O'Neill**. The meeting was one of the best attended for many years, with over 45 MPs and Senators present. After seven hours of discussion, a Motion of Confidence in the Prime Minister was passed unanimously by the House of Commons MPs and with only one abstention by the Senate Unionists. The News Letter reported that, during the meeting, only one person had called for O'Neill's resignation (NL 28.9.1966).

After the meeting, O'Neill emerged to declare that the crisis was over and that the Unionist Party was "now a united Party". He also revealed that at the end of the meeting "nearly all" the rebel MPs had shaken his hand and wished him good luck (ibid). James Chichester-Clarke, the Government Chief Whip, told the News Letter:

> "The rebels are now satisfied. There will be closer liaison between the Government and the party. There will be a good deal more discussion and more party meetings." (ibid.)

One of the leading "rebels", Captain Austin Ardill, said after the meeting, "Everyone is very happy — the matter has now been fixed up"; and the former Premier Lord Brookeborough said, "I think the Prime Minister has now got the entire party behind him" (ibid).

This book will not attempt to provide an in-depth analysis of the leadership crisis within the Unionist Party in 1966. But it can point to a number of the factors which appear to have been behind the moves to depose O'Neill. These include: lack of liaison between the Government and the backbenchers; concern that the Prime Minister was not a "true blue Unionist"; personal dislike of O'Neill; external pressure from the Paisleyites; and dissatisfaction with some of the Government's domestic policies.

There is no doubt that the inadequate liaison between the Cabinet and the back-benchers was a factor in the leadership crisis of September 1966. This was admitted shortly after the Parliamentary Party meeting by O'Neill himself, who revealed that a committee might be formed to deal with the problem (NL 29.9.1966). This occurred the following month, when Unionist backbenchers set up the 1966 Committee with the aim of facilitating consultation and co-operation between the Government and the backbenchers. Another of the leading "rebel MPs", Mrs. Dinah McNabb, became the Committee's first Chairman, and O'Neill was invited to its first meeting (NL 20.10.1966).

The suspicions about O'Neill's "true blue Unionist" credentials did not primarily arise because of specific Government policies. After all, the entire objective of the plot was to replace O'Neill with Brian Faulkner who, as Deputy Prime Minister, had been closely identified with all the Government's major decisions. Faulkner had, for example, backed O'Neill over the Lemass visit, and had himself been actively involved in the Ministerial co-operation between North and South which took place after 1965. Similarly, the decision to permit the Easter Rising parades in 1966 (which was raised during the leadership crisis) was taken by the Government's Security Committee whose members included Brian Faulkner and Bill Craig. In short, therefore, there is little basis to the accusation in O'Neill's autobiography that what "the conspirators... really wanted were different policies." (P85.)

Unionist suspicions about Captain O'Neill were probably mainly due to Protestant gut-reactions to his "hands across the border" rhetoric and his hyped-up political ecumenism. As has already been stated, O'Neill's failure to communicate with the Party rank and file helped to breed mistrust and suspicion.

Some of the opposition to O'Neill undoubtedly came from the backwoodsmen within the Unionist Party who resented the very idea of their leader trying to be 'nice' to the 'other side'. But it is equally true that it was O'Neill's obnoxious personality stirred up antagonism within both the Party and the Protestant community. This can be illustrated by the following remarks from John Laird, the one-time rising star of the Unionist Party, who became the Stormont MP for St. Annes in 1970:

> "Captain O'Neill was the most egotistical man I have ever met and was altogether quite the most unpleasant personality I have ever encountered." (Fortnight, 30.11.1973.)

The influence of Paisley on the developments within the Ulster Unionist Party in 1966 is difficult to evaluate. It was certainly not the case that Paisley was manipulating the Unionist rebel MPs like puppets. What is more likely is that some of the backbenchers at Stormont wanted to guard themselves against being challenged by the Paisleyites at the next election. But it is important not to overestimate the threat which Paisley and his supporters posed to the Unionist Party in 1966. Paisley, it should be remembered, backed away from a confrontation with the Unionists in the Westminster election in February 1966. And shortly after the collapse of the anti-O'Neill plot, Paisley's wife, Eileen was well beaten by an archetypal, apolitical O'Neillite called Harold Smith in a by-election in the Duncairn ward of Belfast City Council. For the record, Smith received 4,390 votes to Eileen Paisley's 2,488, and his comment on his victory was: "I support Captain O'Neill but I was determined to omit all political matters from my campaign [sic]. I believe everyone in Belfast is equal, irrespective of their race and religion, and I will be concerned solely with the economic good of the people of the Dunacirn ward" (NL 6.10.1966).

Paradoxically, Paisley may have actually helped to keep O'Neill in Office. Shortly before the Parliamentary Unionist Party meeting on September 27th, it was reported in the British press that the Party was reluctant to ditch O'Neill because it did not want to be seen to be giving in to Paisley (NL 26.9.1966). This reluctance was exploited by the Prime Minister and his supporters. O'Neill, for example, said on one occasion that his resignation would give "encouragement to a certain gentleman who has been carrying certain suggestions on his banners" (ibid). And the News Letter claimed in an editorial that the ousting of O'Neill "could be interpreted as a return to introspective thinking and backwoods programmes, tainting the whole Province once more with the smear of bitter, outdated sectarianism. Further, it would give satisfaction... to those who feed so greedily on the emotions of the mob, its fears and suspicions. It would be well to remember who first carried the placard 'O'Neill must go'" (NL 24.9.1966).

The only evidence that the leadership plot in 1966 was connected to dissatisfaction within the Party over specific economic policies can be found in the News Letter's first report on the anti-O'Neill petition. It stated that "at least four" of the petition's signatories had signed in protest at the domestic policy of individual Government Departments, and the Ministry of Development in particular. And it quoted John Taylor, the MP for West Tyrone, as saying that he had signed the petition "as a protest against Government policy towards the West, particularly with regard to motorway projects" (ibid).

Overall, it is clear that the 1966 plot did not have a single coherent objective. Nor was it inspired by an alternative vision of Unionism. It is this lack of coherence which explains why the attempt to oust Captain O'Neill failed so miserably. The plotters may have been dimly aware that something was amiss with the O'Neillite strategy. But their quarrel was with the style and emphasis of O'Neill's leadership and not the political philosophy which underpinned it. When it came to their commitment to Stormont and the 'Our Wee Ulster' mentality, the rebel backbench MPs and Terence O'Neill were as one. Consequently, if the Unionist Party had decided to ditch O'Neill in 1966, it would have been the equivalent of a plane crew dropping the pilot and then continuing to fly into the sea. This is what eventually happened when O'Neill was forced to step down in 1969.

Needless to say the total collapse of the 1966 plot against O'Neill was greeted with delight in the pages of the News Letter. Its editorial on the Parliamentary Party's vote of confidence in the Prime Minister said:

"Captain O'Neill said he would fight it out. Yesterday he did just that— and to a triumphant victory. Today, unchallengeable, he stands firmer than ever before at the head of the country and as leader of the Unionist Party." (NL 29.9.1966.)

Captain O'Neill and his supporters, therefore, tried once again to shrug off their problems and act as if nothing had happened. By the middle of October, O'Neill was once again boasting about the benefits of Stormont and confidently predicting that "the day will come when Scotland, at least, will have a parliament and government of its own and, indeed... when other regions will have similar administrations of their own" (NL 19.10.1966).

Almost immediately, however, reality was unkind enough to put in another appearance. During a debate on Northern Ireland in the House of Commons at Westminster, the Labour MP, Kevin McNamara, drew attention to a serious anomaly in the Stormont/Westminster relationship:

> "There is considerable concern on this side of the House that whereas Mr. Robert Chichester-Clarke [Unionist, Londonderry] can ask questions about building schemes in Salford, we cannot ask questions about discrimination about housing matters in his constituency" (NL 16.11.1966).

The Labour Prime Minister, Harold Wilson admitted that there was "a certain logicality" to McNamara's complaint but added that the situation was "part and parcel of long standing arrangements between the two countries" (ibid). This was all too much for the News Letter which whinged:

> "It has never been contested that under Clause 75 of the Government of Ireland Act the overriding responsibility for 'all persons, matters and things in Northern Ireland and every part thereof' lies with the Parliament at Westminster. The practice of successive Governments there has been to exercise minimum interference in those matters which have been transferred to Stormont" (ibid).

At the end of 1966, therefore, the Unionist Family was still getting very touchy over the slightest hint of interference in the affairs of Stormont. Two years later, its delusions about Stormont power rendered the Unionist Party totally incapable of coping with the Civil Rights movement.

Chapter Eight

1967
FAULKNER
AND THE SOUTH

In comparison to 1965 and 1966, 1967 was a fairly uneventful year. For some reason, Brian Faulkner featured prominently in the first major developments of 1967. The first of these concerned the issue of North-South relations.

In the early part of February, a meeting between O'Neill and Jack Lynch, the Taoiseach, appears to have been very much on the cards. This possibility was put to Faulkner following a meeting between himself and the Eire Minister for Commerce, George Colley. Faulkner replied that it would be "the most natural thing in the world" for O'Neill to meet Lynch and added: "We are determined to promote economic co-operation to the full but this does not involve constitutional affairs." (NL 3.2.1967.) In response to Faulkner's comments, the News Letter urged an early meeting between O'Neill and Lynch and suggested a forthcoming rugby international at Lansdowne Road as a suitable venue for the meeting.

Such a possibility, however, was scuppered by a controversy over a statement allegedly made in the Dail by Jack Lynch. The Taoiseach was due to meet the British Prime Minister and was challenged in the Dail to tell Harold Wilson that Partition would have "no means of continuing without British support" (NL 9.2.1967). According to a Dublin journalist working for the News Letter, Lynch replied to this challenge by saying that he never lost the opportunity of pointing this out to Wilson. The paper passed this information on to Faulkner who responded by criticising the Dublin Government:

> "Northern Ireland is part and parcel of the United Kingdom and we are prepared to accept all the responsibilities that our position entails, as we always have done. We receive benefits from being part of the U.K., just as Cornwall, Wales, Scotland etc., receive the same benefits, including sharing in the British standard of living. But it should be clearly understood in Dublin that Ulster Unionists are determined to remain part of the U.K., quite irrespective of material benefits. These benefits are not the sine qua non of Northern Ireland's survival. Even if there were no material benefits and our standard of living slumped, for example, to the level of that which exists in Eire, we would still stay with Britain... It must be remembered that even now, after forty five years of 'independence', Eire is still 90% dependent on the U.K economy." (NL 9.2.1967.)

Faulkner criticised the South again the following week only hours after he had had a friendly meeting with the Eire Minister for Transport and Power, Erskine Childers. He claimed that recent statements from leaders in the Republic did not "make the climate any easier for meetings with the Prime Minister or other Ministers." (NL 17.2.1967.) This was a reference to Lynch's Dail statement and to other anti-partitionist noises that had recently been made by Southern politicians like Frank Aitken and Brian Lenihan. In the wake of Faulkner's comments, a front page article in the News Letter by R.M. Sibbett (one of its top journalists) stated that the chances of another North-South summit had receded as a result of Lynch's behaviour.

All these developments appeared slightly farcical when it emerged that the News Letter had been mis-informed about Lynch's statement in the Dail. The Taoiseach had actually been a good deal more diplomatic in response to the question from the TD. According to the Official Report of Dail proceedings Lynch had replied that he would remind Harold Wilson of "all salient facts" regarding Partition (NL 12.12.1967). Nevertheless, Faulkner stuck to his guns and made it clear that he would have issued exactly the same criticism of the Dublin Government on the basis of what Lynch had actually said. Brian Faulkner's stance received the firm backing of Captain O'Neill in a Stormont Debate on the controversy on February 22nd.

During this Debate, both Austin Currie and Harry Diamond alleged that Faulkner had been acting on behalf of O'Neill and the rest of Cabinet by finding an excuse for O'Neill not to meet the Taoiseach. Diamond also heavily criticised the News Letter for misleading Faulkner over Lynch's comment. "It is deplorable," he claimed, "that we have in our community a journal in which there are people who will interview public figures and deliberately mislead them with statements of this kind" (NL 23.2.1967).

FAULKNER AND WEST

Brian Faulkner was at the centre of the next political controversy to emerge in 1967. But on this occasion, there was precious little evidence of unity between him and Captain O'Neill.

The controversy resulted from O'Neill's decision to sack his Minister for Agriculture, Harry West. The facts which led to this dismissal are quite complicated. They centre on a farm at Rosschilly in County Fermanagh, which Harry West had purchased from his cousin, Victor West. The farmland purchased included part of the disused St. Angelo Airfield, which Fermanagh County Council had been planning to buy and operate as an airfield again with financial assistance from the Stormont Government. Whether or not West had deliberately bought the land in order to benefit from its increased value is a matter for conjecture. If this was his intention, it was a remarkably ham-fisted attempt to make a fast buck. West himself had been lobbying on behalf of those who wanted to make the airfield operational again. At any rate, Harry West was deemed to have broken the code of principles for Government Ministers, brought in by O'Neill in the first year of his premiership. The Prime Minister gave a full account of West's alleged misdemeanours to Stormont on April 26th. West told his side of the story to Stormont on May 2nd. Anyone wishing to know all the facts behind West's sacking should consult the News Letter's relevant reports on April 27th and May 3rd 1967.

Of much more significance than West's Fermanagh farm, however, was the impact the episode had within the Unionist Party. Brian Faulkner was informed of West's dismissal by reporters while he was attending an Ulster Week in Leeds and his response produced an immediate controversy. Faulkner admitted that the news had come "as a bombshell" to him and went on to claim that Harry West was "certainly absolutely blameless" (NL 28.4.1967). When asked whether or not the Cabinet was behind O'Neill on the issue, Faulkner answered:

> "I have not spoken to any of my colleagues on this. It is not really a question of being behind him. It is the Prime Minister's prerogative. Speaking for myself, I want to hear what Mr.West has to say on the situation next week. All of us will have to consider our positions after that." (ibid.)

Aside from Faulkner's response, West's sacking did cause a few rumblings within the ranks of the Unionist Party. On April 28th, for instance, it was reported that four Unionist backbench MPs were trying to persuade the former Leader of the House, Ivan Neill, to challenge O'Neill for the Party Leadership (ibid). Strong support for Harry West was declared by Major Ronald Bunting of the Ulster Constitutional Defence Commitee and at a meeting of 500 Orangemen and loyalists in Derrygonnelly. Bunting claimed that the issue of the Fermanagh farm was merely an excuse and that West had really been sacked from the Cabinet because he was a critic of the Prime Minister.

This accusation received support from an unlikely quarter: Harry Diamond, the Republican Labour MP for the Falls constituency. In a speech at Stormont, Diamond claimed that West had been "framed" for the role he was alleged to have played in the plot against O'Neill the previous year. The Falls MP recalled that when he was leaving Stormont after hearing of Harry West's dismissal, "one of the Prime Minister's supporters said: 'That's one gone and two to go'" The other two, according to Diamond, were Brian Faulkner and the Minister for Health and Social Services, William Morgan (NL 3.5.1967).

In the event, however, the dismissal of West did not lead to serious problems for O'Neill within the Party. Two days after West left Office, O'Neill addressed the Annual Conference of the Unionist Party. His speech received a standing ovation, although the delegates from Fermanagh remained seated.

The entire affair was discussed by 16 backbench Unionist MPs at a meeting of the 1966 Committee on May 2nd. There the following resolution was backed by a majority of one:

> "That this Committee, while agreeing that the Prime Minister's course in asking Mr.West to resign was proper in the circumstances, wishes to add that, in its opinion, Mr. West was guilty of an error of judgement. But the Committee is satisfied that he was not guilty of any dishonesty." (NL 5.5.1967.)

Given that there were at least two abstentions in this vote, the overall tally of backbenchers who backed the Prime Minister was fairly high. Commenting on this, Mervyn Pauley claimed that O'Neill would view the vote as "satisfactory", particularly in view of the strong support for him which existed within the Cabinet (NL 5.5.1967). The controversy over the West affair did not, therefore, develop into another full-blown leadership crisis for O'Neill. Indeed, if anyone's position was put in jeopardy by the affair, it was Brian Faulkner's. He was the object of some veiled criticism in a News Letter editorial published on the day after O'Neill addressed the Unionist Party conference:

> "One of the most regrettable aspects of the situation that has evolved has been the tactless and ill-judged comments of those who could not wait... If the purpose was to undermine the leadership how miserably that purpose has failed. Today with last night's ovation still ringing in his ears the Prime Minister is seen both at home and in Britain as the leader who alone can bring Ulster in full maturity safely through to the rich potential and challenges of the seventies." (NL 29.4.1967.)

(One of the reasons for the News Letter's enthusiastic O'Neill-worship on this occasion was the publication of a favourable article in The Economist about the Unionist Party leader. This article contained the memorable line: "The Prime Minister, Captain Terence O'Neill, approaches Ulster's taboos with a certainty that only an officer and a gentleman of impeccable ancestry could muster" [ibid).)

Faulkner's claim that Harry West was "absolutely blameless" led to speculation that he was planning to lead a 'coup' against O'Neill. This was denied by Faulkner who said: "Under no consideration would I allow my name to be linked at this time with any attempt to usurp the leadership of the Party" (NL 1.5.1967).

When it became clear that O'Neill's position as leader of the Unionist Party was not in jeopardy, attention was centred on Faulkner's position within the Cabinet. In an article entitled, **Faulkner Faces Dilemma**, the News Letter cited the views of an unnamed Unionist MP: "Mr. Faulkner does appear to be in a cleft stick," he said. "To my mind the question is, does he stick by Mr.West and maintain that he was blameless or does he change his ground and say he was premature in his assessment of the situation" (ibid).

Faulkner's use of the words "at this time", when denying that he was plotting against O'Neill, was criticised by the Unionist MP for Queen's, Robert Porter, who implored him to "make it clear where he stands" (NL 3.5.1967). In reply, Faulkner stood by his view that West had not been guilty of dishonesty and added, "If I cannot support the Prime Minister in every single item of policy I would resign forthwith" (ibid).

The Minister for Commerce was put on the defensive again by Major Chichester-Clarke who had been appointed as West's replacement at the Ministry of Agriculture. In a television interview, Chichester-Clarke called on Brian Faulkner to say that he was 100% behind the Prime Minister and that the Unionist Party was a united party. This produced an angry reaction from

Faulkner, who said that if he was being asked to say that he would support every action of O'Neill's at all times, he was being asked for an assurance he couldn't give to the Archangel Gabriel. "What does he want me to say anyway?" Faulkner inquired. "I would remind everybody of what I said after the last crisis, namely that I am 100% behind all the Prime Minister's policies — all of which incidentally, I have had a hand in framing" (NL 4.5.1967).

When asked whether he wanted to be Prime Minister, Faulkner replied:

> "I have no more ambition to be Prime Minister of this country than any other member of the party at Stormont. These long range exchanges are becoming absolutely farcical. Let us get rid of personalities and stick to policies ... All I want is to be left in peace to get on with my work in the Ministry of Commerce." (ibid.)

It appears, therefore, that Faulkner got himself into considerable trouble by defending Harry West, who was a close friend of his. Indeed, a News Letter editorial published on May 4th referred to a "Faulkner must go campaign". The News Letter defended his record as Minister of Commerce and predicted that the campaign against him "would surely collapse once he shows beyond all qualification that he is prepared to be a loyal deputy" (NL 4.5.1967).

Faulkner's troubles were also the subject of an interesting article by Mervyn Pauley in his weekly Stormont Diary column. He claimed that "the Minister for Commerce must be heartily sick of the whole business, if not a little apprehensive at the way the West saga rebounded on him". Pauley referred to "the re-emergence of a power-strugle" within the Cabinet, and contended that Faulkner was "far from forthcoming" when it came to "making a statement on his personal loyalty to Captain O'Neill as leader of the Party". The article contained an interesting remark from a Unionist backbencher, who had likened Captain O'Neill to "the cox in a boat race with one of the crew appearing to row the wrong way". The article's best point, however, came from Eddie McAteer, the Nationalist Party Leader. Referring to the conclusion of the West saga, McAteer said:

> "Now... the leadership crisis has been resolved finally and firmly for another two or three weeks" (NL 5.5.1967).

In the end, the whole controversy faded away without Faulkner having to retract the comments he had made in defence of West. The irony of the whole affair is that, seven years later, Harry West became Unionist Party Leader after Faulkner had been forced to resign over the Sunningdale Agreement.

The whole episode is significant as it gives some indication of the personal animosities and in-fighting which existed within the leadership of the Unionist Party at this time. There were, as Faulkner pointed out, no tangible disagreements between himself and O'Neill in 1967. But there is no doubt that they disliked each other personally. That much is well-known, but the extent to which O'Neill gained the upper hand on his Deputy over the West affair is probably less well known.

O'NEILLISM ALIVE AND KICKING IN '67

There are firm reasons for believing that Terence O'Neill's position as Unionist Party leader was stronger in 1967 than it had been in 1966. And there is no doubt that his political outlook retained its vice-like grip on the Party throughout the year.

On May 15th, Captain O'Neill scored a minor personal triumph while on a visit to Ballynahinch. According to the News Letter, Paisleyites intent on disrupting the Prime Ministerial visit were chased by townspeople and were forced to seek police protection. During his tour of Ballynahinch, O'Neill made another of his grand 'reconciliatory' gestures. He visited the Assumption Convent grounds, and "chatted to Sister Mary Jarlath", while watching a hockey match between a Catholic team and a Protestant team (NL16.5.1967).

Two days after O'Neill's Ballynahinch visit, the results of the Belfast City Council elections were announced. The Unionists won forty four seats, which represented a gain of five. The NILP lost four seats, and only held on to two, while the Republican Labour Party's representation on the Council rose from five to eight. There was no real breakthrough for Ian Paisley's Protestant Unionist Party which did not improve on its tally of two seats. (However, Mrs Eileen Paisley did top the poll in the St. George's Ward.) Perhaps the most interesting result occurred in the Dock Ward, where Gerry Fitt defeated Frank Millar, the Unionist candidate: Millar had been disowned by O'Neill during the election campaign because of his hard-line attitudes (full results — NL 18.5.1967).

There is, as has already been stated, a myth that Terence O'Neill's position as Unionist Party leader was always precarious. This fits in with the picture of O'Neill as a mild reformer, who was brought down by Protestant bigots who failed to understand the need to "modernise" Northern Ireland. This simplistic idea provides a very misleading account of the developments within Unionist politics in the 1960s. It was never inevitable that O'Neill would end up being forced out of office. And the problems which finally led to his downfall were largely caused by the inadequacies of his own political outlook rather than his attitude to North-South co-operation, "reforms", or community relations within the North.

Looking at the speeches made by Terence O'Neill during 1967, it is difficult to believe that they were made by a man under siege from hordes of bigots. The rhetoric was much the same as it had been in 1963 and 1964 and, if anything, even more confident. On June 14th 1967, for instance, O'Neill told the South Tyrone Unionist Association: "We can build a really strong and successful Ulster, using where necessary our regional powers to blaze a trail for the rest of the United Kingdom." (NL 15.6.1967.)

THE TWELFTH

Once again, the speeches made at the various Twelfth of July demonstrations in 1967 provide some indication of the state of play within Unionist politics at the time. This time, the Orange Order's traditional resolutions did contain a declaration of full support for O'Neill and his Government:

> "We pay tribute to our Brother, Captain The Right Honourable Terence M. O'Neill, Prime Minister, for the policy of his Government, whereby Ulster's position has remained strong and viable within the United Kingdom.
>
> "We believe that Ulster is proud of her achievements, and we are therefore resolved that the approaching fiftieth anniversary of the constitution of N.Ireland will be marked by a suitable occasion, showing, not only our History but the vigour and purpose that lies within the agricultural and industrial community of the whole of Northern Ireland." (NL 13.7.1967.)

At the demonstration at Fintona, County Tyrone, an amended version of this resolution was read out, which paid tribute to the Government but omitted O'Neill's name. And, according to the News Letter, the resolution was greeted by organised heckling at "less than half" of the demonstrations in the province. The most serious incident of the day occurred when anti-O'Neill hecklers clashed with the Unionist MP, George Forrest, who ended up in hospital after being struck unconscious (ibid).

There was much less evidence of opposition to O'Neill in the speeches made by leading Unionists at the various demonstrations. The only reported criticism was made by former Government Minister, Harry West, who claimed that "changing attitudes within the Unionist Party" had not gone unnoticed in Nationalist circles, and that the changes had encouraged Nationalists in their "quiet waiting game" (ibid). For the most part, however, there was a mood of confidence about the future particularly among members of the Government. The Minister for Education, Captain Long, for example, declared in a speech at Dundonald: "Those who say Ulster isn't going places must be blind" (ibid).

While vociferous opponents of Captain O'Neill may not have been too difficult to find within the Ulster Protestant community in 1967, it is clear that his delusions about the political life of the province were still shared throughout the Unionist Party. On July 30th, for example, Brain Faulkner, O'Neill's Deputy Prime Minister and supposed arch-rival, made a speech about the virtues of Stormont and the 1920 Government Of Ireland Act. He told a meeting of East Down Unionist Asscociation that Stormont had been created to "solve the Irish problem", which had "bedevilled British politics" for generations. "It has done more than that," he asserted, "it has brought prosperity undreamt of to the whole population" (NL 31.7.1967). Faulkner's speech to the East Down Unionists also claimed that Northern Ireland was witnessing a "slow growth", which was "assimilating two strong religious faiths, two historic traditions", and "two political loyalties" (ibid). Presumably, no one at the meeting thought to ask him what would become of politics in the province once full assimilation of political loyalties had occurred.

In September 1967, the Unionist MP, John Taylor, came up with a particularly deranged O'Neillite project. He urged the Stormont Government to create a separate postal system for Northern Ireland in order to "emphasise the individuality of the Ulster people and State [sic]." (NL 30.9.1967.) This highly impractical suggestion emphasises the extent to which elements within the Unionist Party were moving in a vaguely Ulster Nationalist direction in the 1960s.

NORTH-SOUTH RELATIONS

In the latter half of 1967, the issue of North-South relations again came to the fore and, in December, the Taoiseach, Jack Lynch, paid a visit to Belfast. Referring to this event in his Autobiography, Terence O'Neill stated that, "some time after Mr. Lemass's retirement", he "got the Cabinet to agree that a meeting would be arranged at some propitious moment with Mr. Lynch" (p75).

No doubt aware of this Cabinet decision, the News Letter reported on June 15th that a North-South summit was on the cards for later in the year. The report noted that the last "high level conclave" had occurred on February 9th, 1965, when O'Neill and Lemass had met in Dublin. Since then, according to the report, there had been "sustained contact between the the two governments at ministerial level and... significant developments in the educational, agricultural and electricity spheres." (NL15.6.1967.)

In October 1967, the most tangible achievement of this ministerial contact was achieved: Brian Faulkner and Erskine Childers, the Eire Minister for Fuel and Power, reached agreement on the North-South power pact. The signing of this pact was described by Faulkner as "an important and significant occasion in the history of Ireland". O'Neill's verdict on the electricity agreement is also worth recording, if only to illustrate his pomposity. He wrote in his Memoirs:

> "today when a militant Protestant housewife fries an egg she may well be doing it on Catholic power generated in the South and distributed in the North as a result of that first O'Neill-Lemass meeting." (P75.)

There is no record of any dissension within the Protestant community over the Faulkner/Childers North-South power pact. The same cannot be said, however, for Jack Lynch's visit to Stormont House two months later. The Lynch visit was not an exact re-run of the Lemass visit of January 1965. In 1967, O'Neill decided to let more people know in advance, although he appears to have later regretted it:

> "To some extent we were influenced by the press criticism about undue secrecy over the first meeting, so with the approval of Mr. Jack Lynch... we decided to release the news of Mr. Lynch's visit as he crossed the border into Northern Ireland. Someone or other decided to pass on the information to Mr. Paisley, possibly in order to get some good pictures and sensational news, and as a result as Mr. Lynch's car circled round Carson's statue at Stormont it was snowballed by Mr. Paisley and some of his ministers who had just time to assemble there." (P74.)

The snowballing ministers referred to by O'Neill were the Rev. Ivan Foster (who afterwards became a DUP Councillor in Fermanagh, but left politics in 1989) and the Rev. William McCrea (now DUP MP for Mid Ulster). Their leader, Ian Paisley, said of the Lynch visit:

> "Captain O'Neill has broken his word. He promised that there would be no meeting with the Premier of Eire until the South recognised Northern Ireland's

constitutional position. I am going to push this thing as far as I can. I do not object to anyone coming to Northern Ireland who recognises the constitutional position. Jack Lynch does not and he is therefore an intruder." (NL 12.12.1967.)

Within the Unionist Party, the Government was criticised over the Lynch visit by Court Ward Unionist Association and by the Westminster MP for South Antrim, Sir Knox Cunningham. The Court Ward Unionists accused the Government of placing a "cloud of secrecy" over the proceedings, while Cunningham said:

"I condemn this summit meeting in Belfast. So long as Mr.Lynch continues to voice territorial claims to Ulster and so long as he encourages the Ministers in his Government to attack Northern Ireland at the United Nations and elsewhere, he is not welcome in Ulster.

"These views are held by many thousands of people in Ulster and the Northern Ireland Government would be wise to take notice of them." (ibid.)

In the event, public protest at the Lynch visit culminated on December 19th with a Paisleyite rally in the Ulster Hall. According to the News Letter, 2,500 took part in a march from the Shankill Road to the rally at which Paisley promised that O'Neill would be opposed by a Protestant loyalist candidate in Bannside at the next election (NL 20.12.1967).

There were, in fact, no major ructions within the Unionist Party over the Taoiseach's visit. The extent to which O'Neill and his Cabinet colleagues felt at threat over the issue may be gauged from a report published in the News Letter on December 13th. This stated that meetings between Northern Ireland and Eire Government Ministers would become more frequent, including meetings between the Prime Ministers.

On January 8th, 1968, Captain O'Neill travelled to Dublin to meet Lynch again. There was very virtually no protest in the North about this meeting although Paisley did comment on O'Neill's arrival home. "It is regretted that he returned," Paisley said. "I would advise Mr. Lynch to keep him." (NL 9.1.1967.) The News Letter editorial writer, however, had a very different outlook on the meeting:

"Comings and goings between Stormont and Iveagh House are now almost part of the normal run of politics and soon may cease to make front page news. The sooner the better." (Ibid.)

CURRIE'S WARNING

A good deal of self-satisfaction can be detected in the editorials of the News Letter and in the speeches of leading Unionists at the end of 1967. It is obvious that no one in the Unionist Government was aware that there was the slightest thing wrong with the way they were governing Northern Ireland. In the midst of this smugness, however, the Government was warned that all was not well in Captain O'Neill's "new Ulster". It totally ignored this warning, and within twelve months their cosy political set-up had crumbled down around them.

The warning was made in October by Austin Currie, the Nationalist MP for East Tyrone, at a meeting of the Economic and Political Studies Society in Magee University College, Derry. Currie spoke on the topic of O'Neillism and said:

> "No politician in the history of this state has aroused hopes and expectations to the same extent as has Captain O'Neill. For the first time we seemed to have a Prime Minister who could shake off the shackles of the past and look to the future." (NL 24.10.1967.)

Currie predicted that O'Neill had a twelve month deadline in which to "weed out injustice and intolerance", and that, if he failed, a "growing militancy" would develop within the Catholic community. "There will be more squatting," Currie claimed, "more acts of civil disobedience, more emphasis on 'other means' and less on traditional Parliamentary methods... And Terence O'Neill and his Government must carry the responsibility. The Prime Minister could leave a record of real achievement or, if he refused to act, he will be recognised as the political confidence trickster of and stuntman of this generation." (Ibid.)

Terence O'Neill raised within the Catholic community an expectation of progressive change. He stirred up activity around the administrative routine at Stormont and he indulged in rhetoric about "changing the face of Ulster". But the boycott of Northern Ireland by the political parties which governed the UK state meant that the province lacked a party political means of realising this expectation of change. And rather than attempting to develop alternative political structures, O'Neill actually increased Unionist Party command of the local political scene.

In October 1967, Austin Currie served notice that the Catholic community was not prepared to limit its political activities to the election of a handful of Nationalist MPs to the Opposition benches in Stormont every five years. And, just as he did twelve months later, when the Civil Rights marches began in earnest, O'Neill made no attempt to respond coherently to the criticism of his Government. He did not, for example, ask Currie to elaborate on his vague call for the weeding out of "injustice and intolerance". And he certainly did not concede that Catholics might just possibly be less than 100% happy at their political isolation under the Stormont arrangements. The Prime Minister's response to the warning delivered by Currie on October 22nd was made on November 3rd. He simply dismissed it as "a very ugly, a very intolerant and potentially a very dangerous speech." (NL 4.11.1967.)

ONE MAN ONE VOTE

Coincidentally in December 1967, the Unionist Government did address itself to an issue which was to play a very prominent role in the civil rights movement: the demand for universal franchise in Local Government elections. The issue arose following the announcement of the Government's programme for the new year in the Queen's speech and the publication of a White Paper on Local Government re-organisation.

The Queen's Speech was delivered on 19th December, and contained the following commitment:

"A Bill will be introduced abolishing the University constituency and its representation in the House of Commons and creating four new territorial parliamentary constituencies, each returning one member to the House of Commons. Provision will also be made for the establishment thereafter of a Boundary Commission to keep the boundaries of all 52 parliamentary constituencies under review. This Bill will also abolish the business vote at parliamentary elections." (Hansard, Vol 68, 19.12.1967, Col 61.)

Commenting on the final sentence in the above paragraph, the Unionist MP for West Down, John Dobson, brought up the issue of Local Government franchise:

"**Mr. Dobson:** On the face of it a debate on that particular sentence would seem to be strictly limited to parliamentary franchise but I doubt it is not beyond the powers of the Opposition to succeed in widening it to bring in once again the question of local authority franchise.

"**Mr. McAteer** (Foyle): I never thought of it until now.

"**Mr. Dobson:** I may be wrong. About the only safe forecast anyone can make about this House is that any forecast one makes is almost certain to be wrong but on the verbosity stakes for the Session my bet is that particular item. My own view is, and I may as well open the betting when I have an opportunity, that while there are arguments for and against on both sides on this particular question, the strength of the arguments lies in favour of the existing system and this should be left as it is.

"On one point I am certain. There is no validity whatsoever in the argument that has been... advanced... that a change should be made in the system because it could benefit political parties other than the Unionists. I cannot see that any Government could possibly be under any obligation to make changes merely to ensure that more of its political opponents are elected.

"**Mr. Taylor** (South Tyrone): Hear, hear." (Ibid.)

On December 20th, the Minister of Development, William Fitzsimmons, produced a 24-page White Paper on the Local Government franchise. This White Paper represented the first major re-shaping of local government in nearly seventy years (NL 21.12.1967). On the same day, William Craig, the Home Affairs Minister, indicated at Stormont, "that the Cabinet would review local government franchise in N. Ireland but not until after there had been a streamlining of the system." (Ibid.) He claimed that the fact that no firm commitment had been entered into did not imply that the Government regarded the "present system as beyond criticism or incapable of improvement." Craig's speech also revealed that he had some sympathy with those who defended the existing ratepayers' franchise:

"'One man one vote' sounds very well, but it is not always and necessarily the only proper system... Let us remember — and I emphasise that I am not attempting to prejudge the issue — that contrary to the impression one sometimes gets it is not actually shameful or sinful to be a ratepayer or to feel that one's influence in electing those who spend the money should not be entirely unrelated to the amount one contributes.

"Certainly some aspects of local government are cracking at the joints today. But no one could seriously suggest that a change in the franchise would instantly restore the patient to health." (Ibid.)

The Unionist Government could have introduced universal franchise for local government elections in 1967 without much difficulty. The reform could have been justified to the Party rank and file on the grounds that it was bringing Northern Ireland into line with the rest of the UK. And despite the comment made by John Dobson MP (quoted above), it is unlikely that "one man one vote" would have harmed the Unionist Party electorally in the 1960s. The ratepayers' franchise actually disenfranchised more Protestants than Catholics.

In reality, Local Government elections were of little consequence in Northern Ireland and the turn-out for them was notoriously low. Nevertheless, the failure of the O'Neill Administration to deal with the anomaly in the franchise had very serious repercussions. Within eighteen months of Craig's speech on the issue in December 1967, divisions within the Cabinet on how to respond to the demand for "one man one vote" had led to the resignation of both the Prime Minister and the Deputy Prime Minister.

Chapter Nine

1968
THE YEAR OF THE BIG
TRUTH

O'NEILL AND THE CATHOLIC COMMUNITY

In 1968, a number of significant truths were revealed. The first of these concerned Terence O'Neill's attitude to the Catholic community. In January 1968, the News Letter published an editorial entitled, **The Double Barrier in Ulster**, which dealt with the connection between religion and politics in Northern Ireland. The editorial drew attention to the failure of the Unionist Party to attract significant numbers of Catholics into its ranks and asked:

"Is the reason to be found in the special relationship which exists between the Unionist Party and the Orange Order?

"Under the constitution of the Ulster Unionist Council there is provision for the Order's official representation and affiliation. Further, in the constituencies Orange Halls are in many places the most suitable, sometimes the only, buildings in which Unionists can meet.

"The Orange Order has an honoured place and an important function to fulfill in the life of the Ulster community and this newspaper would neither decry its purpose nor suggest that it had outlived its usefulness.

"Nevertheless, the question must reasonably be asked if this is not an appropriate moment in time for the Unionist Party to look again at the constitution of the Council and to emerge as a political party in which no other organ holds a place of privilege?

"Until this has been done Unionism, for all the benefits it has conferred on the people of this Province irrespective of their political creed or religious faith, cannot broaden the basis of support which is essential to its future growth" (NL 15.1.1968).

The editorial also highlighted the debilitating influence of sectarianism in Northern Ireland politics:

"Religious belief, in its highest and purest form is a deeply personal experience; it has no basis in politics.

"One of the tragedies of this country is that politics and religion combine to create a double barrier within the community. If political parties were gauged and assessed apart, the first step would have been taken to eliminate the bitterness and suspicions now so closely allied with religious differences." Ibid.)

Within the context of Unionist politics, this editorial was a radical development. To follow it up, the News Letter asked a number of political figures for their reaction to it. Sam Napier, the Secretary of the NILP, welcomed the editorial as "an attempt to highlight the imperfections of Ulster's political life" (NL 16.1.1968). The leader of the Ulster Liberal Party, the Rev. Albert McElroy, said:

> "Had N. Ireland been really an integral part of the U.K., the Labour Party, for instance, ought to have held at least half of the Belfast seats. The fact that it has not underlines the abnormality of the local political situation. At its best the Unionist party, emancipated from its tradition of sectarianism, might prove a respectable Conservative Party" (ibid).

A very different response, however, was made by Roy Bradford, who at that time was Parliamentary Secretary to the Northern Ireland Minister of Education. (He is now an Official Unionist Party councillor on North Down Borough Council). On the question of Catholics joining the Unionist Party, Bradford stated:

> "I have said before that all doors are open and should properly be open to a Roman Catholic who, in good faith, and not as a gesture of political expediency, will accept the Constitutional conventions, and, indeed courtesies, of the State of which he is a citizen, and who also will acknowledge the Royal Warrant and symbol which is the authority of the Government of N. Ireland.
> "I can see the difficulty which Roman Catholics feel in the association of Unionism with the Orange Order, but the roots of Unionism and those of the Orange Order are so inextricably interwined that the renunciation of its formal links with the Unionist Party might be a matter for decision within the Order if it felt that such a matter would be for the good of the Party as a whole.
> "Until there is an official recognition on the part of the Roman Catholic Church of the same Constitutional conventions, I foresee little chance of change in the present political climate." (ibid.)

Roy Bradford was the only member of the Government quoted by the News Letter in connection with its editorial of the previous day. When he was promoted to the office of Chief Whip later in 1968, the paper described Bradford as a "firm believer in the progressive policies of the Prime Minister" (NL 3.9.1968). In January 1968, however, this firm believer in O'Neillism could be found rejecting the idea that the Unionist Party should do more to attract Catholic support. Of course, Catholics could join the Party, he asserted, provided they weren't infiltrators and were prepared to bow down before the "Royal warrant and symbol". No doubt, wrapping themselves in the Union Jack every night before going to sleep would have helped as well.

On the issue of the Unionist Party link with the Orange Order, Bradford admitted that it might be a "difficulty" for some Catholics, but claimed that it was a matter for the Order rather than the Party. The fact that every single member of O'Neill's Cabinet was in the Orange Order was obviously felt to be irrelevant. And, anyway, according to Roy Bradford, the Orange Order was not the problem. Everything was the fault of the Catholic Church which was brainwashing its members into rejecting the "Constitutional Conventions".

Captain O'Neill did not comment on the News Letter editorial of January

15th. But just over a fortnight after it, he delivered his most significant speech on the subject of Ulster Unionism. This speech was made at a meeting of the Carrick Unionist Association on January 31st 1968. It outlined O'Neill's belief that Unionism was a coherent political philosophy which was superior to anything that existed in the rest of the UK. Throughout it, O'Neill never once conceded that Catholics might just possibly have genuine reasons for not joining or voting for the Unionist Party. In short, O'Neill's speech to the Carrick Unionists represented an attempt to refute the charge that the Unionist Party was a Protestant Party. In terms of its content, timing, and influence, it is probably the most reactionary speech ever made by any Unionist politician. As such, it should be quoted in full.

"Unionism is often so unfairly and inaccurately described by its critics and opponents that those of us who believe in it have the duty, from time to time, to describe it as it is. And the first point to be made is that, unlike a great many political parties, it exists not to divide the community, but to unite it [sic].

"I have said it before, and I will say it again: Unionism is more than just a political party, although a political party is its instrument in central and local government. It is a movement, a way of looking at things, a frame of reference which can bring together people from very different backgrounds, many of whom have no formal connection with the party as such.

"Unionism has been called sectarian. But I ask those who attach that stigma to us to consider the Manifesto on which we fought the last General Election, and to decide whether there is a single proposition in that policy statement offensive to any religious denomination.

"Our policy, as stated in that Manifesto — and it remains our policy up to the next General Election — is to work, through the British connection, for greater economic strength and for the creation of an 'opportunity State' in which no one will be held back by his environment from realizing his full potential.

"It was stated yet again in the booklet "Ulster Today and Tommorrow", which the Ulster Unionist Council published very recently. May I read you a few words from it? After setting out all that we propose to do to improve Northern Ireland in a physical sense — through houses and factories, hospitals and roads — the booklet says:

"'But there is another dimension of a community's life — the quality of its living. Unionism in the years which lie ahead must be concerned with this also. There is no good reason why the unhappy divisions of the past should be perpetuated. Certainly this Ulster of ours will not be as strong, as prosperous and as happy as we would wish until the community is united in essentials.'

"These are the things that modern Unionism is saying, and people should consider them rather than the words which our enemies try to put into our mouths. I repeat, there is nothing sectarian in the policies of the Unionist Party today, and I welcome the support of anyone who finds in these policies the right and hopeful course for our Province.

"Moreover, Unionism sets its face against any division on class or occupational ground. There is no more sad and revealing expression in current use than the one we hear every day about 'both sides of industry', as though the two were drawn against each other in a cup-tie. The expression is symptomatic of strongly-entrenched and very damaging attitudes in Britain, which have had not a little to do with the economic plight in which we now find ourselves.

"I would like to see the word 'worker' applied to every man and woman who works, whether for a wage or a salary, whether he wears a white collar or a blue collar or overalls. I refuse to be told that someone like Sir Donald Stokes, chief of Britain's vast new motor empire, and a man who will travel at a moment's notice to Tokyo or Tehran to win export orders, is not as much a 'worker' as the man on his company's assembly lines. Somehow or other we must break down the old, rigid divisions between 'bosses' and employees, and begin to regard all of them as workers with different skills to contribute to the success of the same enterprise.

"Someone referred to our country recently as 'Britain Ltd.'. His purpose was to suggest a kind of businessman's Cabinet, and I do not really endorse that idea, because government, like business, has its professionalism. But the idea of 'Britain Ltd.' or for that matter of 'Northern Ireland Ltd.' is sound in a wider sense: that we are all involved in the life of our country, that all of us have something to contribute, that none of us will prosper by leaving it to the other fellow.

"It is for reasons such as these that modern Unionism is attached neither to unions nor to employees, but to a concept of the national interest. Increasingly in all the bodies which deal with our economic and industrial affairs — bodies like the Economic Council and Industrial Training Boards — our aim has been to get both 'sides', or as I prefer to put it, both 'parts' of industry sitting around a common table and working together.

"Such an approach would be impossible if we were a doctrinaire party. We believe in private enterprise which has built here the greatest industrial complex in this island. But that belief does not mean we totally reject public enterprise in special cases where this technique has something to contribute. We showed this, for instance, in setting up the Agricultural Trust to explore and develop new growth-points in our agricultural industry. And if nationalisation of transport undertakings has not been altogether a happy experience, no one can say we have reached that conclusion without giving the idea a lengthy trial.

"Some may say, since Unionism covers such a wide range of interests and — except on the fundamental question of our links with Britain — is far from being dogmatic in its views, that it lacks the purpose and dynamism of a wholly coherent political philosophy. I do not accept that. I never want to see the comfortable and ample jacket of Unionism converted into a straitjacket. Nor should we accept that a party system based on sectional or class or economic interests is vital to the health of a nation. Many countries are well governed by coalitions, and in the United States both great Parties encompass an extremely wide range of views.

"As I said at the beginning, Unionism welcomes the support of all, whatever their background or affiliations, who seek through our link with Britain to build a better and more prosperous Ulster. We look always for progress, but we take no narrow view of the way it is to be achieved. We seek no: the lowest common denominator but the highest common factor in the life of our community and Province." (NL 1.2.69; see also, Ulster At The Crossroads, p59-62.)

This speech represents a very clear expression of Terence O'Neill's political philosophy. In it, British politics and the British party system are condemned as divisive, and "modern Unionism" is held up as a higher form of politics. The suggestion that Unionism in the 1960s lacked the "purpose and dynamism of a wholly coherent philosophy" is firmly rejected. In O'Neill's eyes, Unionism was a "movement...which can bring together people from very different backgrounds", because it was "attached... to a concept of the national interest" and to protecting "Northern Ireland Ltd."

In attempting to prove that the Unionist Party was not sectarian, the speech ironically cites as evidence the Party's Manifesto for the 1965 Stormont General Election — the Election in which O'Neill played the Orange Card for all it was worth against the NILP, and used the full weight of his Party machinery for one purpose only: getting the Prods out to vote Unionist.

O'Neill never came to terms with two basic facts about Unionist politics. Firstly, he failed to understand that the Unionist Party was formed simply to give expression to the opposition of the Ulster Protestant community to Irish Unity. It has, therefore, always been a sectarian Party which is to say that it has always been a Protestant Party. (Calling it sectarian in this sense does not imply that its members have all been raving bigots.)

Secondly, O'Neill could not recognise that the Unionist Party was nothing more than a single-issue pressure group; an all-class alliance representing people with very different ideological and political perspectives. As such, it could not possess a "coherent political philosophy of its own" and, consequently, Unionist Governments at Stormont were able to rubber-stamp the policies of British Governments, whether they were Tory or Labour.

The timing of O'Neill's speech to the Carrick Unionist Association is very significant. He could have used the News Letter editorial of January 15th, two weeks earlier, as an opportunity to begin a debate on how to attract Catholics into the Unionist Party. This he failed to do and, if anything, the message of his Carrick speech was that the Party was doing all it could on the matter. The persistent denials that the Unionist Party was sectarian imply that there was nothing to stop Catholics joining and that their failure to do so was due to shortcomings on their side.

Throughout his premiership, O'Neill never once broached the subject of the Unionist Party links with the Orange Order. And even in his Autobiography, there is no indication that he ever thought about the subject for a second. Severing the links between both bodies in the 1960s would not have resulted in hordes of Catholics marching to Glengall Street to get their Unionist Party membership cards. Nevertheless, it would at the very least have represented a gesture of good-will by the Unionists and a genuine attempt to address the problem of the political isolation of the Catholic community under the

Stormont arrangements. O'Neill, the self-styled liberal, never once even acknowledged the existence of this problem.

If O'Neill and his Cabinet colleagues had made a sustained attempt to break the Party's link with the Orange Order, they would have undoubtedly encountered strong opposition from some Unionists. But it was O'Neill who decided to stir up provincial political activity in Northern Ireland, and to copper-fasten Unionist Party domination of this politics. Having taken these steps, he should have tried everything possible to make the Unionist Party more attractive to Catholics. He did precisely nothing. And the fact that he did precisely nothing makes him by far the most reactionary Prime Minister in Northern Ireland's fifty-one years of Stormont rule. His predecessors at least made no pretences, and raised no expectations.

The issue of Unionist Party links with the Orange Order re-emerged in early February 1968 in the run-up to the half-yearly meeting of the Grand Orange Lodge of Ireland on February 7th. On February 1st, the News Letter published a front page article entitled, **Orange Link May Be Scrutinised**. This article reported that the meeting on the 7th would be discussing the proposed expulsion from the Orange Order of Phelim O'Neill, a Stormont MP, and a cousin of the Prime Minister, for attending a Roman Catholic "community week" service in Ballymoney in 1967 . In light of this news, the News Letter published an editorial, entitled, **Towards a Broader Unionism**, which said that if Phelim O'Neill was expelled "there will clearly arise more immediately than many might have thought the need for a re-examination of the links between his Party and the Order. In such circumstances the case would be pre-judged and the verdict would not be favourable." (NL 2.2.1968.) The editorial concluded:

> "The principles of Unionism are well-known. So, too, are those of the Orange Order. There is a place for each, but they need not necessarily run in harness." (Ibid.)

The Grand Orange Lodge of Ireland's half-yearly meeting on February 7th was addressed by the Deputy Prime Minister, Brian Faulkner. His speech made no reference to the Order's relationship with the Party. The meeting decided to postpone taking a decision about Phelim O'Neill until June. In June, the Grand Lodge expelled him from the Orange Order for attending a Roman Catholic Church (NL 13.6.1968). The News Letter expressed annoyance at the expulsion but, by this time, it had backed away from its earlier demand for a re-examination of the Orange Order's links with the Unionist Party.

When the News Letter was demanding a re-examination of these links in January and February 1968, O'Neill remained silent. Shortly after the first editorial on the subject, he made the speech at Carrick which denied that there was anything remotely sectarian about the Unionist Party. In the wake of the second News Letter editorial on the Party's Orange Order links, O'Neill made a major speech on the subject of community relations. It made absolutely no reference to politics, let alone to the need to break down sectarian political divisions.

The speech was made on February 19th at an Irish Association meeting in Belfast. In it, O'Neill quoted from his Corrymeela Speech of Easter 1966 to outline his apolitical vision of the future:

"...we have people, genuinely trying to be helpful, who advocate a kind of reciprocal emasculation. No National Anthem or Loyal Toast to offend one side; no outward signs or symbols of Nationalism to offend the other. This approach ... I believe to be misconceived; it is rather like trying to solve the colour problem by spraying everyone a pale shade of brown. Moreover, as I said at Corrymeela, and I think it bears repeating:

"'I believe we have a right to call upon all our citizens to support the Constitution. The whole basis of constitutional government would be debased if the State were not to expect of its citizens at any rate the minimum duty of allegiance.'

"I expect, therefore, neither total surrender of one point of view to another, nor a sweeping under the carpet of major differences on points of principle. What I see is rather an occupation of a broad area of middle ground by reasonable men and its steady widening in the course of time." (Ulster At The Crossroads, p128-129.)

This extract shows yet again that, despite his liberal reputation, O'Neill never tried to alter the sectarian framework of Northern Ireland politics. The only political change he wanted was to see the Catholic community becoming more acquiescent. Catholics, of course, were quite entitled to be Nationalists in O'Neill's 'new Ulster', so long as they supported the Constitution and followed a "minimum duty of allegiance". They would also be more than welcome in the Unionist Party, provided they were prepared to put up with the Party's Orange trimmings, and accept the fact that they had little chance of ever becoming MPs or Councillors, let alone members of the Cabinet.

O'Neill's attempts to improve community relations were totally unconnected with politics. He simply wanted to encourage more expressions of 'goodwill', 'niceness', and 'moderation' between the two religious communities. Thus, later in his speech to the Irish Association, O'Neill said:

"I believe there is particular scope for... co-operation across denominational boundaries in the field of voluntary effort for the good of the community. Voluntary Service Overseas receives a proper acclaim; but voluntary service at home could serve not only its own ends of service, but the wider cause of communal understanding.

"Is it, for instance, too visionary to look forward to Protestant young people helping to re-decorate a Youth club in Andersonstown, or a young Catholic reading to a bed-ridden old lady on the Shankill Road? The firmest links can only be forged at the basic level of ordinary, warm, human contact." (Ibid p131.)

These sentiments are still prevalent. The British Government is currently spending a great deal of money on a host of schemes designed to promote greater 'communal understanding' and to produce 'goodwill between the Protestant and Catholic communities'. But abstract notions of goodwill are still proving to be no substitute for politics, and with the two communities still looking upon each other as political enemies, progress remains impossible.

Terence O'Neill was in fact criticised within the Unionist Party over his failure to tackle the problem of sectarian politics. The criticism was made by a Queen's University student, James Simpson, in a speech to the Annual Conference of the Ulster Unionist Council, at the end of April 1968. Simpson proposed a resolution, in the name of the Young Unionist Council, which called upon the Unionist Council Executive and on the Constituency Associations to carry out an examination of the structure, organisation and financing of the Party to meet present day arrangements.

He began his speech by asking what it was that prevented people actively participating in the Unionist Party. One of the main obstacles, he asserted, was the Party's image. He claimed that the Unionist Party was presenting the image of a sectarian party and said that he found this "saddening almost to the point of heartbreak". To back up his claim, he pointed out that the Party had a tendency to hold its meetings in Orange Halls and that Unionist MPs often made speeches from Orange platforms. (The reference to meetings being held in Orange Halls provoked cries of "hear, hear" from the Conference floor.)

Simpson's most significant comment was levelled at the Prime Minister. During his speech, he said to O'Neill: "I feel you ran away from the situation. My generation is fed up with sectarianism. We want a non-sectarian party where Protestant, Roman Catholic, Jew or Atheist can be accommodated." At this point a delegate in the hall called out: "We don't want any Roman Catholics" (NL 27.4.1968).

The reaction to Simpson's speech illustrates how difficult it would have been to develop normal politics in Northern Ireland in the 1960s. Then, as now, the people of the province had no access to the left-right politics of the UK state; they could not vote Labour and Tory at election time. Developing normal politics under the Stormont system would have entailed turning the Unionist Party into a "non-sectarian party where Protestant, Roman Catholic, Jew or Atheist can be accommodated". Such a task would, in all probability, have proved impossible. But at least people like Simpson wanted to try. Simpson wanted non-sectarian politics. O'Neill didn't, and the fact that he didn't exposes his carefully cultivated liberal reputation as a sham.

THE TRUTH ABOUT STORMONT

In 1968, the Unionist Party had to come to terms with an unpalatable truth about the importance of Stormont. In February and March 1968, there was, as usual, no shortage of vague, O'Neillite rhetoric about the benefits of devolution in Northern Ireland. On February 27th, for example, a News Letter editorial stated:

> "For some time, envious eyes have been cast on Stormont from Scotland and Wales and the working of devolution has come under examination. It has been assessed for its merits and faults and the verdict would appear to be a favourable one.

"The Ulster experiment began as an expedient and pragmatically has been moulded into a form of government which is at once more intimate and less bureaucratic. But it has never claimed to be perfect" (NL 27.2.1968).

Within a week of this editorial, the Home Affairs Minister, William Craig, addressed a Young Unionist Conference in Derry on the subject of devolution. Craig said that he could "see Northern Ireland enjoying increased decentralised powers from Westminster and Whitehall in the future." (NL 4.3.1968.) His speech referred to a "strong desire to stimulate regional activity at present", which, he said, would increasingly be seen in the context of decentralised power, and would be a "good thing" for Northern Ireland (ibid).

On March 13th, O'Neill was questioned in Stormont about Craig's speech and the Government's attitude to devolution. He was asked if he was "in favour of Home Rule" by Harry Diamond. "I have always been a convert to Home Rule," replied O'Neill. "I have always been in favour of regional government in N. Ireland. I have always been in favour of making full use of our powers and, indeed, this is what I have been trying to do in the last five years." (NL 14.3.1968)

The NILP MP, Tom Boyd, then asked the Prime Minister if he was in favour of Dominion Status. O'Neill replied:

"I am not in favour of Dominion Status. Anybody who has had experience as Minister of Finance in Northern Ireland would not be in favour of such status. It would really mean giving up our Ulster heritage." (Ibid.)

Later in the same month, a much more significant speech about devolution was made by Roy Bradford at a meeting of the Portadown Chamber of Commerce. This speech marked the beginning of a debate within the Unionist Party about the independence of Stormont. The News Letter described Bradford's speech as a call for greater use of the freedoms given to Northern Ireland under the Government Of Ireland Act. In it, he asked:

"Are we in N. Ireland making full use of the transferred powers conferred on us by the Government of Ireland Act?

"Are we exploiting to the full the latitude allowed to us in the disbursement of the residual share of the reserved taxes, which forms the bulk of our public revenue and which is annually remitted to us by the Treasury? Are we organising our expenditure to further those economic and social ends which the Unionist Government was elected to pursue?" (NL 26.3.1968.)

Bradford's speech also referred directly to the area of social services. He claimed that the Government had "surrended their freedom too easily", and had become "strapped... into the hidebound socialist conception of welfare services — which all elements in the community agreed need urgent re-fashioning" (ibid). And he asked:

"Can we not offer a more inspiring vision than a reserved place in the queue for welfare dole and another house in a council estate, however well planned?" (ibid.)

The most striking phrase in Bradford's Portadown speech was his assertion that the policy of parity between Northern Ireland and Great Britain was a "sacred cow" which had "run out of milk". Needless to say, such statements provoked an immediate political storm. Tom Boyd, the NILP MP, tabled a Parliamentary question on the speech, while NILP Secretary, Sam Napier, described it as a "very grave departure from Government policy" on parity. "The statement holds great dangers," said Napier, "in view of the fact that the social services agreement between Stormont and Westminster will be coming up for review." (Ibid.)

According to the News Letter, Bradford was reported to have paid a visit to the Cabinet Offices at Stormont Castle before issuing an "explanatory statement" on his speech. In this statement, he backtracked from his criticism of the policy of social services parity. He said that the whole point of his speech was, not to question the policy of social services parity, but to "stress the continuing need for a vigorous and imaginative use of existing powers in those fields in which parity considerations are not involved and to emphasise that the qualities of personal initiative and individual enterprise which are deep rooted in the Ulster character ought to be encouraged." He stressed that there was "no conflict" between his views and "existing Unionist policy" (ibid).

Bradford, of course, had very good personal reasons for maintaining the "sacred cow" status of the policy of social services parity: he represented the strongly working class constituency of Victoria in East Belfast. This was touched upon in his explanatory statement. "As member for Victoria," he said, "no one is more aware than I am of the great benefits which my own constituents enjoy through the operation of social service parity" (ibid).

Aside from his subsequent back-tracking on the issue of welfare services, Bradford's Portadown speech was applauded by the News Letter in an editorial entitled, **Parity At Too High A Price:**

"Mr. Roy Bradford has thrown a bombshell into the political life of Northern Ireland in his speech at Portadown in which he has called into question the policy of parity with Great Britain in the application of Socialist priorities... His comments were blatantly in conflict with what has been for long the foundation of Northern Ireland's welfare programme...

"... But time does not stand still. The Reinsurance Agreement assured parity in one sphere of welfare services; the Social Services Agreement in another. Both are essential to the needs of the province and here Mr. Bradford was moving in controversial territiory. Wisely he has retraced his steps.

"This apart, his speech is a significant advance in outlook and he has shown himself not to be hidebound by outworn phraseology. In this he is in line with the most progressive concept of the future of the economy and with new developments in regionalism in Britain. Pressures are increasing for a greater degree of selectivity so that the real needs of the people are met.

"Regional opinion has become keener and more aware of the discrepancies which blanket taxation imposed from London, can have on areas to which it is ill-suited...

"...Who could defend the application of Selective Employment Tax in

Northern Ireland? Its object was completely irrelevant to the prevailing conditions in Ulster.

"So too is the recently proposed 50 per cent increase in duty on heavy vehicles and that of 33 and a third per cent on light goods vehicles. Yet it would cause no surprise and very little protest if Mr. Kirk were to follow unquestioning in the footsteps of Mr. Jenkins [Chancellor of Exchequer] or if, having reduced some years ago the period of tax liability on gifts made inter vivos, it was now extended if only to preserve the existing differential.

"All these are fields for the closest examination by Stormont so as to ensure that too great a price is not paid for parity. Here is the room for manoeuvre that Mr. Bradford implied and the opportunity for Mr. Kirk to adapt his Budget to local needs rather than conform throughout to doctrinaire Socialism.

"If Mr. Bradford has succeeded in drawing attention to the flexibility which is already allowed to the Northern Ireland Government — and which ought to be used to the full — he has done a good job of work." (Ibid.)

Support for the sentiments contained in Bradford's Portadown speech was also expressed by the Unionist MP, John Taylor, in a speech to Londonderry Young Unionists. Taylor argued that the people of Northern Ireland should be concerned at the "subtle diminution of Ulster's constitutional authority" desired by those who "glibly supported" parity with Great Britain in all matters. "It was regrettable," he said, "that some politicians were so devoid of ideas that they were content if Stormont became a rubber-stamp Parliament." Taylor continued:

"It might be the desire of both Socialists and Nationalists to maintain everything in an identical manner to that in Britain, but the large majority of Ulster people surely were not content to be a rubber-stamp people."

Taylor also argued that "a universal implementation of step by step policies would only stagnate political progress in N. Ireland." He concluded his speech by stating that his criticism of step by step policies was not an attack on social services, but a "broader attack" on other policies which, it appeared, were being introduced "without any consideration of their particular relevance to local affairs." (NL 1.4.1969.)

Bradford and Taylor's speeches reveal the extent to which the Unionist Party had become attached to the idea of "Home Rule for Ulster" by 1968. Both Taylor and Bradford had entered Stormont in 1965 and as 'Young Turks' within the Party, it is hardly surprising that they wanted to see some action and were not content with the O'Neill Government's vague pro-devolution rhetoric.

Both men undoubtedly thought of the Unionist Party as a Tory Party and therefore resented the fact that the Stormont Government was consistently implementing the policies of the Wilson Government. Taylor also seems to have been motivated by another delusion: the belief that the Stormont Government had complete control over the future destiny of Northern Ireland. Hence his claim that step by step policies were a threat to "Ulster's constitutional authority".

In the first half of 1968, the Unionists were particularly irritated by a number of the Labour Government's fiscal policies, some of which were referred to in the

News Letter editorial on Bradford's speech (quoted above). Chief of these was the Selective Employment Tax (SET), which was designed to transfer labour from service industries to the productive sector. There is no doubt that antagonism towards SET within the Unionist Party was partly responsible for the criticisms of parity that were made in March and April 1968, especially since the Tax was due to be increased in Northern Ireland by the Ulster Budget at the end of April.

The man responsible for this Budget was Herbert Kirk, the Minister for Finance at Stormont. Soon after Taylor's speech to the Londonderry Young Unionists, Kirk delivered a speech to the Belfast Committee of the Institute of Bankers. In it, he strongly defended the Government's policy of parity with Great Britain in the areas of expenditure and taxation. Having explained how Northern Ireland had received more than £62 million in 1967 as a result of various arrangements with the Westminster Government, he said:

> "We believe that parity with Great Britain is what the people of N. Ireland want and an unbroken succession of elections have proved us right.
>
> "Perhaps you could try a test and ask yourself, if you are a family man, whether you would think it fair to get family allowances at half the Great Britain rate or if you drive a car that I should announce car license duty at twice the Great Britain rate.
>
> "I am not being fanciful in choosing such large differences. If we were to throw overboard the idea of parity and the generous assistance which has come from it we should have to make really drastic reductions in our expenditure and really painful increases in the restricted range of taxation under our control.
>
> "Parity is purely voluntary but it is also a bargain between two Governments and we on our side must be prepared to carry out our part of that bargain." (NL 8.4.1968.)

Kirk, therefore, did his best to introduce an element of reality into the debate on parity. As he pointed out, government expenditure in Northern Ireland exceeded the amount of revenue raised in the province through taxation. Consequently, the province, like other parts of the UK, was subsidised by the British Exchequer. In the case of Northern Ireland, the subsidies resulted from a number of Agreements reached between the Stormont and Westminster Governments. Under the principle of parity established by Lord Craigavon, the people of Northern Ireland, generally speaking, received the same state benefits and paid the same taxes as everyone else in the UK. Some differences certainly existed, the main one being the "leeway expenditure" provided for Northern Ireland by the Treasury to allow it to catch up with the the rest of the UK in various areas. This 'exception', in fact, simply reinforces the fact that throughout the history of Stormont the principle of parity dominated the scene particularly in the areas of taxation and the social services.

Herbert Kirk, as Minister of Finance, was well aware of what the consequences would be if the Stormont Government openly and deliberately moved away from the parity arrangements. It would, in all probability, have led to the Westminster Government cutting off the subsidies which Northern Ireland received from the British Treasury.

Kirk's speech, however, did not satisfy the News Letter which published an editorial, entitled **The Limits Of Parity**, in response. While agreeing with Kirk that "by and large there must be parity of taxation with Britain", the News Letter drew attention to the "transferred taxes", which were supposed to be controlled by Stormont:

> "Stormont controls a limited number of taxes — those on betting, stamps, motor vehicles and estates — and it is within its rights in varying them to suit local needs...
>
> "...Northern Ireland, with Treasury Agreement, has secured substantial departures from parity, mainly in relation to assistance to industry, private enterprise, housing and leeway expenditure on hospitals, roads, and universities.
>
> "Such concessions have taken into account the special circumstances of the Province... It is the continuing duty of the Government, while adhering to the broad principle of parity, to ensure that it is not misapplied to the detriment of N. Ireland." (ibid.)

Ten days later the News Letter returned to the subject in a more forthright manner in an editorial entitled, **Away With The Rubber Stamp**. It dealt with the forthcoming budget and claimed that it was not surprising that pressure was building up for a "close re-examination of Ulster's fiscal structure and against a rigid financial policy that follows Britain step by step all the way."

Having conceded that "there should be no variation in the social services", the editorial went on to criticise recent economic measures taken by the Labour Government in the wake of its decision to devalue the pound. These included increases in the Selective Employment Tax, increased transport costs for freight vehicles and the extension of estate duty liability on "inter vivos" gifts. The News Letter then turned its attention to the entire basis of the existing Stormont-Westminster relationship:

> "When Northern Ireland entered into full partnership with the rest of the U.K. through the Reinsurance Agreement and the subsequent social security agreements it could not have foreseen that future legislation at Westminster, some of it idealistic, would be detrimental to the progress of N.Ireland's industry and the economic growth of the Province. Clearly this is what has happened and it is for Mr. Kirk to act in that light.
>
> "He has stressed the voluntary nature of the partnership but he can scarcely have failed to notice that one of the partners is insisting on socialistic and confiscatory measures which are damaging to the other... That being so, the need for re-adjustment becomes all the more urgent. It will not be met by yet another rubber stamp Budget." (NL 18.4.1968.)

The News Letter's hopes for the Budget were not realised: Herbert Kirk introduced the measures devised by the Labour Government, with only minor concessions. These concessions were secured by Kirk during what were quite lengthy negotiations with Roy Jenkins, the Chancellor of the Exchequer. Traditionally, Stormont Finance Ministers had one meeting with the Chancellor to discuss the Ulster budget; Kirk had two.

The concessions did little to satisfy the Unionist backbenchers. The increases in the hated Selective Employment Act were introduced with only a "temporary partial easement" to give employers a six month breathing space to adjust themselves to the changes. Announcing these increases, Kirk himself confessed to having "no love for this particular tax" (NL 1.5.1968). Despite this, and despite the fact that no one on the Government benches had had a good word to say about SET, the increases were still introduced.

Similarly, the rates for goods vehicles were increased by roughly the same percentages as in Great Britain, although easier rates were introduced for vehicles under 12 cwt. As for the matter of "inter vivos" gifts, Kirk extended the vulnerable period for one year, although it had been extended by two in Great Britain. The whole tone of the Budget was captured in the title of the News Letter's editorial, **Just A Little Out Of Step**, which commented ruefully:

> "In a Stormont budget which ran true to form, with a little gravy here and a little icing there but with a notable absence of a significant change of diet, Mr. Kirk has resisted pressure that has built up in recent months for a new look at the menu." (Ibid.)

Kirk's Budget Statement vividly highlights the extent to which parity rendered Stormont irrelevant in the policy making field. The section of his speech quoted below should be compulsory reading for those who believe that the return of devolution in Northern Ireland would put "power in the hands of local people".

> "[Mr Kirk] It is essential to have as the main theme throughout my Budget speech this conception of parity with Britain but today at this point of time I make an exception because if I were to follow the Westminster Chancellor's speech my words would run for 2 1/2 hours whereas I hope I will run for about 40 minutes.
>
> "**Mr. McAteer:** Very commendable.
>
> "**Mr. Kirk:** So there are some useful changes between parity and what we do here. [Laughter.]
>
> "**Mr. McAteer:** Why have we a speech at all?
>
> "**Mr. Kirk:** I will tell the hon. Member that in just a couple of minutes.

FINANCIAL ARRANGEMENTS

"I will not weary the House with a recital of our financial arrangements but will attempt to summarise the main points. It is necessary for Northern Ireland to have a broad financial agreement with the United Kingdom Government for two reasons: first, because the Reserved Revenue raised in Northern Ireland has to be divided between the Northern Ireland Exchequer for our purposes and the United Kingdom Exchequer as a contribution towards Imperial Expenses; secondly, because in most years since Northern Ireland has existed as a separate entity even the whole of our Reserved Revenue, without any contribution to Imperial purposes, would not have been enough to provide what the Government wanted: a British level of social services and agricultural support, extensive schemes to provide social capital and assistance to maintain and expand industrial employment. If our Reserved Revenue is not enough one of three things must happen: we must raise those taxes which we control ourselves; or we must let our spending fall below British standards, or we must seek help from the United Kingdom Government.

GUIDING PRINCIPLES

"There must obviously be guiding principles on which these matters are to be decided and parity has been the guide since the earliest days. In 1938 it was made explicit in the Simon declaration under which the United Kingdom Government agreed that it would be equitable for them to find means of meeting a deficit in Northern Ireland finances which did not arise from a higher standard of expenditure or a lower standard of taxation than applied in Great Britain. Note the last words: the standard of expenditure and the standard of taxation are firmly linked. Since 1938 the principle has been refined in various ways but in essence has remained unchanged.

FREEDOM OF VARIATION

"It is, of course, literally correct that a Northern Ireland Minister of Finance has a right to vary transferred taxes as he wishes, subject always to the approval of Parliament, but any such freedom is the freedom to throw over an extremely favourable bargain and unless such variation is agreed with the Treasury or compensated in some way it puts in jeopardy that agricultural support which our farmers enjoy and the whole scale of our expenditure on social services, economic and social development and industrial expansion.

"Let me make it quite clear that neither the Constitution nor the arrangements with the United Kingdom Government gives us the right to spend as much as we like, tax as little as we like and send the bill to the Treasury. We have always received the most generous help from the Treasury whatever Government may have been in power, and have by arrangement been able to go far beyond parity in many ways but there can be no surer way of forfeiting the goodwill on which we rely than to assume that we have a right to an unlimited subsidy.

TRANSFERRED TAX CHANGES

Against this background there is only a limited scope in the field of transferred taxation for proposing lower taxes than in Great Britain. No Minister of Finance likes to increase taxation. But on any view of the situation it is clearly necessary for me to propose substantial tax increases this year; if we consider the overall economic strategy of the United Kingdom Budget then Northern Ireland must play its part in reducing home demand; if we consider only the arithmetic of the Northern Ireland Budget then we must raise taxes to meet the £38 million of extra spending this year. If we look at the more general financial arrangements then we must increase transferred taxes as part of the bargain under which we receive so much financial assistance from the United Kingdom Exchequer." (Hansard 30.4.1968. Cols 786-788).

Towards the end of his Budget Statement, Kirk again drew attention to the assistance that Northern Ireland received from the Treasury:

"It is an inescapable fact that we need to spend considerably more than the total of revenue raised in Northern Ireland even at present high levels of taxation. I have shown that to meet this expenditure, create a modest reserve of £3 million for industrial development and pay a token Imperial Contribution of £2 million we need to receive from the United Kingdom Exchequer £19 1/2 million under the Social Services Agreement, £2 million under the Agriculture

Act and £10 million for additional employment premiums — a total of £32 million.

"This underlines not only the advantages of the financial arrangements which we have made with the United kingdom Government but also the magnitude of the development programmes which we have undertaken." (Ibid, Cols 800-801.)

Herbert Kirk's realistic speech contrasts sharply with the Stormont Debate on the Budget. A host of Unionist backbenchers conveniently ignored the facts he had outlined and called on him to step out of line with the British Exchequer. Carrick MP, Captain Austin Ardill, for example, complained that Kirk was "too closely tied to a Socialist system of taxation" (NL 2.5.1968), and claimed that the Budget would have an adverse effect on small businesses. Joseph Burns (N. Derry) expressed annoyance at the increase in car tax and called for the abolition of the Selective Employment Tax. The Woodvale MP, Johnny McQuade, advocated more taxation on petrol and had to be told by Kirk that this was a "reserved matter" over which the Stormont Government had no control.

SET was also criticised by Opposition MPs. The Nationalist MP, James O'Reilly, for example, said that he could not "see how any more money could be squeezed out of the N. Ireland taxpayers" (NL 2.5.1968). O'Reilly's leader, Eddie McAteer, also expressed opposition to SET, but he did point out that the Minister of Finance was "handcuffed very tightly indeed", and that his handling of the "petty cash book" had been "completely predictable" (NL 1.5.1968). McAteer went on to say that the business of financial government in Northern Ireland was "rather incongruous", and that Stormont did not really need a Ministry of Finance. He suggested amalgamating at least two or three of the existing Stormont ministries (ibid).

The speech by the sole representative of the Ulster Liberal Party, Sheelagh Murnaghan, proved that delusions about Stormont were not confined to the Unionist side of the House. As the early part of her speech indicates, the Liberals also had difficulty accepting a "rubber stamp Budget":

"Once again we must acknowledge that the presentation of the Budget and the debate on it tend to be a rather academic exercise in Northern Ireland. The Minister has been at great pains to explain why that should be. He has explained at great length and repeated over and over again, no doubt for the benefit of the people who have recently been making speeches, that we are, as it were, irrevocably bound by the financial arrangements for the rest of the United Kingdom. He went on to state that the Northern Ireland Government have not really got control over the transferred section of our revenue.

"One must accept that those revenue matters which were reserved under the Government of Ireland Act are out of our jurisdiction but we were supposed to have some jurisdiction over transferred revenue matters. In fact what the Minister has said is that we have really no taxation powers because we must not do anything that is not vetted and o.k'd by the United Kingdom Treasury. He explains that the reason for this is to maintain parity. This raises a big constitutional question. It is very relevant to the present discussions which are taking place in Great Britain about the development of regional government for

Scotland and Wales and the development of a federal system. This is actively under discussion and the experiences of Northern Ireland are extremely relevant here.

"I accept the realities of the situation that we cannot expect the United Kingdom Treasury to subsidise us if we reduce revenue raising in those fields within our jurisdiction. However there is still scope for experiment..." (Hansard, 30.4.1968, Col 806.)

In his response to the Budget debate, Kirk replied to Murnaghan's demand for more experimentation with transferred taxes:

"The hon. and learned Member for Queen's University (Miss Murnaghan) agreed that the general standard of our transferred taxation must be the same as in Great Britain but suggested that we might experiment by having differences in detail which raised the same amount of revenue. This sort of variation has always been open to us and it has been done in the past. For instance, we had for many years a private car license duty 10s above the Great Britain level in order to balance rather lower rates for the smaller pre 1947 cars. If Minsters of Finance have not gone in for this sort of experiment to any great extent it is not out of mental laziness or doctrinaire views on parity.

"There are, however, often difficulties in departing very far from the Great Britain system of tax; first, in some cases, there are practical obstacles. For instance, if we raised our Betting Tax too far above the Great Britain level we should merely divert betting business to Great Britain and get no extra revenue. Secondly, those who had to pay tax above the Great Britain rate would regard themselves as being unfairly treated. If I had decided to make no increase of tax on goods vehicles but to raise all the extra revenue from private cars then I should have had to raise the tax on them to £27 10s or £28 per annum" (Hansard, 1.5.1968, Cols 868-969).

The scope for variation in the area of transferred taxes had been one of the main points raised in the News Letter editorials which preceded the 1968 Ulster budget. But, as Kirk pointed out, it made practical and political sense for the Stormont Ministry of Finance not to depart very far from the levels set in Great Britain.

Kirk's response to the Budget Debate was not prominently featured in the News Letter's coverage of the proceedings. His summary of the true facts of the situation was overshadowed by the contribution to the Debate from Captain John Brooke, Unionist MP for Lisnaskea, and son of former Premier Lord Brookeborough.

Captain Brooke attacked the policy of parity with none of the reserve of his Party colleagues. He began his speech by commiserating with Herbert Kirk over the fact that he had to "enunciate Socialist policy... given to him from London" (ibid, Col 835). He then called for a complete re-examination of the financial relationship between Stormont and Westminster:

"In these days when there is so much talk of regionalism it seems appropriate that we should experiment — we are a regional Government as it is — to a far greater extent in the form of taxation or in the form of alignment with Westminster, from which we are presently suffering, even if this meant the use of block grants or a completely different form of financial arrangement with

Westminster." (Ibid, Col 836.)

Brooke's speech touched on a number of policy areas. There was the inevitable condemnation of the Selective Employment Tax, which he decribed as "pernicious". He also advocated the abolition of death duties in Northern Ireland, which he claimed would attract "tens of millions of pounds" into the province from "private companies in England" (ibid, Col 838). The most controversial part of the speech, however, dealt with the policy of parity in the social services:

"This brings me to the apparent sacred cow of social services. I accept that our social services should equate with those in the rest of the United Kingdom, but after so many years is it not time we re-examined the whole lot to see how we can bring them up to date so that the benefits can be given to those who really need them? The fact that it pays a man better to remain in bed than to work appears to me to be eating at the very vitals of our country and the determination of our people. What sort of people are we going to be in years to come if this goes on?

"...The fact is that the social services are out of date. This has been widely accepted and the Opposition at Westminster is determined to review them. We should carry out a review ahead of time so that we can have social services which fit our own special circumstances. We want welfare and not waste." (Ibid, Col 837.)

This speech was the subject of a lengthy editorial in the News Letter which claimed that Brooke "was voicing the views of a growing section of opinion", which believed that Ulster was "too rigidly bound to the Westminster pattern and vulnerable to the ill effects of Socialist legislation." The paper re-iterated its call for a reappraisal of the financial relationship between Stormont and Westminster and added:

"At least no loss would be incurred if this review were undertaken and the air would be cleared. Unless it is the call is certain to become more insistent and the divisions between a number of backbenchers and the Government wider."

The News Letter, however, was quick to distance itself from the more controversial elements of his speech:

"Not all of the suggestions for a change are sound and Captain Brooke indulged in a spell of wishful thinking when he suggested the abolition of death duties in Northern Ireland, visualising a substantial inflow of money to the Province as a result.

"He failed to take account of the other side of the picture — the loss sustained by the Treasury in London. And he did not suggest any means by which this could be made good from revenue raised in N. Ireland.

"Nor did he show a full appreciation of the value of the social services. They were in essence designed to ensure that there would be a stoutly built wall against poverty and the consequences of ill-health. This they have provided and the nation would not lightly relinquish the protection they afford.

"If there are loopholes — and Captain Brooke named one when he declared that a man could make more lying in bed than by working — then it is for Parliament here and in Britain to discover means of stopping them. Perhaps this would be the best point at which experimentation might begin." (Ibid.)

Captain Brooke's speech was also dealt with by the News Letter's Political Correspondent, Mervyn Pauley, in his "At Stormont" column. On the key issue of social welfare parity, Pauley concluded:

> "Nine out of ten Unionist M.P.s — and a fair sprinkling of Opposition members if they would only admit it — are convinced that the social services are haywire and out of tune with modern needs... The only point is that the Ulster Government, by choice and design, is irrevocably committed to social services parity with the rest of the United Kingdom and there is not a thing it can do about this 'sacred cow' even if it wanted to." (Ibid.)

Captain Brooke's speech in the Budget Debate represented the last hurrah in the controversy about parity which had developed within the Parliamentary Unionist Party in the first half of 1968. That is not to say that everyone in the Party became reconciled to Stormont's role as a "rubber-stamp Parliament". The controversy might have re-surfaced had the year not taken a nastier turn for Unionists and given them something other than the Selective Employment Tax to think about.

Overall, there were two factors at work in the debate which surrounded the 1968 Ulster Budget. The first was quite simply the existence of frustrated Toryism within the Party. The policy of parity with Great Britain certainly produced stresses within the Party when a Labour Government was in power.

Secondly, and more importantly, the debate about parity was a product of serious delusions about the independence of Stormont. It is interesting to note at this point that, according to Mervyn Pauley, Captain Brooke "was observed making a deeply attentive Mr. Craig privy to his thoughts" shortly before he rose to make his controversial speech (ibid). Craig was a firm believer in the independence of Stormont and, by the end of 1968, these firm beliefs were to get him sacked from the Cabinet.

It is significant, too, that O'Neill made no contribution to the Debate at all. There can be no doubt that he had done a great deal to stir up the kind of sentiments expressed in 1968 by Roy Bradford, John Taylor, Captain John Brooke and in the News Letter editorials. In 1965, for example, O'Neill had told the Court Ward Unionist Association that "the Parliament of Northern Ireland" was not a "kind of pet dog trotting at its master's heels". In the same speech (quoted in full above), he had also declared:

> "With our own Parliament and our own Government machine, we have built-in advantages over any region of Britain. We are close to the needs and desires of our own people, and can seek within Northern Ireland suitable Ulster solutions to the problems which face Britain today."

Just two weeks before Bradford had made his speech to the Portadown Chamber of Commerce, O'Neill had told Harry Diamond in Stormont that he had always believed in "Home Rule for Ulster" and making "full use of" the powers available to the Northern Ireland Government. "Indeed," he had added, "this is what I have been trying to do in the last five years".

Yet there is no doubt that O'Neill was well aware of the realities to which Herbert Kirk had to point in his Budget statement. (Kirk was a close ally of the

Prime Minister and stuck with him when the Party split in 1969.) As later events in 1968 were to prove, O'Neill was under no illusions about Stormont's dependence on Westminster and, when the crunch came, he immediately obeyed his master's voice. Indeed, he was trotting at Harold Wilson's heels like a pet dog almost before Wilson had time to whistle.

O'Neill's rhetoric about Stormont was as fraudulent as his 'goodwill' gestures towards the Catholic Community. Genuine policy initiatives during his premiership were few and far between. His love for devolution stemmed primarily from his 'Our Wee Ulster' mentality and his hatred of British, class-based politics.

The Premier's reactionary little Ulster outlook was displayed to the world again on May 20th, at a meeting of the Woodvale Unionist Association. (This meeting witnessed a very hostile anti-O'Neill demonstration: 500 protesters gathered outside and threw stones, eggs and flour at the Prime Minister as he left. Inside the meeting, however, O'Neill received strong support: of the 170 present, only 12 refused to back a vote of confidence in him.)

In his speech to the Woodvale Unionists, O'Neill compared "one party rule" of Northern Ireland by the Unionist Party to the dominance of Fianna Fail in the Irish Republic. "The fact of the matter," he said, "is that in Ireland, North and South, we have a rather stable political situation, without the swings which are characteristic of politics in Britain. Stability may not be as exciting as change, but it is not necessarily any less democratic" (NL 21.5.1968).

Only fourteen months after this speech was made, the 'stability' generated by single party politics in Northern Ireland was getting people killed. But the speech didn't finish there:

> "Happily, Ulster people can see for themselves what is going on in other parts of the world — the huge and disturbing upsurge of violent protest which is shaking so many of the great nations of Europe... Ulster people can see, too, the steady rise of violent crime, of drug addiction, of a whole complex of social evils. Some of these trends are evident here, but by and large Ulster lags behind in this Gadarene rush to moral destruction.

> "Our Ulster virtues are not very fashionable; they do not seem very smart to the long-haired brigade who are the self-appointed trend setters and who judge a free society by its permissiveness... The truth is that we have kept alive in Ulster something which is of infinite value — the standards of a Christian society. We have faults, certainly, but we have merits too. There are lessons we can teach as well as learn." (Ibid.)

It is clear from these excruciatingly awful statements that the good Captain had no idea that his beloved, insulated Ulster was about to experience a "huge and disturbing upsurge of violent protest" of its own.

THE TWELFTH IN '68

The developments within Ulster Unionism during the first half of 1968 neatly illuminate the mess which the Party was in on the eve of the first Civil Rights marches. The short-lived debate about the links between the Party and the

Orange Order in January and February revealed O'Neill to be a complete fraud when it came to dealing with sectarian politics. It also showed that, under his leadership, the Unionist Party did not perceive the need to end the political isolation of the Catholic Community.

The inner-Party debate about parity in March, April and May also showed O'Neill up as a fraud on the question of devolution. While he was aware of Stormont's real status, his pro-devolution rhetoric had helped to generate widespread delusions on the subject throughout the Party.

By the summer of 1968, therefore, two major delusions were rife within the Unionist Party. The first was the assumption that Catholics would be content to be without functional politics forever. The second was the belief in Stormont's independence from Westminster. The significance of both cannot be over-estimated: they combined to totally disable Ulster Unionism in the face of the Civil Rights assault.

Both false assumptions were also on display in the early summer of 1968. At the beginning of July, for example, Bill Craig attacked the Catholic comunity for daring to complain. Speaking at a meeting at Desertmartin, Craig said:

"We have given a fair and generous deal to every citizen of this community and the Roman Catholic minority have no grounds whatever for feeling that they get less than justice.

"It was time the Nationalist people realised that if they did not accept the democratically elected Government of Northern Ireland they cannot expect much consideration or generosity from those who do believe in it." (NL 8.7.1968.)

Unionist Party links with the Orange Order became an issue again in June when Phelim O'Neill was eventually expelled from the Order for attending a Catholic service. Shortly after his expulsion, a number of leading figures in the Unionist Party made it their business to defend the Orange Order's role in the politics of Northern Ireland. These included Brian Faulkner (NL 22.6.1968), Harry West and Roy Bradford (NL 13.7.1968). Bradford's comments, which were made at a Twelfth of July parade in Newtownards, were the most pointed. Some of them bear repeating, not least because the man still portrays himself as a 'liberal Unionist' today.

Bradford told the assembled brethren at Newtownards that it was unrealistic to "pretend that the Orange Order was not political". The Order, he claimed, had always been political; it was dedicated to "the maintenance of the Throne and the Union" and had "always used its moral authority to influence legislation". Furthermore, he added, the Order had been part of the "social fabric" in the "Ulster countryside" and, as the "foundation stone of the Unionist Party", it "reflected and echoed the feelings of the Ulster Unionists" (ibid).

The message could hardly have been clearer: the links between the Unionist Party and the Orange Order should remain. And if this dissuaded Catholics from joining the Party then so be it.

Bradford's speech was not the most newsworthy of those made at the various Twelfth celebrations in 1968. That honour went to the Westminster MP for South Down, and Imperial Grand Master, Captain L.P.S. Orr. His speech was a response to comments made by the British Prime Minister, Harold Wilson, on July 11th.

During a House of Commons debate on July 11th, Gerry Fitt and others had challenged Wilson on the convention which prevented discussion of Northern Ireland affairs in Westminster. The Liberal MP for Hampstead, Ben Whitaker, for example, asked why members of the Orange Order had been allowed to vote on the Race Relations Bill (England and Wales) at Westminster when Westminster was unable to do anything about "religious prejudice and discrimination in Ulster" (NL 12.7.1968):

> "That is a very good question," replied Wilson, "and I have tried to ask it myself... It is a matter which will have to be discussed in the fullness of time." (Ibid.)

That answer was bad enough but it was Wilson's reply to a question from Gerry Fitt that caused the most bother.

> "Are you aware," asked Fitt, "that there are a number of people in the U.K. and in Northern Ireland who look to this House to redress the wrongs in Northern Ireland?"

Wilson replied ominously that "the present situation could not continue indefinitely" in Northern Ireland, and that O'Neill and his colleagues were well aware of this.

Inevitably, this comment brought Unionist delusions about Stormont to the fore. These delusions were referred to in the News Letter's report on Wilson's comments which stated:

> "The Unionist attitude is that... the U.K. government has no jurisdiction in matters that are the concern of the N. Ireland Government." (Ibid.)

The Unionists might have just learnt a painful lesson about Stormont's lack of power in the economic field, but they still believed that the local Parliament possessed some degree of sovereignty. Consequently, on July 12th 1968, a sadly deluded Captain L.P.S. Orr declared:

> "We will resist with the last breath in our body any attempts by Mr. Harold Wilson, British Prime Minister, or anyone else, to interfere with the just prerogatives of the Northern Ireland Government" (NL 13.7.1968).

Orr's speech was reported in the News Letter under a front page banner headline which said: **Hands Off Ulster, Wilson Is Told.**

O'Neill's Twelfth Day speech did not, of course, voice such strong sentiments. Instead, there was the usual vacuous rhetoric. He claimed, for instance, that there was a "growing interest in the Ulster type of Government" in the rest of Britain. Most of his speech took the form of an attack on Gerry Fitt and other Nationalist politicians. Having declared that he had "tried to be the Prime Minister of all the Ulster people", O'Neill wagged the finger at others:

> "We have men who are unable to see a large new reservoir because they are looking straight ahead at the parish pump; we have men who care more about some squabble over a single house than they do about a housing programme which is booming as never before." (Ibid.)

O'Neill also confidently ruled out the idea that the Catholic community would be as ungrateful as its politicians. He said:

> "Of course, these threats and warnings — to the effect that if the Government does not do this or that the 'minority' will take certain action — are to a very large extent hot air. Most of them are sensible people, who have shown no inclination to follow where some self-appointed leaders would wish to take them." (Ibid.)

At the end of July, O'Neill was asked about Harold Wilson's warning that the "situation" in Northern Ireland could not "continue indefinitely". The great devolutionist meekly replied that it was "the duty of the Northern Ireland Government to get on with the Government of the day in London, whatever party might be in power". He added that, while he did not agree with everything Wilson had said, it was "better to disagree behind closed doors than to wrangle in public". (NL 25.7.1968.)

CIVIL RIGHTS: THE ULTIMATE TRUTH

The final section of this book examines the impact of the Civil Rights movement on the Ulster Unionist Party. It is not a lengthy examination. The politics of the Civil Rights campaign itself is analysed by Pat Walsh in **From Civil Rights To National War**, a companion volume to this book. Analysing the Unionist Party's political response to the campaign is not a big task: there wasn't one.

Once the agitation got off the ground properly in October 1968, Ulster Unionism collapsed and never recovered. This section will simply chart the course of that collapse.

By way of introduction, however, it is necessary to underline the principal causes of this collapse. Some of it can be put down to straightforward political incompetence, particularly on the part of Terence O'Neill. But the main reasons had to do with the political degeneration that had occurred within Unionism under O'Neill's leadership.

It has been stressed on countless occasions in this book that O'Neill's approach to the government of Northern Ireland was predicated on the assumption that the Croppies would lie down; that Catholics would be content to live as a permanent minority excluded from meaningful politics.

When it became clear towards the end of 1968 that the Catholic community was not going to lie down, O'Neillism was finished. The Ulster Unionist Party went down with it.

The Civil Rights movement was the ultimate truth for Captain O'Neill. In the face of it, he was utterly clueless. He called for calm, tolerance and restraint. When that wasn't enough he demanded an apolitical display of 'moderation' from the 'silent majority', presumably in the hope that this would tame the rowdier elements in the society. When this failed, he prevaricated, split the Party and then walked away and left the rowdy elements to get on with it.

The Civil Rights movement posed a serious political problem for the Unionist Party, but its leader never once attempted to respond to it politically.

It was the same with his opponents within the Party: they simply called for unspecified security measures to be taken against the marchers.

An effective political response to the Civil Rights movement would have involved exploiting its contradictions and ambivalences. In particular, it would have involved taking the demand for "British rights for British citizens" at face value and acting accordingly.

The Unionist Party could have pointed out that it had never wanted to govern Catholics in the first place; that Edward Carson had predicted that the political arrangements envisaged in the 1920 Government Of Ireland Act would create sectarian frictions; and that any grievances the Catholic community had about the way it was being governed should not be directed at them, but at the Westminster political establishment which had ignored Carson's warnings.

Such a strategy, however, would have been unthinkable to the Unionist Party in 1968: it would have meant sacrificing Stormont. By this time, O'Neillite devolutionism had spread through the Party like a fungus. Stormont was no longer seen as an unwanted imposition. It had become the jewel in the Unionist crown.

A great deal of this love for Stormont stemmed from a loosely-defined belief that devolution was the only thing that kept Ulster safe. Without it, went the argument, Northern Ireland's fate would again be in the hands of Westminster politicians who had proved themselves so untrustworthy in the past. The fact that Westminster still possessed sovereign power over Northern Ireland was never mentioned; it was widely believed that Stormont possessed a degree of independent sovereignty with which Westminster could not tamper. The shattering of this delusion at the end of 1968 hastened the collapse of Unionism.

In the final analysis, the responsibility for the carnage in Northern Ireland over the last two decades lies with the British political establishment at Westminster. Westminster imposed the provisions of the 1920 Government Of Ireland Act on the province. The political arrangements forced on Northern Ireland — devolution plus exclusion from the party politics of the United Kingdom — have ensured the survival of communal politics. But it has to be recognised that, under O'Neill, Ulster Unionism became firmly attached to these arrangements. Unionism was seen as something that was better than British politics and Stormont as something that had to be defended at all costs.

This attachment to the Stormont political set-up rendered the Unionist Party politically bankrupt in its response to the Civil Rights movement. It also means that the Unionists share at least some of the blame for the outbreak of communal war in Northern Ireland at the end of the 1960s.

DUNGANNON

The first Civil Rights march took place from Coalisland to Dungannon on Saturday, August 24th, 1968. Among the speakers to address the rally in Dungannon were Gerry Fitt, Betty Sinclair, Austin Currie and Erskine Holmes of the NILP. During his speech, Fitt declared, "We want civil rights and a 32-county Republic" (NL 26.8.1968).

Compared to those which followed, the Dungannon march was something of a non-event. Several British MPs had been invited to address the rally, but none turned up on the day. A smaller loyalist counter-demonstration was also held in the town, but the police managed to prevent a confrontation occurring.

The News Letter obviously saw little in the march to get worried about. Its only report of it on the following Monday was carried on page five, while the main editorial of the day dealt with the USSR invasion of Czechoslovakia. Beneath it there was a short comment on the Dungannon march under the heading, **Not So Civil**:

> "The civil rights protest march in Dungannon failed to live up to the expectations of the organisers, both in the attendance it attracted and in the number of bands taking part. Nor did a foolish attempt to involve British M.P.s in the demonstration evoke any response.
>
> "All that may be said to have been accomplished is a stirring up of that kind of sectarian feeling which the sponsors would presumably deplore .
>
> "…A bigger and better parade was promised by another speaker. Unless those taking part in it conduct themselves properly and are given a sounder lead from the platform, it will not have an influence for the betterment of community relations in the town." (Ibid.)

DERRY

The Civil Rights movement did not really get going until October, 1968. The second march was held in Derry on Saturday, 5th October. On Thursday 3rd, the Home Affairs Minister, William Craig, announced that he had decided to ban the march, along with an Apprentice Boys Parade due to take place in Derry on the same day. No doubt thrilled by this propaganda gift, the Executive of the Northern Ireland Civil Rights Association (NICRA) decided to defy Craig's ban.

The Derry march ended in violence. It was baton-charged by the RUC, and rioting broke out. Further rioting was reported over the weekend: the crisis had begun.

On Monday 7th October, the News Letter published a very different editorial from the one which followed the Dungannon march. Under the heading, **Let That Be An End To It**, the paper asked:

> "Where do we go from here, we who love this place, who live in it and depend upon its happiness and prosperity?
>
> "So easily the situation could be exacerbated to a point where the outcome is a spread of trouble with all the dire significance which can be attached to that frightening word in this region.
>
> "It is our responsibility and that of everyone who can exercise influence that nothing is said or done that might further inflame passions." (NL 7.10.1968.)

In the same apolitical vein, the editorial concluded:

> "The position is serious. Let there be no misunderstanding about that. But let it be understood equally that this is a time to cool off and not to blow up." (Ibid.)

The Unionist Party reaction to the events at Derry was entirely negative and defensive. Among the first to comment on the events in Derry were the

Unionist Party's big three: Bill Craig, Brian Faulkner and Terence O'Neill.

Craig simply took refuge in the claim that NICRA had been infiltrated by the IRA, and that "the majority opinion in the IRA Council was Communist". And although he made it clear that he was not suggesting that "all the people in the Civil Rights procession on Saturday were associated with the IRA or Communism", Craig added that he thought "they were extremely ill-advised in becoming involved without doing adequate research." (Ibid.)

Brian Faulkner's first significant comments on the Civil Rights movement were made on the actual day of the Derry march. Speaking at the re-opening of Cordrain Orange Hall, near Tandragee, Faulkner showed that he was aware of the threat posed to the Government by the Civil Rights agitation. His response to it, however, consisted of nothing more than an appeal to the Catholic community to put economics before politics.

Faulkner said in his speech that the Civil Rights movement was being "exploited by determined and ambitious men for other purposes". The term civil rights, he claimed, "conjured up in the mind pictures of oppression, of illegal imprisonment, of ghettoes, of apartheid in the worst meaning of the word, of a denial of liberty." Thus, he said, it was a "very convenient banner for the Republican faction to hoist aloft".

Having stated that he did not believe that the "vast majority of the Nationalist citizens of Northern Ireland believed one word" of the Republican/Civil Rights propaganda, Faulkner continued:

"Unfortunately for Northern Ireland, the attempt to equate Nationalism with civil rights was not only a malicious twist of political policy, it was an effective one in the eyes of the world.

"All the lurid accusations and every bit of sensational political mud-slinging rebounded not only on Orange and Unionist Ulstermen, but endangered the pay packets of every Nationalist citizen of Northern Ireland as well.

"For industrialists there was no Unionist Ulster, no Nationalist Ulster, no West or East of the Bann. There was only Northern Ireland as a place within which the man who builds a factory could count on finding stability, fair dealing and common sense."

Towards the end of the speech, Faulkner admitted that there were people "dedicated to the precept of civil rights who were acting according to the dictates of their conscience and who had no aim or desire to cause provocation or civil strife." These people, he stressed, had his "sincere respect" as did the "openly avowed" political ambitions of the Nationalist Party.

"Criticism," he said in conclusion, "was the very lifeblood of the democratic process and a Government which stifled criticism became a dictatorship. But no Government worth its salt would allow a deliberate provocation to cause civil strife among the people it was elected to protect." (Ibid.)

Terence O'Neill's first public statement on the Derry disturbances were made on October 7th, during a visit to Leicester for the opening of an Ulster Week. When asked about allegations of discrimination, O'Neill claimed that "there had been a tendency in Ireland for a Nationalist local authority not to be overkeen to house people who were Unionists." And he added:

> "I was hoping that the policies we have been trying to adopt in the last few years were beginning to break these things down. That is why I deplore what happened on Saturday because I'm afraid it will have an effect on the more friendly relations which were beginning to grow up between the two sections of the community." (NL 8.10.1968).

While at Leicester, O'Neill also unburdened himself of more vacuous devolutionary rhetoric. He told reporters that the Civil Rights strategy of trying to get the British Government to "interfere" in Northern Ireland would probably be ineffective. "We might," he said, "get back to a situation of 1912 when a Liberal Government tried to interfere in Irish affairs [sic]. I think it would be self-defeating."

STORMONT DEBATE

A special Parliamentary Debate on the Derry disturbances was held in Stormont on 15th and 16th October. It epitomised the entire Unionist Party response to the Civil Rights movement. O'Neill made a fourteen minute speech during which he tried to refute some of the allegations made about Local Government franchise and discrimination in housing allocation. On the latter, he said:

> "A lot of the discussion has been about the allocation of houses. One would imagine that no Roman Catholic has ever been allocated a public authority house. Yet today, something like 600,000 of our total population of $1 \frac{1}{2}$ million are accommodated in post-war housing, and everyone knows perfectly well that the religious minority are occupying a very substantial proportion of these. In Londonderry itself, some two-fifths of the population are in post-war housing...
>
> "...My colleagues and I accept that the provision of adequate housing conditions for all remains the most pressing social need. That is why we set a new housing target in the forefront of our last election manifesto, and — as I have already said — that target is being reached. But we recognise that no single factor could do more to reduce tensions and improve the entire condition of life in many areas than further improvements in the housing situation. I have therefore decided to summon representatives of housing authorities to meet the Minister of Development and myself at a conference to be held at the earliest possible date. The aim of that conference will be to seek as a matter of urgency ways in which the housing programme may be further accelerated in areas of special need throughout Northern Ireland." (Hansard, 15.10.1968, Cols 1003-1004.)

On the question of Local Government franchise, O'Neill stated:

> "Local government is already under review... It is a big job and a long job, but it is one we will carry out with a desire to undertake a genuine and lasting reform. The question of the local government franchise is obviously tied in with this, and cannot be considered in isolation from it." (ibid, Col 1004.)

The concluding paragraphs of the speech contained sentiments that were to become very familar in the next few months:

"For more than five years I have been trying to improve relations between the two sections of the community. What happened last weekend has certainly set us back a bit, but I will continue to hope, and to work for better times ahead. But if we have further violence, further disorder, there will inevitably be on both sides a retreat into traditional attitudes, and the slender bridges men of goodwill have tried to build will tumble into a chasm. If these bridges should fall, many years may pass before they could be built again. Above all else, at this critical moment, we want a pause, a period of calm, an interval of restraint in word and action. This to my mind is more important than anything else.

"This very day there is being published the results of a national [sic] opinion poll conducted amongst the young people of Northern Ireland — the 17-24 age group. They were asked at one point to place in order of priority the things which they considered the Government should do. The result of this poll, conducted in a calm atmosphere before the events in Londonderry, is revealing. It shows that their first priority is a demand for more industry to be brought to the Province. The second request is for more houses. And such things as alleged discrimination and the franchise, which form the political catch-cries of politics — all these other things come far behind.

"Here are our young people asking us for bread — for the bread of jobs and houses, a decent prosperous life — and are we to offer them instead the stone of discord? For, unless the Province rapidly returns to sanity, future progress is gravely at risk. I call above all for peace. The place for argument is in Parliament, not in the streets. Disorder is the way, not to equal rights, but to an equal share of misery and despair." (ibid, Cols 1004-1005.)

This most striking thing about this speech is its sheer political emptiness. This emptiness is perfectly illustrated by the pious declaration that "the place for argument is in Parliament, not in the streets". Ironically, when O'Neill was speaking, there was just one non-Unionist MP in the House: Sheelagh Murnaghan of the Ulster Liberal Party. The Nationalist Party did not attend the Debate at all, and the two NILP MPs had withdrawn before O'Neill made his speech.

It still never dawned on O'Neill that Stormont was a sham Parliament; that it was completely cut off from the real business of governing the state; and that it therefore lacked the dynamic of a party system capable of uniting diverse elements in society in the struggle for state power.

The Stormont set-up, by its nature, had an in-built Unionist majority. That was hardly the fault of Unionists, for the Union had been made to depend on it. But O'Neill was fooling himself if he seriously believed that Catholics would swap effective street action for "argument" in a sham Parliament with an in-built Protestant majority.

It is obvious that O'Neill had no idea how to cope with the events in Derry. His speech does not contain even the faintest trace of a coherent counter-strategy to the Civil Rights agitation. In particular, he did not address the question of what Catholics were supposed to do if they didn't take to the streets. He talked yet again about the building of slender bridges. But the reality of communal politics meant that a Catholic who crossed an O'Neill bridge was going over to "the other side".

The Parliamentary Unionist Party was obsessed by the fact that the "Red I.R.A." and other "Revolutionary Socialists" were heavily involved in the Civil Rights movement. In his contribution to the Stormont debate on the Derry disturbances, Bill Craig actually gave the names and addresses of three leading members of the Irish Workers' Group — Gerard Lawless, Eamonn McCann and Rory McShane — who, he said, were involved in organising the agitation. Similarly, John Taylor MP recalled that among those who led the Dungannon march in August had been Sinn Fein President, Thomas McGiolla, and "other leading members of the I.R.A. and the Communist movement" (Hansard, 16.10.1968, Col 1067).

However true such claims were, they did not actually get the Unionist Party anywhere; whinging about insurrectionary infiltration proved to be no substitute for a political response to the Civil Rights's campaign.

There appears to have been a vague awareness within Unionism that the marchers were not all IRA volunteers, and that the Catholic community was ready for a break with Nationalism. Captain John Brooke, for instance, said in the Stormont Debate:

> "There is no doubt that a proportion of the civil rights movement was genuine in its desire to get what to it were genuine grievances put right, but the organisation was taken over by some malicious and evil-minded men and the organisers — maybe not the ostensible organisers but the actual organisers — were following the Communist-I.R.A. doctrine." (ibid, 15.10.1968, Col 1007.)

This statement shows just how little has changed over the last twenty years in the apolitical world of Ulster Unionism. In 1968, the Civil Rights movement was held to be the work of "malicious and evil minded men". Nowadays, Unionist politicians blame the ongoing IRA campaign on the "evil men of violence", and avoid examining the underlying political conditions which keep this campaign going.

Later in the Stormont Debate, John Taylor said:

> "We ... must make it clear that Roman Catholics have a full and proper part to play in the development of the State of Northern Ireland [sic]...
>
> "...One of our failings as a Unionist administration in recent years has been that we have not emphasised the distinction between people as Roman Catholics and the role they can play in the progress of Northern Ireland and Nationalism." (ibid 16.10.1968, Col 1069.)

These words have a hollow ring to them in the light of the debate earlier in the year about the links between the Unionist Party and the Orange Order. It was clear from that short-lived debate that the Unionist Family was not in the least concerned about the Protestant nature of Stormont's governing Party. John Taylor never gave any indication that he was in the slightest bit concerned either, despite his belief that Northern Ireland was a state. It can, therefore, be assumed that when he was talking about the Catholic community's "role... in the progress of N. Ireland", he was not talking about a political role.

Taylor's Stormont speech was nevertheless interesting, particularly when it castigated the Unionist Party for its failure to counter the allegations of discrimination that had been made against it. Following on from the statement quoted above, Taylor said:

> "Secondly, another failing for which we are all alike responsible with the exception of the Prime Minister, the Minister of Home Affairs [Craig] and the Minister of Commerce [Faulkner] is that so many of these allegations have gone unanswered and have created in many parts of Northern Ireland and outside it a false impression of the true facts of life in this Province.

> "There could be a more co-operative and united effort by all the members of the Government and by the backbenchers to explain clearly what we are trying to achieve and what we are achieving and to explain what the local government franchise is and that indeed there is a property qualification for local government franchise in the Republic of Ireland, for instance. This is the type of thing we must answer back. By failing to do this in recent years we have to a certain extent created the situation which we find today. The policies of co-operation between Roman Catholic and Protestant in this State are right. The policies of economic and social development at present being embarked upon by this Government are in the best interests of all sections of the community. I only hope now we all get out and explain these policies to the people of this Province." (Ibid, Cols 1069-1070.)

This lavish praise for the Government is worth recording, as it reveals that Taylor was captivated by the O'Neillite vision. Less than four months after he had made this speech, Taylor was calling for O'Neill's resignation. But, as the rest of his political career has shown, he remained an O'Neillite in spirit.

The failure of the Unionist Party to 'answer back' on the charges of discrimination will be touched upon again in this book. It was undoubtedly partly due to sheer political incompetence; to the fact that Ulster Unionism was incapable of responding politically to the Civil Rights movement.

The only detectable hint of a political response can be found in a single article published by the News Letter on November 4th. Written by the senior journalist, R.M. Sibbett, the article dealt with the Parliamentary Unionist Party's attitude to the continuing Civil Rights agitation. In it, Sibbet said:

> "Mr. Faulkner and Mr.Craig, I learned from a leading Unionist source last night, far from being 'hard line' members of the Ulster Cabinet 'resisting reform' as has been alleged in recent weeks, are actually pressing for earlier and complete implementation of the big reorganisation and recasting of the local government system in the Province that the Government has been planning for the past two years.

> "Most progressive elements in the Unionist Party regard the current trend of the Roman Catholic minority towards claiming the full rights of British citizenship (in spite of the fact that it is being exploited for different purposes by certain people) as a natural and healthy one.

> "Members of the Government are believed to be disposed to see in their projected major reform of local government the means to remove any remaining obstacles to all sections in the Province enjoying the full rights of British citizenship that is undoubtedly theirs." (NL 4.11.1968.)

This report is, to say the least, puzzling. It may have simply been a piece of wishful thinking on R.M. Sibbett's part, or an attempt to inject some politics into the situation. The only other rational explanation is that someone seriously misinformed him.

The fact of the matter is that no one within the Unionist Party in 1968/69 ever had the political sense to welcome the "trend of the Roman Catholic minority towards claiming the full rights of British citizenship".

Such a move could have formed the basis for a positive response to the Civil Rights movement. The Unionist Government should have welcomed the demand for "British rights for British citizens", as a "natural and healthy one". That would have been the most effective way of dealing with those who were trying to exploit the demand for what R.M. Sibbett called "different purposes".

Despite Sibbett's predictions, that approach was never tried. It was never tried for one very good reason. A genuine attempt to secure the "full rights of British citizenship" for the Catholic community would have entailed more than a major reform of local government: it would have meant dismantling the Stormont set-up. To the Unionist Party of 1968, that would have been inconceivable.

Unionists could have used the Civil Rights movement to pressurise the Westminster Establishment into undoing the harm done to the province by the 1920 Government Of Ireland Act. They could have called for an end to the political arrangements whereby Protestants governed Catholics, and demanded instead that everyone in the province be given access to the normal party politics of the UK state. It can be safely assumed, however, that the O'Neill Government never considered such an approach for one second.

LYNCH DISAPPOINTS

O'Neill's calls for calm and restraint went unheeded: Civil Rights agitation continued throughout October. The student, People's Democracy group, based at Queen's University, played a prominent role in this agitation, holding sit-ins and other demonstrations. On Saturday, 26th October, violence again occurred when Civil Rights marchers on their way to Strabane were attacked by Protestant counter-demonstrators.

Against this background, the Irish Premier, Jack Lynch, made his first intervention in the developing situation. Addressing an Anglo-Irish Parliamentary Group lunch in London on October 30th, he said:

> "As you are all aware, it has been the aim of my Government to promote the reunification of Ireland by fostering a spirit of brotherhood among all sections of the Irish people.
>
> "The clashes in the streets of Derry are an expression of the evils which partition has brought in its train." (NL 31.10.1968.)

Needless to say, this piece of anti-partitionist pot-stirring came as a great disappointment to Captain O'Neill — bringing Taoiseachs to Stormont had not solved the National Question after all. The following day, O'Neill commented:

"I had hoped that the bad old days were over. I had hoped that this sterile argument could cease, but apparently Southern Irish politics have taken a lurch back into the past." (NL 1.11.1968.)

ENTER MR. WILSON (STAGE LEFT)

Shortly after Lynch's provocation, the Unionist Family had to undergo another traumatic experience: the direct involvement of the Westminster Government. On November 4th, O'Neill, Faulkner and Craig travelled to London to discuss the situation in the province with the British Prime Minister, Harold Wilson. The four hours of talks at Downing Street dealt with issues such as the recent events at the Derry Civil Rights march, the reform of the Local Government franchise, the allocation of housing and the appointment of a Parliamentary Ombudsman.

Predictably, Wilson's involvement was deeply disturbing for the Unionist Party. Indeed, Unionists appear to have been more concerned about the possibility of Westminster interference, than about the chaos being generated by the Civil Rights protests. Thus, after the discussions with Wilson, Faulkner tried to reassure Unionists that "there was no suggestion of Westminster interference in Northern Ireland domestic affairs" (NL 5.11.1968).

On the same day as the Wilson visit, the Unionist Party's touchiness over Stormont's independence allowed Gerry Fitt to dance rings round Unionist MPs at Westminster. To groans from the Labour side, Captain L.P.S. Orr and Sir Knox Cunningham repeatedly asked Fitt:

"Do you think that the power to decide local government boundaries should be a matter for the local Parliament or should be a matter for this one?" (ibid.)

In response, Fitt said: "I want this to be clearly understood. I want the local government franchise and the Parliamentary franchise to be operated from this House". And he received cheers and laughter from the Labour benches when he commented: "I think I have made my position quite clear. I would be the last man in the world to inflict a Stormont on Scotland or Wales" (ibid.)

O'NEILL'S SPEECH

Following his meeting with Wilson, O'Neill spoke at a meeting of the Commonwealth Parliamentary Association in London. In his speech he complained again about North-South relations.

"In 1965, in spite of the continued unwillingness of Southern politicians to face up to the actual position in Ulster, I decided to take the initiative of meeting the then Dublin P.M., Mr Sean Lemass.

"...What I must emphasise is that from my point of view, the object of such talks was to promote a decent, sane, neighbourly relationship. Canada is no less an indepedendent country and a member of the Commonwealth because of her friendly links with America.

"But if such a relationship is to flourish, it demands sensible restraint and common prudence. You cannot go on talking business with someone who comes blundering into your back garden, kicking over the plants. Mr. Lynch can have a friendly relationship based on mutual respect, or he can have the luxury of allowing hinmself to intervene in the affairs of Northern Ireland and the United Kingdom. He cannot have both." (Ibid.)

The speech also tried to counter the allegations that were being made about electoral arrangements in Northern Ireland for the Stormont Parliament. On the franchise for Stormont, O'Neill outlined the insignificance of the two main anomalies: the business vote and the university seats. The former, he explained, accounted for 12,954 votes out of an overall total of 925,041 while the latter made up 4 seats out of 54. And both anomalies, O'Neill pointed out, were being abolished "under legislation now passing through our Parliament".

The Northern Ireland Prime Minister also addressed the specific allegation that the Unionist Government had gerrymandered constituency boundaries to ensure the election of Unionist MPs. He said:

"There are some undue disparities between the sizes of constituencies for the N. Ireland Parliament. Electorates vary between three of under 10,000 and two of over 40,000; but the 15 seats with the largest electorates are all held by Unionists, mainly very comfortably, while 4 of the 6 with the smallest electorates are held by Opposition parties.

"Mr. Gerry Fitt, for instance, represents the tiniest electorate in N. Ireland at Stormont. At the last Ulster General Election his poll of 3,326 votes in an electorate of 7,620 compared with 14 Unionist majorities of more than 3,000 in average electorates of almost 23,000." (Ibid.)

This statement is worth recording as it represents one of the few occasions when Unionists attempted to refute some of the charges of discrimination and gerrymandering that were being made against them in 1968/69. In general, Unionists stayed silent, perhaps because they believed themselves to be guilty of everything that was alleged. Only one man made a concerted effort to counter the civil rights propaganda: the historian, Hugh Shearman. He wrote a number of letters and articles for the News Letter on the specific allegations of gerrymandering. For the record, the contents of two of them are recorded below.

SHEARMAN ON GERRYMANDERING

On January 14th 1969, the News Letter published an interesting article by Shearman entitled, **Gerrymandering — It's Not So Bad In Ulster**. It began:

"We may be good at things like shipbuilding, but not really at rigging an electorate. The ward boundaries of Londonderry are, of course, our exhibition performance, our tour de force; but it is possible that they are evidence of a naive ineptitude rather than of any advanced degree of skill."

Shearman then pointed out that it was the Northern Ireland Government which arranged the ward boundaries for Stormont:

"There is a tendency in some quarters," he said, "to assume that their boundaries must be drawn very much so as to favour the party in office.

"The curious thing is that this party [the Unionist Party] gets a far higher degree of electoral success when constituency boundaries are laid down by an outside authority; as is the case with the constituencies which elect our members of parliament to Westminster."

Shearman certainly had a point here.   In the Stormont elections, the Ulster Unionist Party normally won around two-thirds of the seats (between 34 and 38). In the Westminster Election of 1966, the Unionist Party won 11 out of 12 seats; in 1964, it won all twelve.   Shearman continued:

"Another curious feature is that when an electoral procedure is retained in Northern Ireland after it has been dropped in Britain, it is usually a procedure which tells against the Unionist Party.   A good example is the retention of the Queens University constituency long after university constituencies had been ended in Britain."

This was also true: the Unionist Party won two of the four University seats in the 1965 Stormont Election; while in the overall election, it gained over two-thirds of the Stormont seats.

The article then focussed on the issue of Local Government franchise.   In Great Britain, the Local Government franchise became identical with the parliamentary franchise after World War Two.   In Northern Ireland, it continued to be limited to occupiers of rateable property and their spouses.   Approximately 250,000 voters were thereby only able to vote in Westminster and Stormont elections in Northern Ireland, and had no vote in Local Government elections.

Shearman posed the question, "Who makes up the 250,000 approximate potential local government voters?".   His answer was simple:

"In fact, in all respects, they must form a pretty average cross section of the whole community.   And since there is a Unionist majority in the province at large, it may be presumed that a majority of these people would be likely to vote Unionist at local government elections if they were allowed to do so."

It is a fact that the property qualification for Local Government elections actually disenfranchised more Protestants than Catholics.   But, throughout the Civil Rights campaign, no Unionist, other than Hugh Shearman, managed to point this out.   Shearman returned to the issue of electoral arrangements again in a letter to the News Letter published in February 1969.   It said:

"Constant references to 'gerrymandering' have created an impression that the authorities in Northern Ireland have been constantly tinkering at the constituency boundaries to secure electoral advantages for the party in office. This has not been the case.   What has actually been wrong with our electoral boundaries is that they were left unchanged too long."   (NL 12.2.1969.)

The letter noted that the Local Government boundaries had been established in 1923 and only five changes in the boundaries had been made since.   It also countered allegations of gerrymandering in Stormont elections.   Echoing the point made by O'Neill at the Commonwealth Association in November 1968, Shearman highlighted the fact that the Unionist Party held the fifteen largest Stormont constituencies.   To a party hell-bent on gerrymandering as many safe Unionist seats as possible, these fifteen constituencies would have represented wasted votes.

These extracts from Hugh Shearman's writings provide an interesting counter to some of the charges of malpractice that were levelled at the Unionist Government in the late 1960s. It is, however, beyond the scope of this book to properly evaluate the charges of discrimination and gerrymandering made during the Civil Rights period. The most important fact to note is that accusations of discrimination are inevitable in a majority-minority situation. The blame for whatever went on in Northern Ireland between 1921 and 1972 lies with the Westminster political Establishment, which forced the Protestant community to govern a sizeable alienated minority under devolved arrangements. But, having become attached to these arrangements, the Unionist Party found itself having to defend Protestant majority rule over the Catholic minority. It is hardly surprising, therefore, that it lost the propaganda battle.

STORMONT COMES TO HEEL

Virtually every development within Unionist politics in the late 1960s had at its root illusions about Stormont. Harold Wilson's intervention in November 1968 caused immense turmoil within the Parliamentary Party. The day after his meeting with Wilson, O'Neill was asked "if he was satisfied that there would be no 'unwelcome interference' from Westminster". The arch-devolutionist replied: "I have no idea" (NL 6.11.1968).

The mood of at least a section of the Parliamentary Unionist Party at this time can be gauged from a speech made by John Taylor on November 11th. Speaking at Castlewellan, Taylor said:

> "No useful purpose was served by the automatic rejection, or acceptance, of suggested reforms, be they from Unionists, civil rights agitators or Harold Wilson. All ideas must be considered on their merits, but by no means could affairs in Ulster be settled by the imposition of demands by English socialists or Southern Irish anti-partitionists."

> He also warned that some Unionists, "including several with positions of responsibility", appeared to be prepared to "compromise the rights and privileges of the Ulster Parliament and Government" in order to overcome criticism from political opponents.

> "This being the case," said Taylor, "it was essential that members of the Unionist constituency associations should be alerted as to the trend of thinking among some Unionists and the need for a resurgence of Unionist support for the defence of Ulster's Constitution." (NL 12.11.1968.)

The day after Taylor's Castlewellan speech, the Parliamentary Unionist Party met at Stormont to discuss the previous week's meeting between Wilson and O'Neill, Craig and Faulkner. The Party was informed that Wilson had demanded the introduction of a number of reforms in response to the Civil Rights protests, and had "reminded" the Unionist Government of the subsidy it received from the British Exchequer.

According to the News Letter, O'Neill and his Finance Minister, Herbert Kirk, spelt out to the Parliamentary Party "the serious financial implications for

Northern Ireland in a continued confrontation between Stormont and Westminster", and "left the Party in no doubt that a trimmming of the financial sails is in the wind in the absence of significant steps towards social and political reform." (NL 13.11.1969.)

In his speech to the Party, Bill Craig "concentrated on matters relating to the franchise and touched on other points which were raised at the Downing Street discussions and which directly affect[ed] his department" (ibid).

The News Letter report on the Parliamentary Party meeting also revealed a significant, but unsurprising, fact:

> 'There is still an element in the Unionist Party clinging to die-hard attitudes. They represent the group commonly referred to as the "UDI" section of the Party." (Ibid.)

Events continued to move quickly. On Friday November 15th, with an illegal Civil Rights march and counter-demonstration in Derry planned for the next day, O'Neill again appealed for restraint.

"What we need now is calm," he said. "No rational discussion of any matter can be expected against a background of communal violence and it is well known that the Government are closely examining the underlying causes of the present unrest." (NL 16.11.1968.) In the event, a 15,000 strong civil rights march in Derry on the following day passed off peacefully.

On November 22nd, the Parliamentary Unionist Party held another meeting. Over 40 MPs and Senators were present and, after $4\frac{1}{2}$ hours, they agreed to give unanimous support to a five-point Government reform package. The details of the package were announced by O'Neill after the meeting. It involved:

> the appointment of an Ombudsman;
> the creation of a points system for the allocation of housing;
> the replacement of the Londonderry Corporation by a Development Commission;
> a review of the Special Powers Act; and
> the abolition of the company vote in Local Government elections.

On the general question of Local Government franchise, the Government said:

> "We are concerned at the widespread misunderstanding and confusion which exists on this issue. It is not generally appreciated that in any event the triennial local government elections will not be held again until April 1970.
>
> "It is our intention that a comprehensive reform and modernisation of the local government structure should be brought into effect within a period of three years — that is by the end of 1971.
>
> "As already announced, once the Government have arrived at their decisions on the basis for this re-structuring, consideration will be given to a review of the franchise, in the context of the organisation, financing and structure of the new local government bodies.
>
> "Meanwhile, whatever developments emerge, it is accepted that the company vote no longer has any place in local government and accordingly it will be abolished at an early date." (NL 22.11.1969.)

The Stormont Government's five-point reform package addressed most of the original demands of the Civil Rights movement; the main exception being the demand for "one man one vote" in Local Government elections. Consequently, Local Government franchise assumed a great significance, despite the fact that turn-outs in the elections were always low. Brian Faulkner, the then Deputy Prime Minister later noted in his memoirs:

"It was becoming obvious even then that 'one man one vote' was being allowed to build up into a sort of sacred cow for both sections of the community — for the Unionists a concession which they must not make, and for the civil rights agitators the most crucial gain to be wrested from the government. The whole thing was getting totally out of proportion." (Memoirs Of A Statesman, p49.)

According to Mervyn Pauley of the News Letter, Government success in gaining unanimous backing for its reform package from Unionist backbenchers generated a new mood of confidence within the Party.

"Delighted Party officials," said Pauley, "were looking on the crisis of the past few weeks as definitely over and hoped now for an atmosphere of co-operation throughout the Province behind the Government's programme of reform and communal justice and harmony" (NL 22.11.1968).

One "leading Unionist" told the News Letter that the Parliamentary meeting represented "a complete triumph for Captain O'Neill and his policy with a united Cabinet and a united Parliamentary Party behind him." (Ibid.)

Significantly, Mervyn Pauley also reported that there was some dissatisfaction within the Party ranks, particularly over Wilson's economic pressure. George Currie MP, on behalf of the Grand Orange Lodge of Ireland, was quoted as accusing Wilson of attempting to "dictate by economic sanctions what is to be done on matters within the responsibility of the Parliament and people of Northern Ireland." (Ibid.)

The delusions about Stormont were never far away. Within three weeks of the announcement of the five-point reform package, they had ended the ministerial career of Bill Craig.

CRAIG UNDER FIRE

At the end of November, the first signs of Bill Craig's estrangement from O'Neill were clearly visible. On November 28th, Craig, the Home Affairs Minister, made a very controversial speech at a rally at the Ulster Hall. The rally, which was also attended by Brian Faulkner, was held to launch a campaign to win back the West Belfast seat for the Unionist Party. A candidate, Brian McRoberts, had already been selected to oppose Gerry Fitt in the next Westminster election.

It was Craig's speech, however, which made all the headlines. In it, he attacked the Civil Rights movement and the Catholic Church. He also appeared to be criticising, by implication, some of the reforms that the Government had just introduced. In one of the most controversial statements of the speech, Craig said:

"When you have a Roman Catholic majority you have a lesser standard of democracy. I have no doubt that whatever might happen between us and Great Britain and God forbid that anything might happen, it would not follow that we would unite with the rest of Ireland." (NL 6.12.1968.)

On the Civil Rights agitation and the Government's reform package, Craig said:

"Now I cannot see much merit in an ombudsman, except perhaps one thing — it will expose those who are making reckless and unfounded allegations. And I also think that there is much to be gained too from having a housing points system, because what we used to do is to see that there is no discrimination against the ordinary people of this community because the way some people have been talking is that you should only be entitled to a house if you have failed in your social obligations and have got a family that you cannot look after.

"At least a points system will see that there is a fair basis for all the wide range of needs on how houses should be allocated. This civil rights movement is completely bogus; it has two aspects. You have on the one side a lot of misguided, ill-informed radicals. On the other side, you have a Republican movement who are seeking an opportunity to undermine the constitution of this country. The IRA use civil unrest as an opportunity to resume the campaign of violence.

"It would be the very negation of democracy to over-rule the elected will of the people of Northern Ireland. These affairs that are within our control will be controlled by us and any interference will meet with a much greater resolve than is obvious here tonight." (Ibid.)

Later in his speech, Craig also said:

"There are people who have been suggesting that pressures might be applied, that our powers might be infringed upon, that there might be financial pressure... It is in the the Parliament and Government of Northern Ireland that our future will be decided." (Ibid.)

Despite the incoherence of some of his statements, Craig won a standing ovation from the Ulster Hall audience. His speech quickly fuelled suspicions that he was plotting against O'Neill. The next day, however, Craig told the News Letter that he was "fully in agreement" with the programme of the Government. "What I object to," he said, "is the talk that there is something rotten in the State of Northern Ireland which is nonsense." (NL 30.11.1968.)

The Home Affairs Minister was sharply criticised in the News Letter's editorial column which referred to his "facility for saying the wrong thing", and accused him of giving the impression that the Cabinet was not united (ibid). The Ulster Liberal MP, Sheelagh Murnaghan, announced that she would be tabling a Parliamentary question on Craig's speech for O'Neill and added, "Mr. Craig must resign after this" (ibid).

On Saturday, November 30th, a Civil Rights march in Armagh witnessed further disturbances: marchers clashed with supporters of Paisley, who were holding a counter-demonstration. The following Monday, the News Letter called for firmer action from the Government, and suggested that O'Neill might have to take over from Craig at the Ministry of Home Affairs.

A more direct call for the replacement of Craig was made by the Queen's University Unionist Association. Its former Chairman, a Catholic named Louis Boyle, accused Craig of trying to exploit sectarianism for political ends.

> "In doing so," added Boyle, "he has deeply offended the Roman Catholic community. By implication he has reiterated that Northern Ireland is a Protestant state and must remain so and similarly the Unionist Party.

> "It is because of Captain O'Neill and the knowledge that many in the Unionist Party are firmly behind him, that I have been able to join and take an active part in the Party. Mr. Craig has made this position very difficult to maintain." (NL 3.12.1968.)

On December 4th, O'Neill was asked for his opinion of Craig's Ulster Hall speech. He replied that he regretted "some of the tone — not so much the content" of what his Home Affairs Minister had said. O'Neill also claimed that Craig was fully behind the Government and tried to make excuses on his behalf.

> "The Minister has been living through a period of considerable strain," O'Neill said. "I have noticed him fairly tired lately. I think we must bear that in mind when we consider the tone of his remarks" (NL 5.12.1968).

O'Neill's fairly mild criticism in Stormont still managed to annoy Craig. That night he addressed the Clogher branch of the South Tyrone Unionist Association. He began his speech with the words:

> "I am going to do something that perhaps I should not do. I am not making the speech that was intended to be the speech for Clogher Unionists, but a repeat of the speech taken from a tape recording of that evening in the Ulster Hall." (NL 6.12.1968.)

The Clogher speech was reported by the News Letter under front page banner headlines, **Craig Says It Again**.

The following day, Friday, November 7th, 300 "grass roots" Unionist delegates met at Glengall Street to discuss the Government's five-point reform package. The meeting agreed to back the reforms after receiving assurances from O'Neill that there would be no more movement by the Government, particularly on the issue of "one man, one vote".

By this stage, there was growing speculation about Bill Craig's position within the Cabinet. On December 9th, the News Letter published an editorial entitled, **End Of Line For Mr. Craig**. The paper alleged that the Home Affairs Minister was "setting hmself up as the standard bearer of right wing dissidents from the Stormont backbenches to the Paisley platforms who are either lukewarm or openly hostile in their attitude to the Government's reform programme." The editorial urged O'Neill to dismiss him, stating:

> "It is obvious now that the facade of unity which was presented after the meeting in Glengall Street on Friday has deceived no one. In the eyes of the world, the Unionist Party is divided at the top." (NL 9.12.1968.)

The usual accounts of Craig's behaviour at this time invariably paint him as an ultra-bigot, who was trying to oust O'Neill and install his own brand of sectarian Unionism. These accounts invariably fail to mention that O'Neill and Craig were very close allies for most of the 1960s. In 1963, for example, Craig, (then Government Chief Whip) is said to have played the role of kingmaker for O'Neill: he worked behind the scenes to secure acceptance of O'Neill as Prime Minister within the Parliamentary Party (see, for example, Bleakley: **Faulkner**, Mowbrays 1974, p65).

In his Autobiography, Terence O'Neill tries to suggest that his once loyal ally simply underwent a metamorphosis. He claims that Craig "gradually changed from a forward looking person, interested in continental and international affairs, into a narrow-minded sectarian" (p104). No explanation for this metamorphosis is given, leaving the impression that Bill Craig simply woke up one morning and found himself to be a bigot.

The truth is that Bill Craig's estrangement from O'Neill was caused by the intervention by the Westminster Government in "the internal affairs" of Northern Ireland. Craig was an O'Neillite who took O'Neillism in earnest. Like O'Neill, he believed that Ulster Unionism had a separate destiny to realise, and that it was capable of realising it. But, unlike his leader, Craig took all the rhetoric about the power and the glory of Stormont seriously. In particular, he thought that Northern Ireland had federal status within the UK. Naturally, therefore, he was unable to stomach being told what to do by the British Government, particularly a Labour one.

Craig may or may not have been plotting against the Prime Minister in November and December 1969. But to speak of him planning a "right-wing coup" is simplistic and inaccurate. In reality, Craig was probably no more right-wing or reactionary than his mentor and former close friend, Terence O'Neill. And when he finally left O'Neill's Government, it was because of his views about the independence of Stormont, not the Government's reform package.

The final split between the Prime Minister and Craig was provoked by the most famous of all O'Neill's speeches.

ULSTER AT THE CROSSROADS

By early December, it was clear that the Government's 5-point reform package had failed to halt the Civil Rights agitation, or reduce the rising sectarian tension in the province. On Saturday, November 30th, Civil Rights marchers had clashed with Paisleyite counter-demonstrators in Armagh. Violence had also occurred the following Wednesday in Dungannon.

In this atmosphere, Terence O'Neill made his celebrated **Ulster Stands At The Crossroads** speech on television. He appealed directly to the people to support his leadership. A sizeable section of the speech concentrated on Stormont's subservience to Westminster and was obviously aimed at Craig and the so-called "UDI section" of the Parliamentary Unionist Party. He said:

> "I am aware, of course, that some foolish people have been saying: 'Why should we bow the knee to a Labour Prime Minister? Let's hold out until a Conservative Government returns to power, and then we need do nothing.' My friends, that is a delusion. This letter is from Mr. Edward Heath, and it tells me — with the expressed support of my old friend Sir Alec Douglas Home — that

a reversal of the policies which I have tried to pursue would be every bit as unacceptable to the Conservative Party. If we adopt an attitude of stubborn defiance we will not have a friend left at Westminster.

"I make no apology for the financial and economic support we have received from Britain. As a part of the United Kingdom, we have always considered this to be our right. But we cannot be a part of the United Kingdom merely when it suits us. And those who talk so glibly about acts of impoverished defiance do not know or care what is at stake... Is a freedom to pursue the un-Christian path of communal strife and sectarian bitterness really more important to you than all the benefits of the British Welfare State?

"But this is not all. Let me read to you some words from the Government of Ireland Act, 1920 — the Act of the British Parliament on which Ulster's Constitution is founded.

"'Notwithstanding the establishment of the Parliament of Northern Ireland... the supreme authority of the Parliament of the United Kingdom shall remain unaffected and undiminished over all persons, matters and things in [Northern] Ireland and every part thereof.'

"Because Westminster has trusted us over the years to use the powers of Stormont for the good of the people of Ulster, a sound custom has grown up that Westminster does not use its supreme authority in fields where we are normally responsible. But Mr. Wilson made it absolutely clear to us that if we did not face up to our problems the Westminster Parliament might well decide to act over our heads. Where would our Constitution be then? What shred of self-respect would be left to us?

"...There are, I know, today some so-called loyalists who talk of independence from Britain — who seem to want a kind of Protestant Sinn Fein. These people will not listen when they are told that Ulster's income is £200 million a year but that we can spend £300 million — only because Britain pays the balance." (NL 10.12.1968.)

There was more than a hint of hypocrisy in this attack on Protestant Sinn Feiners, as the logic of O'Neillism was to differentiate Ulster from the the UK. The sentiments expressed in the Crossroads Speech are still shared throughout the Ulster Unionist Party. Modern-day Unionists, like O'Neill, want to remain politically separate from the rest of the UK. But they shy away from full-blown Ulster Nationalism because it would cost them money. Unionists want their own little Ulster, but they want the Brits to keep paying for it. This, above all else, explains why a Protestant separatist movement has not developed in Northern Ireland over the past twenty years.

The main theme of the Crossroads speech, however, was not Stormont's relationship with Westminster. O'Neill's primary intention was to call, once again, for calm and restraint and to ask 'moderates' to demonstrate their support for his Government's attempts to restore order. The entire spirit of the address is captured in its final paragraph:

"And now a further word to you all. What kind of Ulster do you want? A happy and respected Province, in good standing with the rest of the United Kingdom? Or a place continually torn apart by riots and demonstrations, and regarded by the rest of Britain as a political outcast? As always in a democracy, the choice is yours... Please weigh all that is at stake, and make your voice heard in whatever way you think best, so that we know the views not of the few but of the many. For this is a truly a time of decision, and in your silence all that we have built up could be lost. I pray that you will reflect carefully and decide wisely. And I ask all our Christian people, whatever their denomination, to attend their places of Worship on Sunday next to pray for the peace and harmony of our country." (Ibid.)

O'Neill was widely congratulated on his speech. It was welcomed by Eddie McAteer, Sheelagh Murnaghan and Tom Boyd. Gerry Fitt said that the Prime Minister was sincere, but added that Craig had to go and "one man one vote" had to be introduced.

Within the Unionist Party, support was expressed by such people as John Taylor, James Chichester-Clark, Herbert Kirk, Phelim O'Neill, John Andrews (Leader of the Senate), Basil Kelly (Attorney General), William Fitzsimmons, and the Queen's University Unionist Association. Bill Craig said that he supported "everything Captain O'Neill said about improving community relations in the Province" (ibid), while the Deputy Prime Minister, Brian Faulkner said:

"The important thing is that everyone should give priority to: (1) an immediate return to normal conditions everywhere with absolute respect for the rule of law; (2) a continuation of all our efforts to bring more employment and thus greater prosperity to every part of Northern Ireland. These, in my opinion, were the principal objects of the Prime Minister's speech. They deserve wholehearted support." (ibid.)

The News Letter published an editorial entitled **Challenge At The Crossroads**, which declared:

"Since he came to office Captain O'Neill has shown Northern Ireland the way ahead; last night he affirmed his determination not to be diverted. It is for all who want a virile, a progressive and broadening Unionism as he sees it — and a Unionism that will not in the end lead to absorption in an all-Ireland republic — to give their support, or make way for those who will." (Ibid.)

Support for O'Neill flooded in. It is estimated that in all nearly 150,000 people signed messages or declarations backing the sentiments of the Prime Minister's speech. The Unionist Party headquarters was said to have been deluged with messages of suppport, petitions and round robin letters. Unionist MPs also received letters and phone-calls backing O'Neill.

The News Letter threw itself into the cause. It provided "I back O'Neill" posters for its readers to cut out of the paper and display in their cars. It also published pages packed with the names of individuals, organisations, firms, clergymen and Chambers of Commerce who had contacted the News Letter to say that they backed O'Neill.

Members of staff at Stranmillis College, and at schools such as Belfast Royal Academy, and Larne Grammar, declared that they backed O'Neill, as did the Senate of Queen's University and the Assistant Masters' Association. Generally speaking, the messages of support had a middle-class and apolitical flavour. For instance, Belfast Traders from Ann Street, Bridge Street, Donegall

Place, Donegall Square, and Royal Avenue joined together to support the Prime Minister in a statement which included the line:

"The great majority of Northern Ireland people live and wish to live in harmony, regardless of politics and religion."

There can be no doubt that O'Neill's **Ulster At The Crossroads** speech generated a great deal of goodwill in the province. But the underlying political reality remained unchanged: politics was still a question of Prods v Micks. This reality did not take long to re-establish itself.

GOODBYE MR. CRAIG

Within twenty four hours of the Crossroads speech, Bill Craig addressed the annual dinner of the Bloomfield Young Unionist Association. It was to be his last speech as Home Affairs Minister. In it, he expounded his belief that Northern Ireland had Federal Status within the UK by taking issue with what O'Neill had said about Stormont's subordinate position to Westminister. On O'Neill's reference to Section 75 of the Government Of Ireland Act, Craig said:

"I think far too much is being read into that. I would resist any effort by any Government in Great Britain, whatever its complexion might be, to exercise that power in any way to interfere with the proper jurisdiction of the Government of Northern Ireland.

"It is merely a reserve of power to deal with an emergency situation. It is difficult to envisage any situation in which it could be exercised without the consent of the Government of Northern Ireland.

"I would regret very much if we were to sit back passively and see an effort being made to depart from this very fundamental principle touching on our Parliament and Government. It is the duty of every Unionist to stand solidly and defend the Constitution on this basis. To accept any other argument is to make a laughing stock of the whole concept of democracy." (NL 11.12.1968.)

The following day, December 11th, Bill Craig was sacked by Terence O'Neill. In his letter demanding Craig's resignation, O'Neill said:

"Last night you chose to dispute my views on Section 75 of the Government of Ireland Act, and to say that any use of Westminster's sovereign powers should be 'resisted'. As to your opinion of the constitutional position, I can only say that it differs from that of the Attorney General, who is the government's principal adviser on constitutional matters. But it is when you talk of 'resistance' that I must dissent most strongly from you.

"I have said that if we act responsibly here, there will be no case for any intervention in our affairs. Northern Ireland's Constitution is not in danger, for both parties at Westminster are committed to the guarantees we have been given. But what is at risk is the enormous financial subventions which make it possible for us to enjoy a British rather than an Irish standard of living. Unionists stand for the Union, buttressed as it is by these extremely favourable financial arrangements. Your idea of an Ulster which could 'go it alone' is a delusion, and I believe all sensible people will see it to be so.

"Clearly you cannot propound such views and remain a member of the Government. I am sorry to have to say this, for we have :een colleagues for over five years and friends for a longer time, but I must now ask you to place your resignation in my hands. — Yours sincerely, Terence" (NL 12.12.1968).

In his reply to O'Neill's later, Craig said:

"Dear Prime Minister, I hereby submit to you my resignation from the office of Home Affairs. I do so with great regret as I have got much satisfaction in serving in your administration which has pushed forward with a great programme of social and economic change.

"However, I agree we must part company now because it is apparent we take different views on the fundamentals of Unionism and indeed on the management of the Party. You also clearly have failed to understand my arguments; for instance, I have never argued anything of a U.D.I. nature but simply to defend our present constitution which represents the settlement made when our grandfathers and fathers made their historic stand.

"...I stand strongly on my remarks about Section 75. There has never been any cause to suggest that Northern Ireland has used improperly its powers in the past, now or in the future. If Mr. Wilson or anyone else should threaten to interfere in the exercise of our proper jurisdiction it is your duty and that of every Unionist to resist. As far as financial pressure is being applied to a democratically elected Government and Parliament and in order to impose policies to which we are opposed, then it can only be described as blackmail.

"May I also add that with many other members of the Party who take a firm line on our constitutional rights we resent the innuendo that we are opposed to change and advance." — Yours sincerely, Bill Craig" (ibid).

Craig never held office at Stormont again. But he left the Government with his federalist delusions still intact and has been pursuing the Ulster Nationalist/O'Neillite vision ever since.

SHORT-LIVED CONFIDENCE

At the end of 1968, O'Neill had reason to feel quite pleased with himself. In personal terms, his **Ulster At The Crossroads** speech had been an outstanding success and his position as Party Leader had been considerably strengthened.

This was demonstrated on December 12th, the day after Craig's departure, when the Parliamentary Unionist Party decisively backed a vote of confidence in the Prime Minister. Twenty eight members supported the vote, while only four — Desmond Boal, Harry West, William Hinds and Johnny McQuade — abstained. Bill Craig and Tom Lyons left the meeting before the vote was taken.

O'Neill declared that he was "absolutely delighted" with the majority in his favour and later described the Party meeting as a "walkover". After the meeting the Government Chief Whip, Roy Bradford, commented:

"This is a resounding personal success for Captain O'Neill as leader. It also gives an overwhelming endorsement of Government policies under his leadership." (NL 13.12.1968.)

On the same day, however, there was an indication that problems were still looming for the Government. Speaking in the House of Commons at Westminster, Harold Wilson said:

> "We do not feel there is any justification for the prolonged postponement of one man one vote despite the long term propositions which have been made." (Ibid.)

Despite this dark hint, there was still a feeling within Unionist circles that the worst of the civil rights storm had been weathered. The Northern Ireland Civil Rights Association had responded to the new atmosphere in the Province by calling for a period of "truce" without marches or demonstrations. And on December 16th, the Attorney General, Basil Kelly, introduced a truce in Civil Rights cases: all summonses for offences arising out of the Civil Rights campaign were adjourned until May.

But whatever optimism there was among Unionists about the future was quickly dispelled in the new year.

PDs ON THE MARCH

On January 1st, 1969, the People's Democracy march from Belfast to Derry began. Although the Stormont Government's decision to permit this march provoked criticism from Ian Paisley and others, it was firmly supported by the News Letter on the following grounds:

> "If 100 students want to walk to Derry along the raw, windblown highways and brave the rigours of the Glenshane Pass, they should be allowed to do so without let or hindrance. We may be sure that they will arrive in Derry, if not unnoticed, at least with no fanfare of trumpets or the attention of the world. And we would suggest, with the enthusiasm for their cause a little faded." (NL 1.1.1969.)

It did not exactly work out like that. The PD march, which deliberately passed through a number of rural Protestant towns, was repeatedly disrupted by Loyalists, led by Major Ronald Bunting, a close associate of Paisley. Bunting's claim that the People's Democracy group was a front for Republicans was certainly not damaged by the unfurling of a tricolour by marchers as they passed through Toome.

The first stage of the PD march on January 1st ended with the police having to give 80 marchers a four-mile lift to their sleeping quarters to avoid a clash with a 200 strong crowd (NL 2.1.1969). A clash did occur, however, on the following day when the PD supporters were pelted with nails and bolts on the road to Maghera. And, although the marchers decided to by-pass Maghera, violence did flare up between rival groups in the town.

By far the most serious incident of the march took place outside Derry on January 4th, when around 70 marchers were ambushed on Burntollet bridge by Major Bunting's supporters. Thirteen students had to have hospital treatment after being attacked with sticks and stones. More injuries were sustained in Derry when the march was stoned as it passed through Protestant areas.

After the march had ended, Captain O'Neill issued yet another call for calm. "Enough is enough," he said. "We have heard sufficient for now about civil rights: let us hear a little about civil responsibility." (NL 6.1.1969).

His feelings towards the PD marchers were revealed in his comment:

"The extremism of the Republicans, radicals, Socialists and anarchists can only be defeated by the forces of moderation and not by the forces of extremism." (Ibid.)

It is clear that many within the Government were not exactly enamoured with the students who made up the bulk of the PD movement. On January 9th, for example, Roy Bradford suggested that any students convicted of a breach of the peace at demonstrations should have their grants cut (NL 10.1.1969).

O'Neill's feelings about the PD members were also aired later that month in an interview with the **Washington Post**. Referring to the violence which marked their march from Belfast to Derry, he claimed that "if people had been sensible and had left these miserable, long-haired bedraggled students alone everything might have been all right." (See News Letter 22.1.1969).

O'Neill may have had a point here, but the truth is that his Government must share some of the responsibility for the behaviour of Major Bunting and co. Throughout the Civil Rights period, the O'Neill Administration never once showed itself to be in control of the situation. In between fanning the flames of Protestant paranoia by describing the Civil Rights agitation as a Republican/Communist plot, it consistently gave the civil righters the upper hand at every juncture. It could not reassure the Protestant community that it was in control of the situation for a very simple reason: it had lost all semblance of control and had no idea how to regain it. It is, therefore, hardly surprising that Paisley and Bunting were attracting more support by the beginning of 1969.

THE COMMISSION

On Saturday, 11th January, a week after the end of the Belfast to Derry march, violence flared up again at a PD march in Newry. Earlier in the week, Major Bunting had announced that a Protestant counter-demonstration would also be held in the town and the Government had decided to re-route the PD march. In the event, Bunting's planned march was cancelled but a riot developed, following police attempts to divert the march away from the town centre. 24 arrests were made and 10 members of the RUC and 28 civilians were injured.

On the following Monday, the Strabane Civil Rights Association announced that it would be holding a march in the town on Saturday 18th January. And a day later Bunting stated that he would be leading a motorcade through Strabane on the same day in order to hold a "trooping of the colour" ceremony at which he would "show the Union Jack" to the town.

Against this background, the Northern Ireland Cabinet held a special meeting on Wednesday January 15th which lasted from 10am to 6.30pm, with a two hour break for lunch. Following the meeting, the Government announced that it would be appointing a Commission, the official terms of reference of which were to: "inquire into and report on the course of events leading to, and the immediate causes and nature of, the violence and civil disturbances in Northern Ireland on and since October 5th 1968; and to assess the composition, conduct and aims of those bodies involved in the current agitation and in any incidents arising out of it." (NL 16.1.1969; the Commission became known as the Cameron Commission).

The Government's announcement also stated that "in the light of their decision to recommend the appointment of this commission, which will be able to examine the situation without fear or favour, Ministers will not tolerate any civil disorder or other disregard of the law." (Ibid.)

Consequently, the Government declared its intention to introduce amendments and extensions to the *Public Order Act (Northern Ireland), 1951*. The new legislation would make it an offence, not merely to organise, but to take part in an illegal procession; and would prevent counter-processions interfering with legal processions.

Assessing these decisions, the News Letter's political correspondent, Mervyn Pauley, noted that "the Government may be further pressurized, and by its own brainchild, the Commission, into bringing its promised review of the "one man one vote" issue forward in time." (Ibid.)

The Cabinet's decision to appoint a Commission did result in the cancellation of both the Civil Rights march in Strabane and Major Bunting's motorcade. In Belfast, however, a statement from the PDs issued on January 17th said:

> 'There can be no question of any lull in the civil rights campaign while the Commission is sitting. Our struggle will continue and the Commission can, if they wish, watch it in action." (NL 18.1.1969.)

On the same day, Bill Craig returned to the province after a holiday in West Germany, and vowed to "fight and fight and fight again" against "interference with the powers delegated to the Northern Ireland Goverment" (ibid).

It is possible that the Stormont Government had some hopes that the appointment of the Commission would ease its problems. In fact, the reverse occurred. On January 20th, Harold Wilson again added to the pressures on the O'Neill administration. "They have gone some way to meeting what we regard as the minimum that's got to be done to deal with the civil rights question," he said. "They haven't gone the whole way yet. I welcome what they have so far done." (NL 21.1.1969.)

It should be stressed at this point that there was nothing in the least bit principled about Wilson's forays into the Northern Ireland situation in the late 1960s. His interventions can really only be described as meddling, as he had no realistic or coherent objective in mind. Like his predecessors, Wilson was committed to maintaining the perverse mode of government that had existed in Northern Ireland since 1921 and which was at the root of the problem. To put it bluntly, the 1964-70 Labour Government wanted the Catholics in Northern Ireland to continue being ruled by the Protestants until such time as both could be moved into an all-Ireland state. The Labour leaders did nothing towards ending Partition. Their commitment to a United Ireland had no practical effect beyond banning people in Northern Ireland from Labour Party membership. Influential Labour MPs, like Michael Foot, frequently wrote to the papers complaining about the terrible Northern Ireland arrangement, which gave the

Unionists eleven safe seats there, and about the invariable Unionist practice of voting with the Tories at Westminster. At the same time, they refused to stand Labour candidates in Northern Ireland, or to make the Northern Ireland Labour Party a region of the Labour Party, or to accept individuals resident in Northern Ireland into membership. And when, in the forties, Jack Beattie won a seat standing as 'Labour', he was refused the Labour whip at Westminster.

The Labour Party was itself chiefly responsible for the abnormal political situation in Northern Ireland. Its contribution to the unification of Ireland was to ensure that the province remained politically abnormal, and that Protestant and Catholic workers did not overcome their communal antagonism and unite in the class-based politics of the United Kingdom.

Harold Wilson's interventions in the late sixties did not tackle the real problems. He only harrassed the Unionists. And this just brought out the worst in the Unionists, without addressing the most substantial grievance of the Catholic community, namely the Stormont system of devolved government itself.

The Stormont Government's appointment of a Commission did not, therefore, fully satisfy the Labour Government at Westminster. It also earned O'Neill and his Cabinet colleagues heavy criticism from William Craig. Referring to the Commission, Craig said:

> "It is a bad thing because the Government has abdicated its responsibility. It is a political problem and political problems should be dealt with by the Government before the Parliament of Northern Ireland and once you side-step the decision of the elected representatives it is not good democracy." (NL 22.1.1969.)

And on his former Government colleagues, he said acidly:

> "The only conclusion that I can draw is that they have lost their nerve and feel that they can no longer control the events of the day." (Ibid.)

Events continued to move quickly for the Government. By the end of that week, Bill Craig's strong criticism of the Commission had been completely overshadowed by a development of much greater significance.

GOODBYE MR. FAULKNER

On January 23rd, 1969, Brian Faulkner, the Deputy Prime Minister and Minister of Commerce, resigned from the Government over the decision to appoint a Commission to enquire into the ongoing civil unrest. In his resignation letter to Terence O'Neill, Faulkner said:

> "You are aware that I have been unhappy about the setting up of the Commission. It is, in my opinion, a political manoeuvre and to some extent an abdication of authority, and it is misleading to the Parliamentary Party. The Government is better qualified to decide for itself what is to be done.

> "The essential now is strong Government capable of either: 1, gaining the confidence of the Unionist Party for a change of policy and introducing on its own initiative adult suffrage in the local government franchise — which I personally believe to be the right course; or 2, resisting the pressures being brought to bear on the Government.

"In either case law and order must be enforced.

"This administration falls down on both the alternatives I have mentioned.

"I have remained throughout successive crises when resignation might have further disrupted the Party. And for the same reasons I have hesitated now. On reflection, however, I am forced to the conclusion that not only is the Party tearing itself to pieces, but conditions in the country are such that the work of my department is imperilled.

"In these circumstances I feel I can no longer usefully serve in your Government and I ask you to accept my resignation." (NL 25.1.1969.)

Faulkner's resignation seems to have come as a great shock to O'Neill. The News Letter reported it with a large photograph of the Prime Minister looking very distraught, accompanied by a front page banner headline which simply said: **Anguish** (ibid).

O'Neill's reply to Faulkner's resignation provoked another letter from Faulkner, which in turn stirred O'Neill into writing another reply. The full texts of the letters can be found in the News Letter for 25th January, 1969. There is, however, no real need to analyse every point and counter-point made by both men. The acrimonious exchange of letters simply illustrates the extent to which Unionist politics had degenerated by this stage.

The letters also prove that O'Neill and Faulkner disliked each other intensely. In the first of his two letters, O'Neill accused Faulkner of being a disloyal Deputy in the past. He said:

"You also tell me that you remained through what you term 'successive crises'. I am bound to say that if, instead of passively 'remaining' you had on occasions given me that loyalty and support which a Prime Minister has the right to expect from his Deputy, some of these so-called crises might never have arisen."

Faulkner concluded his second letter by referring to this accusation:

"I am hurt by your reference to lack of support during my period of office. There is much I could say, but I would prefer not to indulge in recrimination." (Ibid.)

O'Neill, however, went back onto the attack in his second letter:

"You say you are hurt by my reference to lack of support from you in the past. Yet on television last night you displayed again that ambiguity which has confused people in the past. Thus you said at different times that you had consistently been behind the Government policies, yet on a number of occasions before had been on the point of resignation. If you were, in fact, consistently behind the Government policies I am at a loss to know what was bringing you so often to the fence of resignation which you failed to jump.

"You still seem unable to understand that a Deputy Prime Minister above all can reasonably be expected to show some personal loyalty to the Prime Minister of the day. I do not wish to argue the point. Instead I enclose a transcript of an interview which you gave from America while I was struggling for my political life in 1966. You will see that you were specifically asked to say whether or not you supported me as Prime Minister and that you took refuge in ambiguities about Government policy. Had you been willing to give straight answers to questions such as these on a number of occasions it would have sustained me and, I am sure, increased respect for you."

On January 24th, Faulkner elaborated on the reasons for his resignation. He claimed that the Government was failing to resist the pressure which had come "from all directions" in recent months. He said that it either had to stand up to the pressure over "one man one vote" or to "accept that the question of the franchise was a very important factor in causing unrest, change its policy on this and go to the Party and get the support of the Party" (NL 25.1.1969). Settling the franchise question, he claimed, would have robbed the unrest "of a very high proportion of its raison d'etre" (ibid).

Faulkner also attacked the Government for "shifting responsibility on to a Commission", and claimed that this represented a breach of faith, as the Parliamentary Unionist Party members had been told that there would be no change in the Government's attitude to Local Government franchise.

> "But the Government knows very well," he claimed, "that if the Commission reports that the franchise question was a cause of unrest, then it will have to make a change." (Ibid.)

The following day, at a meeting of his Constituency Unionist Association in East Down, Faulkner expanded on this point:

> "The Government continues to give pledges it can no longer keep because the Prime Minister has told his colleagues that a change in local government was inevitable and that this recommendation could well come from the Commission."

The meeting enthusiastically passed a vote of confidence in Faulkner.

On the same day — Saturday, 25th January — O'Neill lost another member of the Cabinet: William Morgan, the Minister for Health and Social Services resigned from the Government. In his resignation letter, Morgan stated simply:

> "After very careful thought I have come to the conclusion that it would be in the best interests of all concerned that a change of leadership should take place. In view of this I very much regret that I am unable to continue as a member of your Cabinet and ask you to accept my resignation." (NL 27.1.1969.)

Morgan was replaced by Robert Porter, while Roy Bradford took over from Faulkner at the Ministry of Commerce.

CROSSROADS ELECTION

At the end of January 1969, Ulster Unionism slipped further into the morass. On the 28th, Mervyn Pauley reported in the News Letter:

> "There is a group of backbenchers — thought to number about ten — known to be discontented with the party leadership and the state of party unity" (NL 28.1.1969).

At first, Pauley was somewhat dismissive of the backbenchers' challenge. He claimed that "if it came to the crunch", O'Neill "would have a majority of Unionists behind him and Government policy". His report also quoted the Prime Minister as saying:

> "I have every intention of continuing. I am presiding over a united Cabinet... We have all got our tails up." (Ibid.)

The seriousness of the challenge to O'Neill's leadership became apparent two days later, when a letter, signed by twelve backbench Unionist MPs, was sent to the Unionist Party Secretary, Jim Bailie. It said:

> "We, the undersigned, being convinced that the disunity in the Parliamentary Party and constituency associations has reached grave proportions and being dedicated to the principle that the progressive policies of the Unionist Party must be vigorously pursued by a united Party, are satisfied that there must be a change of leader." (NL 31.1.1969.)

The letter, which also called for a meeting of the Parliamentary Unionist Party, was signed by Desmond Boal, Captain John Brooke, Harry West, William Craig, John Taylor, John Dobson, Tom Lyons, Albert Anderson, Joseph Burns, Johnny McQuade, Austin Ardill and William Hinds. In response to it, O'Neill made it clear that he had no intention of going quietly:

> "I understand that some members of my party are stating that they want a change of leadership. The real issue is a different one. What they truly seek is a change of policy, and because I believe our present policies are the right ones, I want to make it absolutely clear that, just as I did in 1966, I intend to stand up and fight, together with those who have supported me in what I believe in.
> "I will not back down. I will not trim my sails. I will do my duty." (ibid.)

It was widely believed, however, that O'Neill's position as Party Leader was becoming untenable. The Nationalist Party Leader, Eddie McAteer, for example, said, "the writing is on the wall for the Prime Minister", while Sam Napier, the NILP Secretary, claimed, "the arithmetic of Parliamentary strength seems to be against the Prime Minister".

Mervyn Pauley, by this stage, had changed his mind about the Prime Minister's prospects. Having estimated that the Parliamentary Party would back O'Neill by 20 votes to 14, he added ominously:

> "Even his closest supporters in the Parliamentary Party regard his chances of remaining in office for any useful period of time as remote." (ibid.)

On Monday, 3rd February, the twelve dissident Unionist MPs met together in the Seagoe Hotel, Portadown. The meeting, which became known as the "Portadown Parliament", called again for a change of leadership. By this time, all eyes were being fixed on a meeting of the Parliamentary Unionist Party which was scheduled for February 5th. But on the evening of February 3rd, O'Neill's Cabinet decided to dissolve Parliament and call a General Election for February 24th. The following day a Cabinet statement declared: "The country now has the choice before it. We are confident of its verdict." (NL 5.2.1969.)

The General Election became, as Faulkner put it, "the most confusing election in history" (NL 14.2.1969). The Unionist Party candidates divided into Pro-O'Neill and Anti-O'Neill camps, and a number of the Anti-O'Neill Unionists were opposed by Unofficial Pro-O'Neill candidates. Ian Paisley fulfilled his promise to stand against O'Neill in his Bannside constituency, while supporters of the Prime Minister formed the New Ulster Movement (NUM) to canvass support for the Pro-O'Neill candidates. In short, the Crossroads Election, as it became known, provoked the first major split in the history of the Ulster Unionist Party.

Given the state of the Party at the time, it seems inconceivable that the February 1969 election could have done anything other than provoke a major split. The holding of the Crossroads Election must go down as another of O'Neill's high-handed political gestures. (During the election campaign, Bill Craig pointed out that the Prime Minister was not President de Gaulle — Sunday News 9.2.1969).

The effects of the split which occurred in Ulster Unionism in 1969 remain to this day. Paisley's near-success against O'Neill in Bannside provided a launching-pad for his Protestant Unionist Party, which became the Democratic Unionist Party in 1971. And the Alliance Party of Northern Ireland grew out of the avidly O'Neillite New Ulster Movement.

The significance of the split was not lost on Lord Brookeborough, the previous Prime Minister, whose son, Captain John Brooke, was one of the twelve backbench dissidents. Speaking on behalf of his son at an election meeting in Ballinamallard, the eighty year old former Premier had some harsh words to say about Captain O'Neill's leadership of the Party:

"I am horrified by this election. It's a terrible tragedy to me to think that after all these years when older ones like myself fought to keep ourselves united, now we are split right down the middle into little bits. Somehow it has got to be put right...

"...Unfortunately, this whole business is so mixed up that nobody knows where they are. In my opinion, the so-called rebels — some people call them the twelve apostles — were quite entitled to have a meeting to decide what they were going to do... They wanted to see the Prime Minister to discuss the situation with him. That happened to me when there was trouble. They used to ask to see me in my room and discuss their difficulties and we usually succeeded in getting over them...

"...The Prime Minister did what he thought was right, but the election, to my mind, was one of the most damaging things that ever happened to the Ulster Unionist Party. I do not want to exacerbate the position. God knows, it will be nearly impossible to get things back to normal. The party is not only split in half, but split in many bits. I am not bitter, but I am merely stating facts as I see them." (NL 14.2.1969.)

SAVE OUR STORMONT

At an early stage in the election campaign, the historian, J.C. Beckett, suggested that the outcome of the crisis in Northern Ireland would be a form of Direct Rule from Westminster. This heretical suggestion provided the News Letter with another opportunity to parade its devolutionary fanatasies.

Direct Rule, it claimed,

"would mean a complete suspension of the democratic process and the control which the people of Ulster exercise over their own affairs — a measure of autonomy which is the envy of Scotland and Wales. In Britain the tide of regionalism is flowing strongly, and a commission has been set up to consider devolution in other parts of the U.K...

"...It is true that Northern Ireland accepted a local Parliament that she never sought. This was a compromise solution, but it has worked better than most compromises and today it has a sure foundation in the Government of Ireland Act, reinforced by Mr. Attlee's legislation in 1949.

"Under these statutes Ulster has the right of decision as to its own constitutional future, which might be placed in jeopardy if the powers were transferred to London.

"There is only one road for the people of Northern Ireland to take and that is to line up solidly behind the programme of moderate and enlightened self-government which is the crux of this election." (NL 10.2.1969.)

It says a lot about the News Letter that, despite all that was happening in February 1969, the paper still saw Stormont as a "compromise solution", which had "worked better than most compromises". The editorial provides a perfect example of Unionist thinking at this time. Direct Rule is rejected on the grounds that Westminster could not be trusted, and Stormont is held up as a bulwark for the Union. The fact that this bulwark could be abolished by one stroke of a Westminster Prime Minister's pen was not recognised.

The way the News Letter, and the rest of the Unionist Family, viewed Stormont in the late 1960s helps put the behaviour of Bill Craig and the other Unionist rebels into perspective. If Stormont is believed to be the guarantor of Ulster's position within the UK, then the last thing Unionists should have done was let someone like Harold Wilson dictate to it. Craig may have been deluded, but at least he was more consistent than either the News Letter or Terence O'Neill.

LOUIS BOYLE: NO CATHOLICS NEED APPLY

O'Neill appears to have expected a significant degree of Catholic support in the Crossroads Election. In his Memoirs, he expresses disappointment that this support did not materialise (p131). But, in the course of the election campaign, the reality of O'Neill's overtures to the Catholic community were once again exposed.

On Wednesday, 12th February, Louis Boyle revealed that the South Down Unionist Association had declined to nominate him as candidate for the election. Boyle was one of the few Catholics within the Unionist Party, and was certainly the most prominent: he had been active within the Party since the mid-sixties and was a former Chairman of the Queen's University Unionist Association. Announcing his intention to write to O'Neill about the matter, Boyle said:

"I feel compelled to express my dismay over the choice of candidate for South Down. I want to make it absolutely clear that I have nothing personal against the candidate and that this is not a question of personal animosity but goes much deeper.

"Ever since the election was announced, I made it clear to Unionist headquarters that I sincerely wanted to contest this seat. I was ready to put my name forward as the official candidate, but South Down Unionist Association decided not to contest, I believe wrongly.

"On Monday [10th February] I informed the Unionist headquarters that I wanted to go forward as a Government candidate, that I had the backing of the Young Unionist Association in Newry and I had received a very favourable reaction from the constituency and wanted to be officially endorsed." (NL 13.2.1969.)

Boyle was informed that the Party HQ wanted the seat contested and was prepared to support and endorse a candidate. He then learnt that an outsider had been asked to contest the seat. Boyle commented:

"As I saw it, I was presenting the Unionist party with an opportunity to translate into practice what 'O'Neillism' should mean. Namely a candidate who was on a completely non-sectarian platform and able to attract support from both sections of the community." (Ibid.)

The outsider approached to contest the South Down seat was a Major James F. Kerr from Groomsport. Shortly after Boyle had made his comments, the Executive Committee of the South Down Unionist Association met in Newry to consider Kerr's nomination. The Committee decided to adhere to the Association's original no-contest decision on the grounds that it was impossible to call a full meeting of delegates to ratify any decision on Kerr's candidature.

This decision was taken despite the fact that the seat was certainly not unwinnable for the Unionist Party. In 1965, the Unionist candidate polled 3,227 votes while the Nationalist polled 6,907. In 1969, the Nationalist candidate received 4,830 votes and only narrowly defeated a People's Democracy candidate who received 4,610. The introduction of a Catholic Unionist candidate into the 1969 contest would, at the very least, have been very interesting.

Louis Boyle's brother, Kevin, was a very prominent figure in the People's Democracy group. He wasted no time using the propaganda gift handed to him by the Unionist Party. He claimed that, although he had never admired his brother's politics, he had admired his courage and his refusal to allow his religion to determine his political views. For Kevin Boyle, the blame for the way his brother had been treated lay with Captain O'Neill. He said:

"If Captain O'Neill was serious in his view that he must persuade more Catholics to vote Unionist, I cannot think of a better way than to endorse a candidate who is a Catholic, ardently pro-O'Neill and who has considerable political experience and local support." (Ibid.)

He claimed that the decision not to nominate his brother had been based on a "conservative fear of reaction among the Unionist faithful that there might be a Roman Catholic Unionist M.P." And he added:

"I have been known in the civil rights movement as someone sympathetic to the view that Captain O'Neill might promote genuine change. My sympathy is now exhausted." (Ibid.)

It is difficult to argue with Kevin Boyle's assessment. As has already been demonstrated in this study, Terence O'Neill never seriously attempted to attract Catholics into the Unionist Party. Even in February 1969, when the Party was fighting the most important election in its history, O'Neill did not lift a finger to help Louis Boyle in his attempts to become a Unionist Party candidate.

The Prime Minister was asked about Boyle's failure to gain the nomination in South Down in an interview with Patrick Riddell of the Sunday News. Riddell put the following question to him:

"The Unionist Party has professed its hope that Roman Catholics will join in and stand for Parliament as Unionists. Yet Louis Boyle, a Roman Catholic Unionist, was refused the nomination for his own constituency. How do you reconcile this seeming contradiction?" (Sunday News, 23.2.1969.)

In reply, O'Neill simply washed his hands of the whole affair:

"This is quite easily explicable. In England the Conservative Central Office has a considerable effect upon the choice of candidates. In Northern Ireland we are very much more parochial. If you arrive in a constituency and say you have the blessing of Unionists headquarters in Belfast, it is equivalent to the kiss of death.

"They like to be able to choose their own people in their own way and in their own time. Therefore it is very difficult for anyone at Headquarters to influence selections.

"I am very sorry if Mr. Louis Boyle feels that he has been spurned. I have written to him about it and told him how sorry I feel. But there is nothing that headquarters can do... forgetting all about religion." (Ibid.)

It should be said that, as a matter of historical record, Unionist Party Leaders have been known to intervene in the selection of party candidates by local associations. Lord Brookeborough, for example, intervened to secure George Forrest's nomination in 1958. More recently, in 1987, Jim Molyneaux expelled the entire North Down Association simply because it had nominated Robert McCartney to stand against the "Unionist Unity" candidate, Jim Kilfedder.

O'Neill's glib dismissal of Louis Boyle's complaints again illustrates the fraudulent nature of his liberal credentials. Constituency associations, he affirmed, had to be "able to choose their own people" (i.e., Protestants). Had O'Neill simply accepted that the Unionist Party was a pan-Protestant, single-issue Party, which Catholics could not reasonably be expected to join or vote for, disaster might have been averted. Such an acceptance would have implied a return to the low-key politics of the Craigavon and Brookeborough periods. But O'Neill stirred up political excitement and expectation. And he represented Unionism as a full-blown political philosophy, superior to British party politics, which could engender general harmony in Northern Ireland as a party of all the people. The onus was therefore upon him to change the Protestant nature of the Unionist Party and make it a Party which Catholics could join and flourish in. But his priorities lay elsewhere, and he did not even try.

The Louis Boyle affair illustrates, above all else, the impossibility of developing normal politics within a purely Northern Ireland context. By July 1969, Boyle himself finally admitted that the Ulster Unionist Party was destined to remain a Protestant Party. He, therefore, resigned from it saying that there was "no possibility" of "creating a non-sectarian party out of the existing Unionist Party". He also stated:

"My views will continue to be Conservative and Unionist. But I know that

I cannot continue to propagate them as a Catholic in the Unionist Party. Nor could any Catholic who thinks likewise." (NL 9.7.69)

LAST WEEK OF ELECTION

The Boyle affair was by far the most significant development to occur during the election campaign. For the most part, the campaign was a complicated mess. The only other developments worth recording occurred in the final week.

Five days before polling day, O'Neill landed himself in deep trouble for supporting the Unofficial Pro-O'Neill candidates who were standing against some of his opponents within the Party. He said:

> "I cannot endorse men who have been progressive in public but reactionary in private. I do not back those who equivocate and hedge. I am unable to support Unionists who reject vital parts of the official election manifesto or whose words or deeds in the past are incompatible with its healing message." (NL 20.2.1969.)

The most prominent critic of O'Neill's decision to support the Unofficial Unionists was Colonel J.G. Cunningham, an Honorary Secretary of the Ulster Unionist Council (NL 21.2.1969). Cunningham had backed O'Neill within the Party at the time of Faulkner's resignation. The Prime Minister's stance on the Unofficial candidates certainly added significantly to his problems after the election.

On the same day as O'Neill's controversial statement was reported, the reality of his "progressive", "healing message" was revealed. The News Letter reported that one of the most prominent O'Neillite Unionists, Roy Bradford, was circulating a leaflet entitled, **"Northern Ireland Labour — What Are Its Real Aims?"**.

The leaflet which had been produced by the Unionist Party headquarters in Glengall Street, stated:

> "Since the Northern Ireland Labour Party officially adopted a policy of loyalty to Northern Ireland's constitutional status, it has given frequent indications that its real attitude is little different to that of other opposition parties." (NL 20.2.1969.)

The evidence of the leaflet for this nonsensical allegation was: that the NILP had joined with the Irish Labour Party in 1968 to form a Council of Labour; that a resolution at the last NILP conference had called on the Wilson Government to set up an enquiry into the administration of Northern Ireland; that the two NILP members at Stormont had voted against the Government's ban on the Republican Clubs; that the NILP had never condemned the "blatantly anti-Ulster activities of some British Labour MPs"; and finally, that the NILP had "clearly shown evidence of solidarity" with the Civil Rights agitators.

Thus, in 1969, the Unionist Party took up where it had left off in the last election in 1965: playing the Orange card against the NILP. With this tactic, O'Neill effectively smashed the NILP in 1965 and, in the process, destroyed the only party which could have provided a non-sectarian alternative to the Unionist Party. By putting the boot into the NILP in 1969, the O'Neillites exposed their 'progressive' posturing as sheer hypocrisy.

RESULTS

In his eve of poll statement, Terence O'Neill declared:

> "Everything is at stake for us today. The world awaits with eagerness to know where we are going; which road our people want to follow. It is a momentous time for us all. Today we decide our destiny." (NL 24.2.1969.)

Despite the Prime Minister's grandiose rhetoric, the election results were, to say the least, inconclusive. O'Neill himself narrowly defeated Paisley in Bannside by 7,745 votes to 6,331. Nine of the twelve dissidents who had provoked him into calling the election were re-elected, although most of them had reduced majorities. Of the other three, two (Tom Hinds and Austin Ardill) had not been re-selected by their local associations. The third, William Hinds, was defeated by an Unofficial Pro-O'Neill Unionist.

A similar fate befell the former Health and Social Services Minister, William Morgan. Faulkner, however, defeated both a Nationalist and a Pro-O'Neill candidate in East Down, but his majority was reduced from 3,367 to 1,709. In Larne, Bill Craig scraped home against an O'Neillite by just 653 votes.

Overall, 39 Unionist MPs were elected, including three Unofficial Pro-O'Neill candidates. Predictably, the Parliamentary Unionist Party remained divided. According to the News Letter, 24 of the 36 Official Unionist MPs were supporters of the Prime Minister, 10 were opponents and two had not declared their position.

The election also witnessed an upheaval in Catholic politics. Three outgoing Nationalist MPs were defeated by independent candidates who had been prominent in the Civil Rights movement: John Hume, Ivan Cooper and Paddy O'Hanlon. Hume's victory over the Nationalist Party Leader, Eddie McAteer, in the Foyle constituency, symbolised what was effectively the beginning of the end for McAteer's Party.

In Belfast, Harry Diamond of the Republican Labour Party lost his Falls seat to Paddy Devlin of the NILP. Diamond's Party, however, maintained its number of seats at Stormont: Paddy Kennedy gained the Belfast Central seat at the expense of the National Democrats, and Gerry Fitt held the Belfast Dock seat. The NILP held on to its Oldpark seat, but lost Pottinger to the Unionists. The Ulster Liberal Party had already lost its single seat as a result of the abolition of the four University seats.

For the record, the overall results were as follows:

FEBRUARY 1969 STORMONT ELECTION: RESULT		
	Seats gained	Seats Before Election
Ulster Unionists	36	37
Unofficial Unionists	3	-
Nationalists	6	9
Independents	3	-
NILP	2	2
Republican Labour	2	2
National Democrat	-	1
Liberal	-	1

THE END

There is not really that much to add about O'Neill's premiership. The outcome of the Crossroads Election certainly did nothing to strengthen his position as Party Leader. In his memoirs, he records his feelings at the end of February 1969:

> "My colleagues in the Cabinet pressed me to stay on. A lot of clever people produced figures to show how well we had done; but I knew in my bones that the game was up. In a month's time I would have been Prime Minister for six years. Quite a respectable stint even by British standards. Why should I soldier on in this impossible situation? In fact, but for certain events in April it is quite possible that I would have carried on till the autumn. I am glad that it did not turn out in that way." (p122.)

On the last day of February, a meeting of the Parliamentary Unionist Party voted by 23 to 1 in favour of O'Neill remaining Leader. The vote against came from Brian Faulkner, while Bill Craig recorded the only abstention. According to the News Letter, ten dissidents walked out of the meeting before the vote was taken (NL 8.3.69).

A week later, a closer vote was recorded at a meeting of the Standing Committee of the Unionist Council. This body passed a vote of confidence in the Prime Minister by 183 votes to 116.

Towards the end of March, O'Neill's position was further undermined when the Civil Rights agitation resumed after a two-month break. Once again, O'Neill's only response to the agitation was to call for calm, moderation and decency. By this stage, these calls sounded more hollow and inadequate than ever. On March 21st, for example, on the eve of PD marches in Enniskillen, Newry, Derry and Armagh, he said:

> "I continue to believe in the stability, decency, commonsense and innate sense of fairness of the Ulster people as a whole. Our extremists of whatever kidney — men and women who want to be their own judges of what is lawful — are minorities insignificant save in the volume of noise they make and the degree of notoriety they attract." (NL 22.3.1969.)

As O'Neill said in his memoirs, "certain events" were to ensure that he would not remain in office until the autumn. The first of these occurred on March 30th, when a power station at Lisnabreeney on the outskirts of Belfast was damaged by an explosion. Two transformers were destroyed and damage was estimated at £500,000.

April 1969 saw five further explosions. At the time, no one appears to have known who was responsible for them. The truth did not emerge until October, when a member of the Ulster Volunteer Force was killed planting a bomb at a power station in County Donegal. The four explosions in April, however, were devastatingly effective, not least because many believed that the IRA were to blame.

That, in fact, was the intention behind them and the bombings, therefore, added dramatically to the feeling that the O'Neill Government had lost all control over developments in the province. In his memoirs, O'Neill claimed that the explosions "quite literally" blew him out of office (p122).

The attack on the Castlereagh power-station occurred on the eve of the annual meeting of the influential Unionist Council. A News Letter editorial on the day of the meeting declared:

> "There can be no excuse for any Unionist worthy of the name failing to stand squarely behind the Government at such a time." (NL 31.3.1969.)

Many at the meeting ignored the News Letter's advice. After three hours, a vote of confidence in O'Neill was passed by 338 votes to 263. The Prime Minister, therefore, secured a majority of 75 in a poll of 601. Only 56% of the Unionist Council had backed him compared to the 61% support he had received from the Council's Standing Committee earlier in the month.

On 4th April, there was an explosion at a water installation at Dunadry, County Antrim. Just over a fortnight later, the situation took a dramatic turn for the worse. On April 19th, Civil Rights demonstrations were held in towns throughout the province, including Dungannon, Lurgan, Newry, Enniskillen, Armagh, Strabane and Dungiven.

A march in Derry ended in serious violence. Clashes occurred, firstly between Paisleyites and Civil Rights marchers, and then between marchers and the police. In all, approximately 80 civilians and 200 policemen were injured.

That night, a bomb wrecked the main supply pipe between the Silent Valley reservoir in the Mourne Mountains and Belfast. An explosion also damaged an electricity pylon at Kilmore in County Armagh. After an emergency Cabinet meeting in Belfast, it was announced that British Army units were being brought into the province to guard key installations against terrorist attack.

Captain O'Neill and his Cabinet chose this time to force through the introduction of "one man one vote". In his Autobiography, he recalls:

> "I felt that my time was running out and that I would, before I went, bring in 'one man one vote' for local government elections." (p124.)

On April 22nd, O'Neill told a meeting of the Parliamentary Unionist Party that, unless it backed the introduction of "one man one vote", he would resign. He reportedly told the meeting that he wanted to go to London for a meeting with Harold Wilson armed with an assurance on the franchise question. Other members of the Cabinet, especially the then Home Affairs Minister, Robert Porter, were set to resign with the Prime Minister (NL 23.4.1969).

The meeting was adjourned until the next day and, overnight, an explosion shattered a four foot main that provided North Belfast with Lough Neagh water. According to the News Letter, Belfast's overall water supply was, by this time, halved.

Before the Parliamentary Unionist Party reconvened on April 23rd, James Chichester-Clark, the Minister for Agriculture, resigned from O'Neill's Government over the timing of the reform of the franchise. In his resignation letter, he stated:

> "I question firstly whether this concession at this time will stop the activity in the streets and secondly I fear that our supporters will lose all faith in the determination of the present Government.

"A Government must have some goodwill if it is to govern and the measure proposed will, in my view forfeit a great measure of the goodwill that remains — I reiterate I am not against the principle but against the timing." (NL 24.4.1969.)

Later in the day, Chichester-Clark told reporters:

"While supporting the principle of universal franchise, I don't believe this decision should have been taken at this time." (ibid.)

He added that he thought there was a danger of encouraging militant Protestants to react, "possibly even to the point of bloodshed" (ibid).

The Parliamentary Unionist Party meeting that day voted in favour of "one man one vote" by 28 votes to 22. Chichester-Clark voted against, as did Brian Faulkner. Afterwards, Faulkner said that, while he was in favour of the principle of universal franchise, he was opposed to its introduction "in the absence of full discussion within the Unionist Party — not just at Stormont but in the country."

He repeated his accusation that the Government had evaded the franchise issue by appointing the Commission. He also claimed, rightly as it transpired, that the franchise reform would not placate the Civil Rights demonstrators. They had already declared that the franchise was "no longer a major issue", Faulkner added.

The former Deputy Prime Minister also warned that the introduction of the measure would "heap fuel on the fires burning" in the Party, and up and down the country.

"But much more serious will be the further risk to the rule of law in Northern Ireland at the present time. It can only be maintained by fairness coupled with firmness. There is neither fairness nor firmness at the present time." (Ibid.)

The introduction of "one man one vote" in Local Government elections was O'Neill's last act as Prime Minister. Thus, the man of destiny secured for himself another mention in the history books. In so doing, O'Neill did the incoming Administration no favours at all. The new Government could have got off to a positive start by settling the franchise question once and for all. O'Neill robbed them of this opportunity.

On the night after Chichester-Clarke's resignation another explosion took place: the third in six days. This time the target was a water main in Annalong, which carried supplies to Belfast; the city was by now experiencing a serious water shortage.

That weekend, rumours about O'Neill's position circulated widely. He gave an interview to the News Letter in which he defended the way he had governed the province:

"I have absolutely no regrets that moves were made to improve relations inside the country and between North and South. But wicked men have seen to it that this movement has been reversed." (NL 28.4.1969.)

Captain Terence O'Neill finally resigned as Unionist Party Leader on 28th April 1969. That night, celebration bonfires were lit on the Shankill Road. He formally resigned as Prime Minister on May 1st, after the Party had chosen his successor.

Before long, O'Neill had also retired from public life and moved to England. He joined the House of Lords at the beginning of 1970.

As a parting gift to Northern Ireland, O'Neill performed one last bungle: he intervened decisively in the election of the Party's new Leader. His intervention is described in his memoirs:

> "The following morning, Thursday, 1 May, was the day the Party was meeting to choose its new leader. I was told that Chichester-Clark would have a majority of five over Faulkner and someone queried whether I ought to attend and vote as the outgoing Prime Minister... I was convinced that as an MP I had every right to attend and vote. In the event Chichester-Clark got a majority of one: Faulkner must have been working very hard. If I had not attended, there would have been a dead heat! In a sense it seemed odd that I should vote for the man who brought me down, but it had been due to worries and doubts in his very unpolitical mind... But in any event, I couldn't have brought myself to vote for the man who had been trying to bring me down for six years. It was as simple as that." (P129.)

Out of spite, therefore, O'Neill secured the accession of a man with a "very unpolitical mind".

Faulkner's account of the leadership contest differs markedly from O'Neill's:

> "Major James Chichester-Clark, Minister for Agriculture, resigned from O'Neill's Government on 23 April 1969... On the surface this seemed to precipitate O'Neill's resignation. But there were many, like myself, who thought it was a scheme arranged between them to ensure that power was kept in the hands of the 'Big House'. Chichester-Clark had strong social and personal ties with O'Neill (both were Eton and the Guards), though he was politically unknown and inexperienced. His resignation placed him in the pubic eye at a time when we were daily expecting O'Neill's resignation. When O'Neill resigned five days later and held a farewell tea party for his political friends at Stormont Castle to which the Major was invited it was clear who O'Neill was backing to succeed him.

> "The 'Pro-O'Neill' faction took up the Major as their candidate. Everyone at that time was labelled as either 'moderate' or 'extremist', 'progressive' or 'reactionary'. It was a destructive and blinkered practice which did littlle justice to the complexity of people and their political opinions. Chichester-Clark, who had resigned in opposition to universal franchise in local elections, was labelled a 'moderate' while I, who had resigned in favour of universal franchise three months earlier, was labelled a 'reactionary'...

> "...On May 1 the election for Leader of the Unionist Party was held... I could not believe that the party would elect someone with no apparent popular influence at such a crucial time for Ulster, but it soon became obvious that it would be a close contest. Chichester-Clark had virtually formed his Cabinet 'designate' before the voting took place... Chichester-Clark won by one vote." (P54-55.)

The News Letter reported the result of the leadership election under the headline, **One Man One Vote Did It.** Whether or not Chichester-Clark's victory was secured by a "Big House" plot, it must go down as one of the stupidest decisions ever reached in the history of politics. By passing over Faulkner, the Unionist Party effectively sealed its fate.

O'Neill's chosen successor lasted just twenty-two months. He had even less idea of how to cope with the crisis than O'Neill. By August 1969, Northern Ireland had completely collapsed into sectarian chaos. When Faulkner replaced Chichester-Clark in March 1971, it was too late: the war was well under way.

O'Neill, by then, was living in England and well away from ghastly things like bombs and bullets.

Chapter Ten

CONCLUSION

Two great myths have grown up around the subject of O'Neill's premiership. One concerns his attitude to Civil Rights reforms, the other his approach to the Catholic community.

· O'Neill And Reforms

Accounts of political developments in Northern Ireland in the late 1960s often explain everything by reference to 'reforms'. O'Neill is held up as a good man who tried to alleviate Catholic grievances by introducing much-needed reforms. This, it is said, provoked a violent reaction from the bad men in the Unionist Party. The Party split and O'Neill was driven out. Unionist failure to introduce reforms is also used to explain the re-emergence of the IRA.

This kind of simplistic reasoning can be found, among other places, in the memoirs of James Callaghan, the former Labour Prime Minister. Callaghan was Home Secretary in Wilson's Government during the Civil Rights period and his comments illustrate just how out of touch with reality the Westminster Government was at the time. (Some things, at least, do not change.)

Referring to O'Neill's downfall, Callaghan states:

> "It was not until April 1969 that the Ulster Unionists could bring themselves to concede the elementary right of universal suffrage [sic]. Even so, as a result Captain O'Neill was forced by his own party to resign and from that time forward events moved towards the disasters of the 1970s and 1980s.
>
> "It is possible that if the Unionist party had been more far-sighted and generous, and had allowed Terence O'Neill to bring forward the reforms that simple justice demanded, the IRA might not have been able in later years to misuse and pervert the genuine anger of the minority." (**Time And Chance**, Collins 1987, p271.)

There is, in reality, no hard evidence to support the view that O'Neill was a great reformer. This myth appears to be based entirely on the fact that he was in charge when the Unionist Party introduced its first package of Civil Rights reforms in November 1968. But by then he was well into his sixth year as Prime Minister. During that time, he never once showed any interest in any of the reforms that suddenly became a priority at the end of 1968. The issue of Local Government franchise was raised on a number of occasions in the 1960s, and was airily dismissed by the O'Neill Administration. A proper reforming Government would have cleared that anomaly up well before 1969 (and with the minimum of fuss).

O'Neill's November 1968 five-point reform package included the appointment of a Parliamentary Ombudsman. Three years earlier, however, O'Neill had made a controversial speech on the subject of parity, which was specifically designed to counter suggestions that Northern Ireland should have an Ombudsman because Great Britain had one (speech to Court Ward Unionist Association — quoted in full in Chapter 5).

In all, it is difficult to avoid the conclusion that O'Neill only became interested in the concept of reforms because Harold Wilson was demanding some kind of 'moderate' response to the Civil Rights agitation.

The importance of 'reforms' in the civil rights period has certainly been over-stated. For a start, 'reforms' by themselves, were not the primary reason for the break-up of the Unionist Party in 1969. Bill Craig, for example, who led much of the opposition to O'Neill within the Party at the time, was mainly concerned about the wider issue of Stormont's independence from Westminster.

As this study has shown, all sorts of factors combined to cause the disintegration of the Unionist Party monolith in 1968/69. Many, if not all, of these factors were related in some way to delusions about Stormont. There was, for example, Craig's belief that Northern Ireland had federal rights within the UK. There was also the notion that defending the Union meant defending Stormont.

But the greatest of all Unionist delusions about Stormont was Captain O'Neill's assumption that Catholics would accept their position as a permanent minority under the Stormont arrangements; that the Croppies would lie down. Once that delusion was shattered by the Civil Rights movement, O'Neill was finished. (Craig too had no idea how to cope with this unpleasant reality other than using the police and B Specials to batter the Croppies down.)

O'Neill's first leadership crisis came in 1966. That attempt to oust him certainly had nothing to do with a five-point package. 1966 was the year of the Easter Rising commemoration marches. Those marches provided a hint that the Croppies might not be meekly lying down. O'Neill's premiership very nearly didn't stand the strain. 1966 was a dry run for 1968/69.

Delusions about Stormont and, in particular, about the Catholic community, provide the real reason for the collapse of Unionism and the downfall of O'Neill. To attribute everything to disagreements about 'reforms' is just simplistic nonsense.

The significance of reforms to the Civil Rights protests is likewise over-stated. If the O'Neill Government had introduced "one man one vote" in local government elections in, say, 1966, Catholics would not have danced in the streets to celebrate. For what it mattered, the absence of "the elementary right of universal suffrage", as Callaghan describes it, actually disenfranchised more Protestants than Catholics.

Issues like the franchise, housing allocation or the need for an Ombudsman were not the driving force behind the Civil Rights agitation. The Civil Rights movement was, above all else, a rebellion by the Catholic community against the Stormont arrangements: it had had enough of being a permanent minority and it had had enough of being ruled by Prods.

The Unionist Government could make concessions on issues like housing allocation or an Ombudsman. But that was just treating the symptoms and ignoring the cause. The cause of all the problems was the form of Government imposed on Northern Ireland by the Westminster Government in 1921.

Under O'Neill, the Unionist Government was incapable of calling for the dismantling of the Stormont arrangements. And to its everlasting shame, the Wilson Government also shied away from dealing with the fundamental cause of the unrest.

O'Neill And Catholics

People like John Hume often claim that Terence O'Neill wanted to be 'nice to Catholics', and was brought down by Unionist backwoodsmen as a result. This claim may be effective as a Nationalist debating point but it is an insult to the self-respect of all Catholics.

The myth that O'Neill wanted to give the Catholic community a new deal is preposterous. Certainly, at times, he gave the impression that he was offering a new deal. But all O'Neill actually did was raise expectations of political change; he never even tried to develop political structures that would accommodate these expectations.

There were two basic themes in O'Neill's approach to Government. Firstly, he stirred up political activity and expectations around the administrative routine at Stormont. Unlike his predecessors, he preached the virtues of "Home Rule for Ulster" and claimed that Stormont gave Northern Ireland an "in-built advantage" over the rest of the UK.

Secondly, O'Neill increased Unionist Party domination of the Stormont political scene. In the 1965 Stormont election, he devoted all his energies into smashing the NILP. This was not done for purely pragmatic reasons, but out of an ideological commitment to one-party politics. O'Neillite ideology was most clearly expressed in two speeches delivered in the first half of 1968.

The first was made at the Carrick Unionist Association on January 31st, 1968. In it, he railed against class-based politics, and held Unionism up as an all-encompassing creed that was superior to anything offered in the British political system. The Carrick speech has already been quoted in its entirety in this book (see Chapter Nine). But the following brief extracts are worth recalling:

"Unionism sets its face against any division on class or occupational ground. There is no more sad and revealing expression in current use than one we hear every day about 'both sides of industry'... The expression is symptomatic of strongly entrenched and very damaging attitudes in Britain ...

"... modern Unionism is attached neither to unions nor to employers, but to a concept of the national interest...

"Some may say, since Unionism covers such a wide range of interests and... is far from dogmatic in its views, that it lacks the purpose and dynamism of a wholly coherent political philosophy. I do not accept that. I never want to see the comfortable and ample garment of Unionism converted into a straitjacket.

Nor should we accept that a party system based on sectional or class interests is vital to the health of a nation."

The second key speech was made to Woodvale Unionist Association on May 20th, 1968. In it, O'Neill outlined his preference for "one-party rule", and compared the Unionist Party position at Stormont to the dominance of Fianna Fail in the Irish Republic. He said:

"The fact of the matter is that in Ireland, North and South, we have a rather stable political situation, without the swings which are characteristic of politics in Britain. Stability may not be as exciting as change, but it is not necessarily any less democratic."

In his televised Crossroads Speech at the end of 1968, O'Neill asked his viewers: "What kind of Ulster do you want?" The kind of Ulster he wanted was one in which the Ulster Unionist Party enjoyed uninterrupted power.

Politically speaking, Catholics just did not feature in O'Neill's vision of the future. He refused to accept the fact that the Unionist Party was a Protestant Party. Not once did he even broach the subject of the Party's institutional links with the Orange Order. When the News Letter suggested a separation of both bodies, he maintained a stony silence, while one of his most enthusiastic supporters, Roy Bradford, poured cold water on the whole idea.

In political terms, Captain O'Neill wanted his New Ulster to be permanently ruled by a single, monolithic Protestant Party. And if Catholics did not like this Protestant Parliament, they would have to lump it.

It is interesting to compare O'Neill's attitude to the Catholic community with that of his former Deputy, Brian Faulkner. O'Neill was Prime Minister for just over six years. In that time, he made no attempt to end the political isolation of the Northern Ireland Catholic community. Faulkner, on the other hand, had a much shorter tenure of office. He was Prime Minister of Northern Ireland between March 1971 and the introduction of Direct rule in March 1972. He was also Chief Executive of the Northern Ireland Power-Sharing Government that lasted from January to May 1974.

Faulkner, however, made two serious efforts to provide meaningful political structures for Catholics. The first was made in June 1971, and involved the establishment of Committees at Stormont, which would participate in the Government's policy-making process. Under Faulkner's scheme, a number of the Committee Chairmen would be members of the Opposition (i.e. the SDLP). Although it initially welcomed the scheme, the SDLP effectively wrecked it by withdrawing from Stormont in the following month.

Faulkner's second attempt to reform the Stormont system was the power-sharing experiment of 1974. At a comparatively early stage in this experiment, he made a very powerful speech to the Assembly. The following extract from that speech, marks Faulkner out from any other Unionist politician of the past twenty five years:

"Virtually everyone of judgement now agrees that it has been a great source of weakness and instability to Northern Ireland over half-a-century that its Roman

Catholic community, representing one-third of the population, has not played a commensurate part in the life and affairs of the Province. We can argue until the cows come home about whose fault that was over all those years. We can go on attributing mutual blame up to and beyond the point where the rest of the world grows sick of us. All I know is that we have now found the means to work together. Are we now to say to that community, 'Democracy is simply majority rule, and if that means you are to sit in opposition for half-a-century more, it's just too bad'? I ask the opponents of all that we in this Executive represent, 'What is your answer?'" (Hansard, 24.1.1974, Col 133.)

This quote should compared with O'Neill's infamous comment:

"It is frightfully hard to explain to Protestants that if you give Roman Catholics a good job and a good house, they will live like Protestants, because they will see neighbours with cars and television sets. They will refuse to have eighteen children; but if a Roman Catholic is jobless, and lives in the most ghastly hovel, he will rear eighteen children on national assistance. If you treat Roman Catholics with due consideration and kindness, they will live like Protestants in spite of the authoritative nature of their Church." (Belfast Telegraph 5.5.1969.)

This unbelievably patronising comment actually sums up the entire nature of Terence O'Neill's 'niceness' to Catholics. He thought that a little bit of economic advancement would make them forget about their political grievances; that a few houses with televisions would reconcile them to being ruled by Prods. He failed.

Faulkner's initiatives also failed but for very different reasons. His efforts in 1971 and 1974 are important enough to require a separate study. But, even at a glance, it is clear that he was not primarily responsible for their failure.

The collapse of the 1974 power-sharing experiment and the way Northern Ireland politics has developed since then confirms one thing: genuine progress is impossible within a purely Northern Ireland context. The provincial communal political structure is incapable of generating a solution. Northern Ireland is, as Charlie Haughey put it, a failed political entity.

Only the British political establishment has it within its power to sort out the mess which it created here in 1921. At present in Northern Ireland, there is a strong and growing cross-community demand for representative government. This demand should now be met in full: Northern Ireland people should be given full access to the party politics of the UK state. If the Westminster establishment cannot bring itself to take this simple step then it should set about expelling Northern Ireland from the UK. Perpetuating the limbo land will simply get more people killed.

David Gordon
July 1989

Bibliography

Adams, Gerry: The Politics Of Irish Freedom, Brandon, 1986.

Arthur, Paul and
Jeffery, Keith: Northern Ireland Since 1968, Blackwell, 1988.

Bleakley, David: Faulkner, Mowbrays, 1974.

Boyd, Andrew: Brian Faulkner And The Crisis Of Ulster Unionism, Anvil Books, 1972.

Callaghan, James: Time And Chance, Collins, 1987.

Clifford, Brendan: The Road To Nowhere (A Review of Unionist Politics From O'Neill To Molyneaux and Powell) Athol Books, 1987.

Deutch, Richard and
Magowan, Vivien: Northern Ireland — A Chronology Of Events, Volume 1, Blackstaff, 1973.

Farrell, Michael: Northern Ireland: The Orange State, Pluto Press, 1980.

Faulkner, Brian: Memoirs Of A Statesman, Weidenfield and Nicolson, 1978

Flackes, W.D.: Northern Ireland — A Political Directory, BBC, 1983.

Lyons, F.S.L.: Ireland Since The Famine, London 1971.

McAughtry, Sam: Down In The Free State, Gill and Macmillan, 1987.

O'Neill, Terence: Autobiography, Hart-Davis, 1972
Ulster At The Crossroads, Faber and Faber, 1969.

Smyth, Clifford: Ian Paisley—Voice Of Protestant Ulster, Scottish Academic Press, 1987.

White, Barry: John Hume—Statesman Of The Troubles, Blackstaff, 1984.

Walsh, Pat: From Civil Rights To National War, Athol Books, 1989.

Index

FROM CIVIL RIGHTS TO NATIONAL WAR
Catholic Politics 1964-74
PAT WALSH

In this pioneering work Pat Walsh traces the development of Catholic politics
in Northern Ireland from the early 1960s, and shows how the Civil Rights
movement became transformed into the shooting war of today.

The decline of the Nationalist Party, the IRA split, the formation of the SDLP
and its moment of truth at Sunningdale are all covered in detail, showing how
the old, when it gave all the indications of dying out, reasserted itself against
the new and fashioned the mould of Catholic poitics for another decade.

This controversial and hard-hitting reassessment of the forces which shaped
contemporary Catholic and nationalist politics in Northern Ireland is published
at a particularly appropriate moment, as we reach the 20th anniversary of the
present phase of the national war.

Pat Walsh is currently preparing a work on Irish Republicanism and Socialism.

THE CONSTITUTIONAL HISTORY OF EIRE/IRELAND
ANGELA CLIFFORD

Published to commemorate the 50th anniversary of De Valera's Constitution,
this book shows that Ireland is governed under three Constitutions. Its
anomalous relations with Britain and with Northern Ireland continue to be
governed by the evolutionary Treaty settlement of 1921. Social affairs are
governed by the Canon Law of the Catholic Church, which also lays down the
form of relations between Church and State. The official Consitution adopted
in 1937 fits between these two informal but preponderant Constitutions

Angela Clifford traces the evolution of the 1922 Constitution; details the
introduction and development of the 1937 Constitution up to the 10th
Amendment; traces the fate of the Treaty; and explains the relations of Church
and State.

The Constitutional History of Eire / Ireland is the most comprehensive review
of Irish Constitutional affairs since Donal O'Sullivan's superb but neglected
'Irish Free State And Its Senate' published half a century ago.

336 pages

Athol Books Publications
July 1989

A Story Of The Armada
　　by Captain Francisco De Cuellar, Joe Keenan and others
　　£3.50

The Constitutional History Of Eire/Ireland
　　by Angela Clifford
　　£15

Northern Ireland And The Algerian Analogy: A Suitable
　　Case For Gaullism?
　　by Hugh Roberts
　　£3

The Dubliner: The Lives, Times And Writings Of James Clarence Mangan
　　by Brendan Clifford
　　£7.50

Thomas Russell And Belfast
　　by Brendan Clifford
　　£5

The Veto Controversy, including Thomas Moore's
　　A Letter To The Roman Catholics Of Dublin (1810)
　　by Brendan Clifford
　　£10

The Life And Poems Of Thomas Moore
　　edited by Brendan Clifford
　　£5

Farm Labourers: Irish Struggle 1900—1976
　　by Dan Bradley
　　£5

Available (mail order only) from:
Athol Books,
10 Athol Street,
Belfast, BT12 4GX.

Selection Of Pamphlets On Northern Ireland Politics:

Parliamentary Sovereignty And Northern Ireland
Brendan Clifford Nov 1985 £1

A Review Of The Party System In The British Constitution, With Relation To The Anglo-Irish Agreement.

Parliamentary Despotism, John Hume'sAspiration
B. Clifford   Jan 1986   £1

The Constitutional Nationalist View of Constitutionalism explained.

Government Without Opposition   Brendan Clifford June '86 £1

How Northern Ireland has been subject to unopposed Government under both Devolution and Direct Rule. With extracts from writings of Harold Laski.

The Road To Nowhere   Brendan Clifford Jan 1987   £1

A review Of Unionist politics From O'Neill to Molyneaux and Powell.

The Unionist Family   Brendan Clifford July 1987   £1

The meaning and implication for Catholics of the phrase, "the Unionist Family".

Integration–A Word Without Meaning Jim Davidson May '86 30p

Queens: A Comment On A University, And A Reply To Its Politics Professor   Brendan Clifford Oct 1987   £2

A survey of academic writing on the party system.

Electoral Integration   Jim Davidson Nov 1986   40p

An Argument on Behalf Of The Catholics Of Northern Ireland
Joe Keenan   Sept 1987 £1

The political biography of a non-religious Belfast Catholic who is defined as a Catholic by the abnormality of political structures in the province.

The Fulham Manifesto   May 1986 £1

The Story Of the By-Election Campaign by the *Democratic Rights For Northern Ireland Campaign in 1986*.

For A full list of publications,
send a stamped addressed envelope to
Athol Books, 10 Athol Street, Belfast, BT12 4GX.